LEAVING MOOSE JAW

TAYLOR LAMBERT

ISBN: 1-48233-668-5

ISBN-13: 978-1-48233-668-9

To C.B.,

with immeasurable thanks and tremendous profanity.

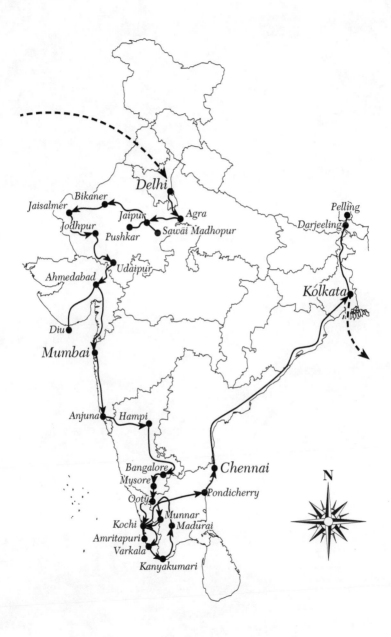

ROAD MAP

AUTHOR'S NOTE

This is a work of non-fiction. Aside from the courtesy of pseudonyms and the unfortunate, inevitable and hopefully rare failure of memory, this is a true story.

The book in your hands is a product of independent publishing. All aspects, from the interior layout to the cover design, were done by myself and a few others (to whom I am hugely indebted). Thank you for supporting our endeavours, and please suggest this book to someone if you enjoy it; keep your mouth shut if you don't.

Finally, apologies may be in order to the fine people of Moose Jaw. My spontaneous flight would, in hindsight, likely have occurred much the same had I been anywhere else, and the story that follows should not be taken as an indictment of the Friendly City, which is quite a lovely town and highly deserving of its moniker. Good Thai food, too.

—T.L.

The drugs had come down hard on me. Sitting on the concrete, looking up at the night sky, I wondered how long I had been there. I couldn't see over the two-foot concrete abutment that ran along the edge of the rooftop I was on, but I knew we were six storeys in the air.

Everything blurred and everything amplified and nothing was stable enough to hold on to. But the night felt cooler over here. Rickshaws honked in the streets below, and the myriad smells of India washed over me. Sitting lower to the ground seemed to help steady my head. I felt more in control, aside from a powerful curiosity about jumping off the building.

...Maybe I should just go take a peek. See the view...

MOOSE JAW

Itchy feet in the vein of screech

I was in a café on Main Street eating a reuben and drinking stale black coffee when I finished reading *The Rum Diary* for the first time. It was a cold and rainy day in early spring, and I left the café and bought two bottles of Newfoundland screech and two packs of cigarettes and went home and started writing. This was the beginning of my departure from Moose Jaw.

That seems so long ago now. I still remember that moment when things were set in motion, though I could not have known the scale of the machinery I was turning. But all that came later; for now, I'm content to remember the sauerkraut soaking through the bread.

I had been working in Moose Jaw as a sportswriter for the local newspaper for the past six months. It had been an exceptionally cold and miserable winter, even by Saskatchewanian standards, but the weather was never really the problem.

Moose Jaw is a quaint, dull little town forty minutes west of Regina. The thirty-some-thousand souls are friendly people who enjoy their junior hockey and high school sports. There are some nice parks, and the downtown has a handful of early twentieth-century buildings with some degree of charm. The local claim to fame is the possibility that Al Capone's bootleggers may have operated for a brief time in the tunnels that run beneath the city. I divided my time between musty arenas and sweaty gyms with a notepad, and the better of the local pubs with a glass.

The newspaper was a ship adrift with too many captains: the editors outnumbered the reporters, and enough of them had accepted the bare minimum for so long that it was no longer seen as such. I had come there fresh out of journalism school in Montreal to start a career and pay my dues. But despite my deep Saskatchewan roots, it wasn't where I wanted to be. I longed for action, for chaos, for things I hadn't seen or even thought much about before. I wanted to run.

I had taken a gap year after high school to travel Europe, as is customary of my generation, but that was years ago and I was restless. I have a chronic case of what is known in some medical circles as 'itchy feet syndrome': a tendency to cut and run once I feel comfort and complacency setting in. There is no cure, merely symptomatic treatment.

Of course, I knew I wanted to leave Moose Jaw before I read *The Rum Diary*; but Thompson turned the whispering voice in my head into a full-on screaming lunatic rant of dangerous persuasiveness: loud enough to make me jump, to spring me into action, to make me buy two bottles of screech and two packs of cigarettes and go home and write and write until I had nothing left inside me but the scraped-clean walls.

I wanted to go to Puerto Rico fifty years ago and join Thompson on his escapades. But it wasn't the drinking: it was the adventure, the unknown, the chance to see and see anew. Eventually I went to sleep, and probably dreamed fright and screech. When I woke up I felt the difference. I was now hungover, but the weight of the burden had shifted: it was in my hands instead of on my back. I already had the bug, but now it had been stirred and awakened, and so had I, and I immediately began planning my escape from Moose Jaw.

Conway was a friend of mine from my days in Montreal. We were semi-professional drunks back then, and our lives revolved around three things: alcohol, women and music. We forged a partnership through that triumvirate with countless nights of bars and bottles and singing in the old rainy streets. He was still there, about to graduate from university and trying to scrape together enough cash to take a trip to India; the plan was no more detailed than that. Once he told me about it, the thought grabbed me and wouldn't let go. The wheels began turning, and the machinery began to gather unstoppable momentum: within a few short months I had acquired plane tickets, vaccines and visas, quit my job, tossed my life into a storage locker and flown across Canada to meet Connie and leave Moose Jaw behind me.

Suddenly I was at a departure gate at Kennedy Airport in New York with no genuine or true knowledge of how I had arrived there. For the first time, the great and looming reality of going to India with reckless abandon and no-plan arrogance hit me.

I knew I was running, even then. If you look on a globe, India and Saskatchewan are nearly exactly opposite each other; I couldn't have picked a farther place to flee to. But I could not manage to understand what I felt, not then, not as I sat waiting for the culmination—really, only the beginning—of the biggest decision of my life up to that point.

Here was the cliff I had run towards; now, balancing on the edge, peering down at the true depth of the plunge before me, reality returned: I had quit my job, the first proper writing gig I'd ever had, and bought a one-way ticket to a developing country with a former-cokehead drinking buddy I had known for barely two years.

But maybe, I thought, maybe this feeling of unreadiness is a good thing. Great adventures are forged from everything except planning. Chaos breeds excitement; bravery is needed. When nothing is certain, anything is possible.

And yet, I felt detached. Surely I was conscious of what was about to happen. Or maybe not; perhaps my mind was so alarmed at the events I had sent colliding into each other that it had pulled some cognitive plugs simply to cope.

DELHI

Squeezing through an undersized looking-glass

L anded, after twenty-four hours in transit…
…O Christ, break down the door. Let me off this thing.
Come on come on come on, okay, out. Staggering down through tunnels and strange corridors leading to more corridors. Immigration check. Next: a baggage carousel. Soldiers assault rifles police. Stay calm. No white faces anywhere. Stay calm, stay awake, look sober. Carousel is stopped. Bags luggage parcels piled on the floor. Connie says ours are there we go and grab them now what. Look up, giant signs for customs… small red sign points down corridor to declare, huge green sign leads out to light to air to exit to not-declare.

We declare nothing and waltz past the soldiers police assault rifles with surging paranoia… outside, into a mass frenzy of dark faces and horrible smells.

Conway: My friend recommended me a hotel, don't worry, I'll call them, don't worry.

He goes to a makeshift kiosk with phones and pays a man two

rupees to make a call. He steps inside a wooden box and dials a number. He comes back and pays two more rupees goes inside dials the number. Comes back and throws the book at me, I go and tell the phone man the number, he demands more rupees. I argue. He argues. I turn to walk away and he gives up and dials the number for me. A voice answers.

> Me: Is this Hotel Xxxxx?
> Voice: Sir, Hotel Xxxxx.
> Me: Where are you?
> Voice: Sir, %%%%%%%.
> Me: What was that?
> Voice: Sir, %%%%%%%. No
> problem. Room you like?

The line goes dead. The phone man demands more rupees. Angermadness. No focus whatsoever. Shouting and smells surround us. Conway, find a map. Conway, wake up, you bastard. Give me that map. Here, Paharganj. (A man overhears and asks if we want to go to Paharganj for one thousand rupees. We ignore him.)

Back inside, to the government prepaid taxi booth. Wait, they all say 'government'. And they all look like villains.

Get in line. Man in vague uniform tells us Paharganj is seven hundred rupees plus sixty-rupee processing fee. I refuse. He says we must. I walk away, he says okay, fill out this form, pay seven hundred twenty, now take this to the driver, you must sign it at the destination or he will not get paid.

We find the driver and go for a long ride into the city. Then he stops and says this is as far as we paid for, but he'll take us the final three kilometres for one hundred rupees cash. I check the slip and this is indeed the address that was written down. I sign it and Conway and I get out and walk in whatever direction we had been driving.

On a corner in front of a dilapidated building: seven people, thin and swollen with hunger, a ragged collection of bodies, various ages, barely clothed, lying on the concrete in the shade of the building. The stark-naked infants lie with the dogs and both babies and animals alike look sickly and are not moving. I can't tell which ones are dead; maybe all, maybe none.

We find New Delhi train station and Paharganj district next to it: filthy, disgusting, decrepit, crowded, dogs, cows, goats, humans all piss and shit in the street. Garbage crunches underfoot. Shouting, everyone is shouting at us, trying to sell us scarves or cigarettes. The three- and four-storey buildings cramp the narrow crooked street and look like they should all be torn down immediately. Barely enough room to walk in the crush of crowding Indians.

(I loved it; this was definitely not Moose Jaw.)

Shit, where are we? Hotel signs everywhere, most written on cheap Bristol board or painted in black on the concrete walls. We march on, looking for the name of one particular hotel, finding one that sounds similar but is horribly overpriced. Then a tout approaches and shoves into our hands a business card bearing the name of the hotel we are searching for. Hey hey, where is this place? He is all too happy to show us, through a maze of alleys with open sewers, and we take an ensuite double room with a television for four hundred fifty rupees per night.

Exhausted and withering, we dump our bags and set out to explore Delhi at nine o'clock in the morning.

Subcontinental spittle, and the Mango Lassi incident

L ooking back on the madness of that first day, those initial steps into the country that would be my home for the following five months, I'm struck by how well we performed given how unprepared we were for the reality of India.

Delhi is, was, dirty. That is putting it mildly: there was no air in the city, only smog and smoke, and almost everyone had some sort of bandana or mask over their face during the morning and afternoon traffic rushes. The streets were crowded and old, and they glimpsed the history of the country by giving the impression that much has and does happen there. Poverty was everywhere, and the poor seemed a special kind of life: lively and colourful, easy-going and fierce at once.

Conway and I wandered through the bazaars and markets for a few wide-eyed hours, electrocuting our senses with each new scene we stumbled upon before finding our way back to the hotel and sleeping away much of the afternoon. After an evening walk and some food from a restaurant (we were still too green to try our hand at street food), we collapsed into bed, exhausted from a mad two days.

But I went to sleep happy that night, happy that I had flung myself halfway around the world, hoping India was ready to catch me.

✿

We woke up early the next morning and headed out. The first goal of the day—and what would become the first goal of every day for the next five months—was chai. Sweet, sensual, truly life-sustaining, masala chai is the entire magic of India in a single glass: hot, spicy, sugary, fresh, with countless variations on a simple idea. We didn't walk far down the main road before we found an old man at an ancient bicycle-wheeled pushcart slinging made-on-the-spot milky tea. Conway and I stood and sipped from burning hot glass tumblers as we watched Delhi get ready for another day.

The scene was at once the same and completely different from every big city I'd been to: boys sat on the sidewalk in their under-wear scrubbing metal pots to prepare lunch at the many food stands; motorcycles and rickshaws shuttled Indians of all ages to work or school or places I could only guess at; ordinary people going about their daily business.

We walked in the direction of the Red Fort in Old Delhi, separ-ated from Paharganj by the rail line. Dust and smog and noise shrouded the city as people worked, or got ready for work, or stood around in groups drinking chai, perhaps discussing last night's cricket match against Australia (which we had watched with several beers before supper, trying to decipher the strange rules and scoring). Piles of garbage smoked in the street as we walked; not far away, a man hand-washed his brand-new blue Suzuki sedan.

We fulfilled our tourist obligations at the fort and paid our respects at Gandhi's grave at the sombre Rajghat. They were remarkable sights, but I left with a sense of boredom; I wanted to get back to the city as quickly as possible. Delhi was not these ancient bricks and mortars, nor a quiet memorial to the father of modern India. I was hooked on the markets, the bazaars, the noise, the filth, the excitement, the people. I wanted to get back to Paharganj and its populace of beat-down, often dirty folks with hard lives and lots of mouths to feed: the working poor. I could never have imagined anything like them. Whatever their situations may have been (I could only speculate), they were always out on the street, selling and laughing and joking and shouting to each other with a remarkable buoyancy. But with the tourists they were all business.

Paharganj is less a proper district than a single main drag with myriad winding tributarian alleys. The primary street is at all hours a hub of activity, and we couldn't walk through the bazaar without being offered t-shirts cigarettes knives wood carvings marble children's toys shoes toilet paper every type of clothing luggage Chinese cell phones books in all European languages good price sir come look my shop sir, all the crap they could drum up and try to gouge tourists for. The hawkers tried all sorts of various methods, sometimes all of them with one potential customer walking briskly by. Passive or polite tactics were the least-used and probably the least-successful, since the rest of the street was so damn noisy and chaotic that anyone trying to speak in this manner would never be noticed.

Then something happened, something that brought me more fully into the world I had, up to that point, only physically stepped into: a rickshaw carrying a middle-aged woman in a sari rattled past us, followed by a young boy (presumably her son) who ran after the vehicle to climb up and in and onto the seat with her. He turned and faced me and met my eyes through the rear window of the vehicle. He could not have been more than six or seven, and I smiled at him; he smiled back, uneasily but so very genuine, and they rattled off together until our eyes could no longer find each other. It was such a brief moment, so unassuming and without any extraordinary circumstances, but it gave me my first personal connection, however small, with these people I knew almost nothing about.

o

It was hard not to notice the stares. No doubt some attention is to be expected when two white men of nearly two-metres' stature venture into a country of typically short and dark-skinned people; but the type and degree of attention caught me off guard.

Many people, particularly young men, will gaze at you so long and hard that you wonder if they might be trying to drill into your skull somehow. Their faces hold looks of wonder and disbelief as though —even in major cities; even with television and magazines; even with the growing number of tourists in India—they had never before seen a person of European descent. I assumed this wasn't the case, but I couldn't figure out the social or historical mechanics behind this unnerving behaviour. It was to be a while yet before I was given my first clue.

Still, the majority of people on the street were only passively interested in our presence. While walking back to Paharganj, Conway and I passed a bus stop where many people were waiting. At the far end was a girl of about fourteen, dressed in a dark red sari with golden trim. I caught her curious eyes as we approached and smiled at her. She returned it nervously and looked away; when she looked up and saw me still watching her, she burst into a great wide grin and I couldn't help but join her.

Back in Paharganj, a woman approached Conway on the street while I was taking a picture of something. When I caught up to them, he was trying to ignore her while she shoved some papers at him. His patience wore thin and he gave her a harsh and direct "No!" and so she turned to me. The papers appeared to be a petition for something, but I wasn't really sure; I politely said, "No, thank you." She spat on me as she walked away.

My first reaction was shock, as I had not done nor said anything improper. But I also, in some way, found myself agreeing with her, for reasons I only partially understood; this was the first moment of the trip in which I felt the Rich Man's Shame, which I liken to survivor's guilt. In both phenomena, the beneficiary of a piece of good fortune—surviving a disaster in which others perish; being born into the middle class of a prosperous nation—feels inexplicable but very real guilt for benefiting while others do not. Of course, the difference between the two cases is that the dead cannot be brought back, but the lives of people can be improved; and yet it almost goes without saying that the imbalance will be with us forever in one way or another, this rich-poor divide, and we comparatively few lucky enough to have been born on the right side of it should remember that it is nothing but cosmic luck.

On the other hand, Indians have a well-deserved reputation for entrepreneurship, and a gaggle of Westerners with cash to burn and subconscious guilt is a juicy apple waiting to be picked. My first experience with this came a few hours after I had wiped the petitioner's spit off of me. Conway and I ate supper at a mid-scale restaurant to reward ourselves for coping so well in the chaos of Delhi.

We had picked a restaurant out of the guidebook that promised high-quality authentic Indian food in a classy setting. Of course, we had no appropriate clothes for the occasion; had we walked into an equivalent joint in Canada dressed in shorts and t-shirts, we would have been quickly and quietly shown the door. But in India, white skin ensures you are perceived as a high roller, both in terms of prestige and purchasing power.

The meal was all right: good, not great; about on par with your average Indian dinner back home. But it cost us twenty dollars altogether, a large and unnecessary sum considering the price of food in that part of the world. As we left with full stomachs and lighter wallets a young street boy followed us for a least two blocks: hand out, eyes wide, fully and knowingly exploiting our sense of full-stomach guilt; it might well have been a coincidence, but I would guess that he had cleverly staked out the restaurant. Regardless, he went away empty-handed and Conway and I pressed on into the smoggy noisy darkness.

We later decided to avoid such restaurants, partly to stretch our budget, but also because the food simply wasn't worth it. We had eaten an eighteen-rupee thali on the street that same day, and it was far superior to our expensive supper...

SCENE: A street-side food stand somewhere in Delhi

Me: Should we eat here?

Conway: I dunno. Looks pretty skeezy.

Me: You're right. Pretty unhygienic.

Conway: What about that place?

Me: Looks exactly the same.

Conway: Right. Look at all those flies.

Me: But the locals are eating it like crazy. It can't be dangerous, right?

Conway: Maybe they're immune to it.

Me: To what?

Conway: I dunno.

Me: Well, it's cooked.

Conway: But they're not cooking anything right now. That stuff could have been made yesterday.

(Long pause as we look up and down the street)

Me: Whatever, I'm starving.

Conway: Yeah, let's just eat it.

We ordered two thalis—stainless steel trays divided into sections for each curry, with flatbread as a utensil—and sat on the curb eating the delicious food with our hands.

☼

The smell in Delhi is really just a concentrated version of the general odour hanging over all of India. In coastal areas it drops off or has salt and fishiness added to it, and other regions have their own slight variations; but everywhere in India there lingers some mutation of this basic aromatic formula, seemingly at its most pure in Delhi, as though the scent was some national fragrance being officially issued from the capital.

Like the bouquet of a fine wine, it is complex and layered. The base of it, the heaviest element that underlies everything else, is urine. You may not be anywhere near it (though you likely are), but the smell of piss lingers and permeates everything on even the subtlest level: sniff the air anywhere in India and you will nearly always find traces of urine; often more.

Next comes garbage, the precise contribution of which varies based on the proximity and type of decomposition, but organic material is always present and generally pretty funky.

Dust and dirt also play a strong role, as do smog and pollution. But the overall smell is not entirely unpleasant: food is a major factor, with the countless street-side vendors adding their own flavours to the mix. The scent of fried dough, a whiff of chai, endless aromas of myriad curries; coriander, cloves, chillies, cumin, turmeric, garlic, ginger all waft upwards and contribute to the nasal palette of the country.

It was into this Smell that we ventured the following morning with the goal of tracking down the government tourism office for advice on booking trains and our hypothetical trajectory through India. We were shortly joined by a young Indian boy; he introduced himself as Ricky, said he was a seventeen-year-old student, and wondered if we would mind if he practised his English with us; he even offered to help us find the tourism office. He was the first local we'd met who spoke enough English to carry on a conversation of any depth, so we were delighted to talk with him.

Part of the reason Conway and I did so well in the early days—never getting significantly ripped off, so far as we could tell—was our skepticism of everyone, particularly people who approached us in the street without invitation. That strong level of distrust was likely deeply ingrained in our conversation with Ricky, but, for my part, I was curious to see what would happen: he may be trying to scam us, but that doesn't make him any less interesting.

And so we walked and talked with him about Delhi, about

Canada, about being a student, about cricket, about girls, and Ricky led us in the direction of C.P.

The heart of New Delhi is Connaught Place: a huge and unwieldy bit of urban planning (apparently regarded as a landmark development in that discipline's history) that is essentially a series of concentric circles radiating out from a centre, each with two- or three-storey block of British Raj-era buildings and arcades; our friend assured us this was the way.

Addresses are useless in a country that lacks street signs and building numbers, but an address was the only piece of information we had to locate the office, and we began to realize that Ricky's route was leading us directly away from where we believed we needed to go. He brushed these concerns off, so Conway and I simply pushed onward in our own direction. Ricky trailed along, telling us confidently that we were wrong and wasting our time; he had nothing to do that day, he said, except go play cricket with his friends, and we would be sorry for not trusting him.

We found the tourism office, precisely at the address we had, and nowhere near where Ricky insisted it was; we pointed this out to him and he shrugged and sauntered away, the poacher having lost his quarry and now in search of another.

Inside the office, we found a lovely young Indian woman who went over our rough conception of a route through her country with fluent English and a decisive pen: skip this town, do no miss this town, go from here to here instead. But the biggest alteration she made was to change the overall direction from clockwise to counter-clockwise: moving west and south from Delhi instead of east. We didn't dispute the logic of this stranger who had just decided the path we would more or less follow in the coming months, though in very unforeseen fashion.

We left Connaught Place and got drunk on beer at the hotel. It was already mid-afternoon and we were worn out from the sun. The bellhops had charged us one hundred rupees (two dollars) for each large bottle of cold Kingfisher, but we were nothing if not cheapskates, and enterprising ones at that: Conway surreptitiously tailed one of the boys to the source of the beer, a tiny general store on the main drag, where he was able to haggle the shop price down to seventy, which meant a savings of thirty rupees on each bottle we drank. Every few rupees saved could mean another day added to our travels; after all, there was a long road ahead.

❧

With several successful days under our belts, Conway and I began feeling quite comfortable in our surroundings; so much so that our natural smartassedness began to re-emerge with free rein.

Instead of simply ignoring persistent touts, we were now emboldened to engage in games of sabotage: terrible in-jokes to counter and defuse their advances. If a rickshaw driver would not stop badgering us, I would aggressively demand transport to Moose Jaw; if we were asked where we were from, we'd say Japan, or Pakistan; if they asked why we wouldn't buy whatever they were selling, we'd trap them in a ridiculous circle of spurious logic; we'd break into song; we'd quack like ducks. This all began as a way to deflect their endless offers and demands, but it became a sort of sick fun, a surrealist experiment to see what our limits were in this country and how far we could go.

I pushed the boundaries of my own sense of decency well before any external repercussions came crashing down. On a particularly hot day, I had a sudden craving for a mango lassi. Conway and I walked around Paharganj until we found two places, side by side, serving the cool yoghurt drinks.

Before I even approached them, both men were calling out to me, offering various food items. I inquired with one about the price of a mango lassi; I was told forty rupees. I went next door, and the answer was thirty-five. So I called over to the first shopkeeper that it was cheaper over here; he replied that he would do it for thirty-five as well.

This is when I backed up into the street and started pointing at the men, auctioning off the right to my business to the lowest bidder. Thirty! Okay, thirty! How about twenty-five? No twenty-five! Okay, twenty-five! Twenty! No twenty!

...And back and forth this went, a complete orientalist humiliation of two men whose lives I could never relate to. The working poor, reduced to public bartering in a foreign language with a white man from a rich country who wanted to save a few cents.

I got the lassi for twenty-five rupees, very proud of myself and thoroughly amused by my own spectacle. Connie congratulated me with some incredulousness, and though I had the sense that I had crossed some lines somehow, it wasn't until later that I realized how petty I had been.

❀

Although we enjoyed simply soaking up the bizarre cultural landscape surrounding us on the street, we still felt obliged to be good tourists and go see some major sites.

India Gate—formerly the All-India War Memorial—is a sort of Arc de Triomphe for the subcontinent. We took the obligatory photos—Conway had decided that every picture of a landmark would have him performing a handstand in front of it—and examined the structure for a few minutes before preparing to walk away...

...And then we were introduced to a part of the Indian experience which would shortly become very familiar to us: some middle-class Indian tourists asked if they could take our picture in front of India Gate. I thought it was a bit strange, but we agreed; they snapped the photo and shook our hands and went off. Then another family approached us with the same request; then another. Most wanted to pose with us in the shot. Eventually, people began queueing up while others were taking photos: we had become celebrities, attractions in our own right. At first, we found it strange and hilarious that these people would want our photos so badly, with such evident excitement.

But then it became tiring: after fifteen minutes, Conway and I started trying to turn down requests, but the people who had been waiting in the impromptu line complained that they had missed their chance with the white men. Okay, last one. Okay, one more. All right, that's it… It was at least twenty minutes before we managed to get the hell out of there, and only then by abruptly walking away from the crowd. It was a baffling experience, and I had no idea what to make of it.

In the rickshaw on the ride back to Paharganj, we were stopped at an intersection when a young girl of about six or seven appeared, wandering through traffic. She was completely filthy, a depressing real-life caricature of Pigpen from the Peanuts comics, wearing nothing but filthy panties and a filthy undershirt. Without word or gesture, she began performing on my side of the rickshaw: handstands and somersaults and backwards arches and snaking through metal rings that she carried with her. The performance lasted perhaps one minute, and was as impressive in its skill as it was disturbing in its degradation.

The girl, approaching us with her eyes wide for effect, stretched out her hand. Conway turned away; but my heart was touched by the girl and I felt obliged to give her something. I dug into my pocket for some change and found a two-rupee coin and placed it in her palm. I smiled at her. She looked at it. She looked at our driver, who said nothing and slowly turned his head away. Then she looked at me with those wide sad eyes, painful and accusatory; I could not miss their meaning: What the fuck am I supposed to do with this? I was caught off-guard: I expected her to be grateful, as all beggars and buskers are in my country when you give them some change. But the girl stood motionless, drilling her eyes into the side of my head while I faced forward and prayed for the traffic to clear so the rickshaw could drive me away from this uncomfortable moment. She said something in Hindi and indicated with her hands that she wanted paper money. I ignored her out of fear and uncertainty and shame. Why aren't we moving, goddamn it? I noticed passengers in other cars and rickshaws glancing over at the girl and I out of idle curiosity. It seemed like an eternity, but the rickshaw finally shuddered forward and we left the girl behind in the middle of the busy road.

Immediately I chastized myself: why only two rupees? What the hell difference does it make to you? Shit, you should have given her a five hundred note: that's only ten bucks! But it could change her life.

I was still caught in self-hatred from the Mango Lassi incident the previous day; I was trying to grapple with the reality of beggars, and the ethics of giving money. With only very limited experience and no informed insight into this problem, it would be some time before I began to understand things in a clearer light. (Children are often forced into begging by their families or 'owners' and can become professional exploiters at a young age; I didn't know this then, but in hindsight that girl had probably practised that face a hundred times.)

As we left our hotel that night, snaking through the labyrinth of alleys to get food and beer, Conway and I encountered the body of an old man sprawled face-down in a side street. He was not moving. There were three or four Indian men standing around, text messaging, talking; nothing about them seemed particularly urgent. We tried to ask if the old man was all right, but no one understood us.

We were faced with the uncomfortable position of being unable to assist these people (who had telephones and spoke the local language), but were blocked by the man from proceeding. And so we found ourselves stepping over the body of a man who may or may not have been dead, trusting that he was in more capable hands than ours; this was a logical, callously practical decision that left me thinking about the man for the next several hours as we wandered through the busy night.

When we came back through the alley later, the man was gone; no one could tell us what had happened.

°

The time had come to press forward with our adventure. We decided to leave Delhi the following day and take the train to Agra. The Indian Railways website supposedly allowed for online booking, but none of our credit cards would work; so we had to seek out the ticket office in the railway station, which was adjacent to Paharganj.

Our guidebook advised that the foreigners' ticket office was located on the second floor, and that many touts dressed as officials or posing as helpful strangers will try to steer tourists away from it—usually with the story that it is under repair or permanently closed—and suggest a nearby travel agent who pays them commission. And so we went with skepticism at the ready and only a vague idea of what to look for.

The ground floor of the New Delhi railway station was packed with Indians standing in line, sitting on the floor, holding children, huddling together; the huge and open station was reduced to a maze of blankets and bodies. Charting a course from one end to the other, we found a staircase and moved up to the second storey. Glancing both ways, we saw very little: no signs or offices, no people, the general ambiance of an abandoned construction site. A man appeared and asked if we were looking for the ticket office; we said yes, and he did not disappoint.

"It has been closed and moved since last year," he said. "Come, I will show you." He began to head down the stairs, but we ignored him and walked to either end of the second storey, searching for clues.

But we found nothing; not even any hints or signs about the location of the phantom office. The man, who was dressed like a generic security guard, was insistent that there was nothing to be found. I began to wonder: maybe it really did close down; maybe he's the real deal; that uniform, after all...

We followed him downstairs and began an investigation of the ground floor, much to his exasperation; it struck me that he was suspiciously persistent for someone offering to take time out of his actual job to help strangers. But, again, we came up empty-handed: not even an information booth or helpful passenger. Our general skepticism of everyone offering to aid us had been validated at every turn up to this point; now we were lost and out of ideas. Conway suggested another search of the upstairs, so we went, with our would-be guide shaking his head and coming along. This time a more thorough search uncovered a small stairwell leading up to the third storey, where we were greeted by a large sign indicating the foreigners' ticket office. Our helpful friend had vanished by this point, so we went inside and booked our tickets onward for the following day, then escaped the station as quickly as possible.

(The office was, in fact, on the second floor as promised: in North America, floor numbering starts from the ground floor, which is called the first floor; in India, as in Britain and elsewhere, the 'first floor' is the one just above ground level. Thus, the office was located on the second floor, which was also the third storey.)

Our errand completed, we ambled towards the Red Fort, where Conway had designs on taking a photo of an especially stunning mosque. But we lost our bearings and, as night fell, we wound up in the depths of Old Delhi, one of the multitude of cities that have existed on the land upon which modern Delhi now stands.

Old Delhi lives up to its adjective in every manner imaginable: crumbling buildings and roads, a mix of the very poor and working classes, completely devoid of anything to draw your average foreign tourist. But that night turned out to be one of the most remarkable experiences of my life, wandering aimlessly through endless markets and bazaars teeming with people, animals, vehicles. There were no touts because there were no tourists; there were, however, a great many children, and Conway and I had four separate occasions when groups of youngsters followed us fervently.

They all yelped with great excitement at seeing our whiteness and our heightness; some would try jumping to reach our level. We continued on, pressing forward through the extremely crowded streets as the sun set and took the light with it.

One gang of kids threw orange peels at us from behind. Some asked for our names. All of them shouted in Hindi as they trailed us. All of them asked for money. A few grabbed onto my arms and legs. The kids were apparently unaccompanied by any parent or guardian, but several adults in the streets showed displeasure at their behaviour; a few berated them sharply, and the kids would immediately retreat, sometimes for good.

The streets were wild and crazy, even at ten o'clock at night. It was hard to tell what was a market and what was just a crowded street. Very few automobiles moved through the sea of bodies; a few motorcycles tried to manoeuver, but mostly it was a crush of people and animals and wooden carts. Chaos was everywhere.

This was India: we had found the nerve centre, the very heart of, well, something; something that struck my North American sensibility as Authentically Indian. The shops were different from other parts of Delhi; there was absolutely no English spoken; no spots of bourgeoisie or modern progress, no middle-class restaurants tucked in here and there. We were the only non-Indians to be seen. Everyone was talking or shouting, trying to push through, moving around the people who had stopped to buy things from the vendors of everything on the sidelines of the madness.

We walked around increasingly disoriented, though Conway swore he knew which direction the train station was; I thought he was wrong, but I didn't really care. I wanted to wander those streets forever. Nothing there could ever be boring; every day must be different. This, the ancient idea of the street market, is pure unadulterated humanity. Who has robbed us of this in the West? Who has pushed it into the corner as a niche novelty experience that too-often requires a car to reach? Have we forgotten something that people in this part of the world have not? And look at them, these people of varying degrees of poverty and employment and respectability: everyone, together, crowded into a street market at night; there is no isolation here, no insular escapism; there is only India, and India is chaos.

Conway's directional sense did steer us back to Paharganj, and as we walked down the main road we saw two policemen talking to two men, with more men standing around watching. One of the two men was shouting at the other; he slapped him, yelled some more, then slapped him again. Then he stepped back and the cops moved in: they beat the second man—the one who was slapped—with batons and fists as he turtled on the ground. A local man next to us noticed that we were closely watching the scene and said with a smile, "Very strict. They are very serious."

AGRA

Marble and feces and cracks in the chain

Our train was supposed to depart the next morning at half-past ten, but an unexplained delay meant that it was already dark when we arrived in Agra six hours later than expected, with the by-now familiar chaos of the New Delhi train station supplanted by the completely foreign madness of the Agra terminal. Our guidebook map told us that we were a long way away from our reserved hotel; it helpfully mentioned that rickshaw drivers at the station would be more than happy to rip us off, and the best option was a prepaid taxi from the government-sanctioned booth.

This is all we were armed with when we got off the train. The moment Conway and I walked outside, we experienced the first of what would be countless ambushes by rickshaw drivers: there is nothing more juicy and saliva-inducing to these men who stake out train and bus stations than a white person with a backpack. All tour-ists pay a skin tax on nearly everything with a negotiable price, but distances are difficult to gauge in a strange city, and the drivers often extract double or triple the local fare from their prey.

We asked the shouting throng where the prepaid booth was; most of the men lost interest in us at this point, but a few determined souls grabbed our shoulders and led us towards a shack in the park-ing lot. The man in the shack was surrounded by drivers talking loudly, and when we gave him the name of our desired destination, a shouting match ensued, apparently for the rights to our lucrative asses. The man who had led us over appeared to win and we were told the price.

But the whole thing felt like a scam: it was far more wild than the prepaid booth at the Delhi airport, and the price given to us kept changing as the drivers argued in Hindi. Meanwhile, we were tired and frustrated, particularly Conway, who had gotten little benefit from his nap on the train. The six-hour train delay coupled with general exhaustion and culture shock did not leave much patience for dealing with situations like this.

It took us nearly thirty minutes of wandering, searching, talking to officials in the station, trying to confirm that this was indeed a legitimate prepaid booth, negotiating with drivers and generally expending as much energy as we could borrow on credit before we secured a fare that seemed somewhat reasonable to us. In the end, our stubborn caution likely saved about twenty cents on the fare.

In the rickshaw en route to the hotel, Conway started griping about lazy Indians and their poor work ethic and why can't they get real jobs instead of harassing him. I tried to ignore him but wound up taking a confrontational stance against his reasoning. Things were tense: the fraying had begun.

We checked into our room, which was not as clean as the one in Delhi, but still quite comfortable for the price. We dumped our bags and immediately set out in search of beer. Once armed with several tall bottles of Kingfisher, we returned to the room and played crazy eights real friendly-like.

"Do you realize we're in India right now?" I said.

"I know." He sipped his beer and looked around the room. "It's insane. Look at this place."

"Did you ever expect you'd wind up in a crummy hotel room in India, drinking beer and playing cards with me?"

"The beer and cards sound about right."

"How did we get here? It's beyond comprehension."

"We just fucking did it."

He was right. I looked at him and raised my beer. "We fucking did it." Connie touched his bottle to mine. "We fucking did it."

Our world felt secure in that moment. But once the beer had worked its magic, the conversation turned hostile once again, this time from both sides: it was shifting and unstable and largely ridiculous, but this heady talk about cultures and societies and philosophy served as our first notice that our world views and personalities may be so different as to be incompatible rather than complimentary.

I couldn't stand to hear my friend lash out with generalizations, judging people he knew nothing about, blaming the poor for being poor. After we argued about these things for some time, the final straw was some absurdly minor argument over something in the card game, which we blew out of proportion to match the mood in the room.

We finished our beers in anger and Conway shut off the lights and went to bed. I sat in my chair at the foot of the bed. As he stirred beneath the covers, he said, "We both realize this won't last six months. Maybe we should just split up now." I said nothing.

My mind started drunkenly humming in the silence of the room. I was frustrated with him, and in that moment I believed that neither one of us would budge an inch from our points of view: we were both built from stubbornness, designed to opine. This clash, which had left a seriously bad taste in my mouth, was sure to happen again.

I went to the bathroom; when I returned, Conway was snoring. I quietly ripped out some paper from a notebook and scribbled This Was Your Decision on it; this I folded around enough cash to pay back my debts from the past week.

I would wait a few more hours before leaving quietly, sneaking out of our partnership in the first light of dawn. I am, and always have been, frustrated greatly by ill-informed or intellectually hostile people. I felt a burning need to get out now.

This was not the Conway I thought I knew: the Connie in Montreal, when our nights were spent playing guitar and drinking Cheminaud all night long, telling outrageous jokes and singing at the top of our lungs in the streets. That Conway made me laugh until my bladder threatened to weaken; this Conway made me want to slip out in the night like a criminal.

I sat there for a long while before I crumpled up the note and hid it in my bag for safekeeping. There were still enough positive points in our friendship to justify sticking around. I knew there would be conflict, but I hoped at the time that they would be isolated blips, brought about by a stressful day and cheap liquor. Six months was an arbitrary number, and we intended to travel for as long as possible.

"But," I confided in my notebook, "six months is indeed a long time, and I wonder how long it will last."

º

We woke up the next day and did what all decent people visiting the city of Agra do: we went to the Taj Mahal. The roads surrounding the Taj are off-limits to motorized vehicles, ostensibly to protect the ageing building from the ravages of smog; never mind that the whole goddamn city is heavily shrouded with industrial pollutants.

Once we bought tickets and entered the grounds, the city faded away and lush manicured lawns took over. We marched forward with hundreds of other tourists, Indian and otherwise. Our first glimpse of the Taj itself was through a large marble archway which, as we neared it, framed the building strikingly. But only after passing through into the main courtyard did the scale and true beauty of the Taj become apparent: it must surely be, without question, the greatest and most poetic structural achievement in all of human history.

Conway had me take the standard photo of him doing a handstand, and we wandered down the long and beautiful walkway to the Taj itself. Removing our shoes and climbing the stairs to the enormous marble landing surrounding the structure, we joined the queue for entry, which doubled back on itself several times as it wrapped around the building. At this proximity, the Taj was larger than I expected, many storeys high and boasting tremendous girth. Inside in the pitch dark, a man with a flashlight showed us how all of the beautiful flowers and designs that covered the interior of the mausoleum were not painted but actually carved from coloured stone—individually and by hand, of course—and then carefully embedded in the marble facade. Each of these is an impressive demonstration of craftsmanship; taken together, they shift the Taj Mahal from the impressive to the incredible, from the stately to the stuff of fantasy. The care and effort and dedication needed to produce it is staggering. Nothing like it could ever be built again; it may be the pinnacle of man's egotistical love of creation.

Aside from the surprisingly transfixing and strangely emotional first sight of the Taj, the most memorable part of my visit there was actually away from the building. As we explored a mosque below and to the right of the Taj, I happened to snap a photograph of a little girl playing by herself in the empty stone square with the Taj Mahal looming behind her. She was all alone, for that moment at least, and she was far more interested in happily skipping along than in the famous testament to love and death behind her.

✳

Feeling strangely peaceful as we returned to the modern world, Conway and I walked back to the hotel to find lunch and take a nap before we opted for a cycle rickshaw to take us the three kilometres to Agra Fort. The cycle rickshaws had caught our eye since our arrival in Agra, but we had thus far only taken the motorized variety.

Our driver was an old thin man who worked very hard to move our large carcasses on his three-wheeled contraption. We tried to enjoy the views of the city from the elevated bench upon which we sat, but our consciences compelled us to focus on the struggles of our human engine. Fortunately, we hit a slight downhill section for the final kilometre, and he sat and coasted. I paid him extra. He said he would wait for us to finish at the fort and drive us somewhere else; we told him not to bother because we didn't know how long we'd be.

The fort was big and red and dramatic, but it had a tough act to follow in the Taj. The structures were empty and endless, with walkways and staircases leading tourists to whole new wings of red stone and marble. It was peaceful and beautiful; but the most memorable part was the wild monkey rifling through the backpacks that foolish tourists had left outside the gate, apparently unattended.

Two and a half hours later, as we exited the fort, the old man on the cycle rickshaw found us. Now feeling obliged to hire him, we asked to be taken back to the hotel; but this time he had to struggle against a slight incline, towing four hundred pounds' worth of able-bodied young men behind him.

"Sir, sir!" we said, "let us pedal for a while!" No-no, and he laughed at the idea. "Yes, sir, come sit. You sit, we pedal. Okay?"

A few minutes of pestering and gesturing, with assurances that we would still pay him, and the old man allowed Conway to take the driver's seat (which was comically cramped for his large frame). The old man refused to sit, however, and he moved behind the vehicle to push from the rear. He tried to prevent me from climbing out and joining him, but I insisted. And so I pushed the rickshaw alongside the driver we had hired while Conway pedalled with no one in the passengers' seats; what a sight for the locals.

The old man asked if we wanted to go shopping. We said no. He said he wanted to be honest: there were several stores that would pay him commission for bringing in tourists, even if they did not buy anything. We agreed to go if it would help him out. The driver (who reclaimed his pedals once the road flattened out) took us to a marble store, which according to the owner was run by the seventh generation of the family that produced the marble for the Taj Mahal. The owner was in his late twenties and very nice: he refused to be pushy, calling us his guests and offering us drinks of chai, which we politely declined. I was making an effort to not be overly cynical of salespeople, but I clearly saw his eschewing of the sales pitch for what it was: another sales pitch.

He took us to his workshop, where we observed his labourers making the inlay designs in the marble: the pieces set into the cut-out are tiny and numerous, as many as fifteen for a single small flower, and I watched in awe as the workers quietly went about their craft. The owner took us inside a showroom and demonstrated the change in the appearance of the Taj's marble throughout the day by lighting various bulbs beneath a marble slab. Once the show ended, we looked around a series of rooms full of sale items before thanking our host and leaving empty-handed.

After a couple more shops hawking jewellery or handicrafts (where our driver discreetly collected his commission, though we bought nothing), the old man took us back to the hotel where I paid him double the fare of the afternoon. He promised to be outside our hotel in the morning, even though we protested with honesty that we had no idea what we would be doing or if we would need a ride.

❖

Agra is not a particularly nice place for tourists. Its touts, corruption and filthiness make the rest of the country seem to sparkle by comparison. As such, while the Taj is an excellent reason to visit, Agra is not a place most travellers feel a desire to linger in.

We ate most of our meals at a resto called Joney's Place, just across the stretch of packed dirt and shit that served as a road in front of our hotel. Every other place near us, including the rooftop joint in our hotel, was very lousy, poorly Westernized and over-priced. Joney's, whose menu did somewhat cater to tourist palettes, nevertheless had sensationally good Indian food. We never had the same thing twice, so we reassured ourselves that we were still being exploratory with our eating habits, despite the fact that we were known as regulars there by the end of our time in Agra.

In the evenings, we got drunk on cola and Indian whisky, which was nearly intolerable to drink neat. Crazy eights and a rooftop terrace with a bottle of three-dollar whisky and a view of the Taj Mahal is a fine way to spend one's time in these surly bonds of Earth. The rooftop was also good for watching the local pigeon wranglers. These fellows—known as pigeon fanciers, or kabootar baz—have whole flocks completely loyal to them, and in the late afternoons they will use sticks, shouts, whistles and gestures to put their flock through aerial paces. It's an old tradition, highly respec-ted in some places. Thoroughbred birds can cost more than five thousand rupees, which is a great amount for these not-rich men.

Anyone familiar with pigeons, supposedly smart birds though they

31

may be, can understand the time and effort and patience it must take to gain the trust and loyalty of a huge flock of these birds and train them to respond instantly to every gesture or call as they swoop about the city. I watched them for hours in a peaceful trance.

Early the next morning, we were ambushed outside the hotel by our old friend the cycle driver. The look on his face, and the knowledge that he would wait for us at any hour for more generous cash, broke our hearts. But we couldn't bear to let him heave us around anymore: we apologized and politely encouraged him to go seek other customers, then piled into an auto-rickshaw in front of him and went off to the central bazaar.

As we bombed along the city streets, our driver engaged in the usual small talk about nationalities and women. And then, turning to Conway...

"Do you want to drive?"

"Hell yes!" and the rickshaw slows and he jumps into the front seat with the driver, who gives him a quick precursory explanation of the controls... and off we go, bombing through the streets in thankfully-sparse traffic as Connie pushes the engine for more speed, whooping and laughing as the buildings and people we pass blur and fall behind us.

JAIPUR

**Small children armed with projectiles,
and how to outrun a goat on a sandy mountain**

Our train to Jaipur left Agra two hours late that night, but apparently made good time en route, so that we arrived one hour late at two o'clock in the morning. Fortunately, our complimentary pick-up from the hotel we had reserved was still waiting. We checked in and took refuge in our room with what was left of the large bottle of whisky and cola we had prepared for the train ride; but we were exhausted and both Conway and I promptly passed out.

In the morning, we searched out the general post office, where we mailed some letters and postcards to loved ones. Then breakfast, which we found conveniently located right in front of the GPO. In Delhi and Agra, our standard street breakfast had been samosas served with chana masala (chickpea curry), and, of course, chai. This meal usually cost us fifteen rupees, or about thirty-three cents and, goddamn, was it good.

But in Jaipur, the standard form of serving seemed to be to tear up the samosa and add the curry on top, eating the concoction with something resembling a tongue depressor. As usual, the whole business was served in a bowl made from dried leaves, which was then discarded into large bins. Chai on the street was most commonly served in glass tumblers.

For a country with such a serious garbage problem, they seemed

33

to have certain things right; although, it should be noted, these choices are made for economic rather than environmental reasons: it's simply cheaper for the food vendors to reuse glass tumblers than hand out disposable cups, and leafy bowls are more expensive than plastic ones. Environmentalism as a by-product of capitalism; food for thought.

The Pink City district is the primary attraction in Jaipur, and Conway and I headed there straight away. The oldest part of the city is a tribute to rigid, logical civic planning. The streets follow a grid system, with each street in the commercial district dedicated solely to one speciality: textiles, jewellery, handicrafts, butchers, and so on, not unlike the aisles of a supermarket on a grander and much older scale. While most Indian cities have specialized commercial districts, the careful order of the parallel streets was a unique novelty in a country marked by its love of disarray.

We wandered through the bazaars before becoming intentionally lost in other parts of the city. This had been our general plan of action everywhere we went, particularly as a method of exploring a new place. We weren't worried about becoming irretrievably lost or wandering into the wrong part of town. This is India: to Western sensibilities, most of the country qualifies on appearance as 'the wrong part of town.' But India's is not a violent culture, religious extremists notwithstanding. Statistically speaking, since violent crime rates in India are well below those in Canada, one is in significantly greater mortal danger on the streets of Winnipeg or Regina than in the slums of India, particularly as two large white men.

As we wandered through the slums—which invariably appeared whenever we broke away from the main city areas—we soon found ourselves being followed by a pack of young children. They shouted and threw small rocks at us (in friendly fashion) as their group grew in numbers and boldness. The adults and those children too old for such silliness smiled and laughed as we passed them. We smiled back and waved and they did the same. As we walked farther, the pack of kids would suddenly stop and disperse, only to be quickly replaced by a new bunch, almost as though each juvenile gang had their own turf and dared not stray into enemy territory.

We weren't walking entirely aimlessly: Conway had his eye on the

Tiger Fort, perched dramatically atop the huge hills that loomed just beyond the slum. The fort was our compass as we tried to make our way through the neighbourhood to, hopefully, some climbable path that would take us to the top.

Eventually, kids in tow, we found ourselves in front of a huge sand dune, nearly eighty metres tall and much wider. As we stood at the base of it with our gaggle of child groupies—now numbering at least thirty—we decided to climb it and gain a view of the city. I removed my socks and shoes as the children watched closely, oblivious to what Conway and I had just spoken about in English.

Then without warning I bolted for the dune, provoking a race and gaining a huge lead that only Connie could match. We reached the top only after a battle with our legs, which were out of shape, and our lungs, which were weak from a cold we both had. But we stood triumphant-though-exhausted and watched the rugrats clamber up the hill.

We soaked up the view of the city, catching our breath. The children had brought a few goats up the sand dune with them, and one tried to eat my shoes out of my hand when I wasn't looking. We tried to talk to the kids, but they spoke no English outside of "Hello" and "I love you" and "money". I pulled out the cheap tin flute I had bought in Agra and played a touching rendition of Michael Jackson's Will You Be There? and the children fell silent in bewildered awe.

After a while of standing around, Conway and I decided to head back down. I pointed to something in the sky, and when the mass of young heads were turned I took off and began swerving down the hill at high speed. My flute, meanwhile, fell out of my bag and a young boy grabbed it. Once at the bottom, I put on my socks and shoes while the kids who had gotten hold of my flute fought over it and snapped it in half.

"You owe me a hundred and fifty rupees!" I shouted at them, palm outstretched for effect. They laughed and I laughed and I let them keep the lousy thing as a trophy.

Conway and I walked through the slums again towards the Pink City as the children pelted us with small rocks and the adults smiled. Women sitting on flat rooftops with their children encouraged their toddlers to wave at us; we were celebrities once again.

Eventually, as we moved into the busier commercial areas, our posse of kiddies gradually vanished. We wandered around until we found a chai stand, and that's where we were standing with our hot glasses when two men approached us with assurances that they didn't want to sell us anything; as sure a sign as any that they were trying to sell us something. One man was a painter and offered to take us back to his studio.

The only real danger for large white men in India is getting ripped off: flat-out thievery and muggings are rare, but cons and scams are rampant. Going, therefore, with strange men to a strange place where they will try to sell you something you do not want is of little danger so long as you keep your wallet in your pocket. Besides, there might be an interesting adventure to be had. (Not recommended for unaccompanied women of any size or depth of courage.)

At the studio, our friends introduced us to the master, who accepted us as his guests. The studio was a tiny, dark room exiting onto the street, covered with cushions on the floor and artwork on the walls. We removed our shoes and stepped into the dimly-lit room.

We were offered chai, which we said yes to and for which someone was sent out. The master also offered us beedis (a cigarette composed of cheap tobacco rolled in a tendu leaf and tied with a string, common across south Asia), which I accepted but Conway did not. There was a ceiling fan spinning at full blast, and I had to ask our hosts to turn it off as I struggled to light my beedi with matches. As I smoked with the master, he showed us the artwork for sale, which was incredibly beautiful. He tried, as expected, to sell us something, but we were not budging no matter how many cups of chai and free smokes he came up with.

"Wednesday is lucky day for business," he said, "and if you buy something, more good luck for me and my family." Whether or not this was true, I didn't much care.

"I don't believe in good luck, I believe in good business," I said. "And if I come back tomorrow and buy, it's still good business for you."

My beedi, meanwhile, kept going out, and I kept asking for more matches.

"It is different than a cigarette," said the master sagely. "A cigarette you can ignore and come back to. But if you forget a beedi, it forgets you."

He laughed uproariously at his own joke and gave me another match.

In the evening, after a good many wobbly pops with some Australian fellows on the rooftop terrace of our hotel, Conway and I headed out after dark to eat dinner at a nearby mid-scale restaurant. It was busy with a nice atmosphere, and we ate expensive thalis and some sort of chicken dish. But that otherwise forgettable meal became memorable as the catalyst for our first dose of Delhi belly.

I spent the next two days staying very close to the bathroom in the hotel. Conway, though, was only out of commission for one day, and he headed back out into the city alone at my insistence: partially because I saw no reason why my illness should interfere with his trip; but also because I thought that some time apart could do wonders for our relationship, which had not significantly improved since Agra.

After about fifty hours of gut-wrenching, toilet-tethered misery, I was feeling sturdy enough to return to the world and so we headed out into the city together once more. The two young characters who had picked us up from the train station when we arrived had told us that they did tours of the city. We had liked them immediately, so we had the hotel manager call them up—he appeared to do so very reluctantly—and they shuttled us around to various Jaipur sights. The highlight was undoubtedly the monkey temple, an old stone structure atop a hill guarded by dozens of monkeys. While our drivers waited in the rickshaw, we fed these simian sentries peanuts from our hands with the encouragement of our 'guides': three young boys who showed up and insisted on showing us the temple with hyperactive nine-year-old gusto. We gave them a solid tip at the end.

Back with our two drivers, a cop pulled our rickshaw over and reprimanded them: neither one was wearing the required uniform; a two-hundred-rupee bribe greased the slippery wheels of justice and we continued on. Conway and I offered to repay our friends for the shakedown money afterwards, but they wouldn't hear of it.

They took us to do some shopping, at their suggestion. We arrived at a textiles factory that produced and sold everything from scarves to tablecloths to bedspreads to suits. Connie and I examined some scarves and shawls with the intention of buying several as gifts to send home. The salesman was shrewd in making us feel shrewd, knocking off several thousand rupees from the total and reluctantly giving us deals. I left with several shawls of very good quality and the sense that I had gotten a good deal for my money.

As we headed back to the hotel, Conway started musing about buying a guitar, something we had agreed upon during our tedious days of illness. All the music stores we had looked at previously had shown us low-quality instruments for unreasonable prices, but our reliable drivers took us to a shop that they promised would be able to help us. We found a small guitar that seemed decent (a 'Givson') and, over the course of an hour, talked the price down and the extras up. In the end, we left with the guitar, two extra sets of strings and a case for half the original asking price. We named it Shiva.

Things seemed to be getting back to normal between Conway and I, and our humours had greatly improved. But after dinner, as we got ready for bed, Conway suddenly said he would offer to buy me out of my half of the guitar.

"Just so there's no trouble when we split up."

I thought about it for a moment and turned him down. He asked if I wanted to buy him out; I said no. Without further comment or argument, he pouted and sulked on his side of the room for the rest of the night, putting in his headphones and ignoring me.

My thinking was that I wanted to try and make our partnership work for as long as possible, my secret aborted escape plan in Agra notwithstanding. We were less than three weeks into our trip and already discussing the possibility of splitting up. My stubbornness would not admit failure so easily; not to mention the fact that when we did get along (which was still a lot of the time), we did so famously. To my mind, having one person buy the other out of the guitar was just conceding that a break was inevitable. It was something we were still partners in: like married couples who stay together for the kids, perhaps we could stay friends over a guitar.

Phantom tigers and friendly celebrities

C onway and I did not speak on friendly terms until we arrived in Sawai Madhopur the next day. Sawai is a tiny village southeast of Jaipur, and the only call for any tourist to go there is Ranthambore National Park, reportedly the place with the best chance to spot one of the world's few remaining wild tigers.

Of course, 'best chance' is a relative term; there are only a handful kicking around, and the park is so big and forested that seeing anything is unlikely.

Upon arriving at our hotel, we were approached by a young white couple with a six-year-old boy; they asked if we wanted to split the cost of a driver to tour the old fort in the park before our arranged tiger safari in the afternoon, and we agreed.

More thorough introductions followed as we rode along in our spacious jeep (not the brand, but a catch-all term for a supersized SUV). The family was from Iceland: she was a journalist, he was a politician, and as they told us stories about their lives back home it became evident that these were Icelandic celebrities. The woman reluctantly admitted this, but they were both extremely grounded and friendly (presumably, being famous in Iceland is even less of an ego trip than being famous in Canada).

Both the fort and the tiger safari were enjoyable—driving around a jungle is usually a memorable experience—though the latter was fruitless, a few deer being our only wild sights. We had already booked our train tickets out of town, to Pushkar via Jaipur and Ajmer, for the following day. The Icelandic duo were heading that way as well, and we noted the name of the hotel they were planning on staying at.

Conway and I left for Pushkar the next day, arriving very late at night after a jeep ride from the train station through the mountains.

The little bit of scenery that we could discern through the cloak of darkness, combined with the twisting, near-vertical climb of the jeep, was enough to keep us awake. We eventually arrived at a road where we were told to get out and walk through a narrow alleyway to Hotel Milkman, our place of lodging.

The hotel was a vertical imagining, nothing but stairs right up to the rooftop. Along the way were a couple storeys of concrete rooms, a restaurant on the third floor, a garden on the fourth floor, and endless friendliness from the family who ran the joint. We checked in and quickly found our Icelandic friends in the restaurant; they were off to bed, but Conway and I sat down for beer and muesli (kept separate, of course, until the stomach). Then we grabbed a couple more beer and headed to our room.

Milkman is a strange place, but undeniably inviting. Like the town itself in some ways, it has adopted the 1960s-era hippie philo- sophy of much of the clientele it caters to. This is superficially evid- ent in the brightly painted walls and quasi-erotic frescoes on the walls: all Indian, to be sure, but of a flavour that appeals to the white folks with dreadlocks.

We dropped our bags in our room—which featured a cozy double bed with a painting of an Indian man becoming very friendly with two Indian women whose breasts had fallen out of their clothes— and wandered up to the rooftop to have a look at things.

The view seemed like it would be nice in the daytime, and the general stoner-pad ambiance was at least a familiar vibe. Some people were camped out on the roof in small tents, smoking joints and playing traditional drums. The cool night made me feel peaceful as I looked out at the sleeping town, dark and quiet at this hour

As we walked back down, I heard singing: it was lovely, two soft female voices singing gently, a familiar but forgotten song. I saw the two girls sitting on a bench swing, their backs to us, playing a small guitar for a few people sitting in front of them. I decided not to intrude, but the singing stayed with me as we walked back to our room.

PUSHKAR

**Young nubile Austrians,
drugged milkshakes,
and poor hash from poor farmers in alleys**

Pushkar is a portal out of India for Western travellers, which is a strange fact considering the many official prohibitions in the pilgrimage town. Yet every amenity is available for weary tourists, one way or another: drugs, booze, Nutella, omelettes, brewed coffee, sit toilets. In short, Pushkar is a drop-out zone, one of many places to go if you want a break from India.

Conway and I wandered around the town, through the bazaars and down to the ghats (large stone steps) by the lake. There was no water in the lake, and there hadn't been for years, apparently. There were, however, plenty of other tourists out and about, and a large number of young couples with babies and children.

As we ambled through the town under the hot sun, a group of three young Indian women, dressed like gypsies, approached and asked if we wanted to come with them to their shop. We said no, but they were persistent. I was firm with them and we turned to continue. One of them grabbed my hand and started drawing on it with henna ink.

"What the hell is wrong with you?" I shouted as I jerked my hand away. She smiled and told us again to come to their shop; the subtleties of advertising were lost on these women.

I looked at my hand: she had branded me with a large ink blob

41

which took the vague shape of a Z on the back of my hand. Conway was laughing his ass off, so I seized his arm and pressed my ink onto him.

"Jesus fuck!" he sputtered, jerking away from me as I had from the gypsy. The ink left him with a shapeless spot on his forearm much like a large birthmark.

I laughed and he glared at me, but I held up my Z hand, which now had smushed into Rorschach weirdness. We both laughed and yelled back at the gypsy women as we sauntered away.

Neo-hippies and clandestine drugs aside, Pushkar is first and foremost a Hindu pilgrimage site and one of the oldest cities in India. There are over five hundred temples in the small town, but the two most renowned sites are the Brahma Temple, which is the only temple in the country devoted to the creator of the universe, and the Savitri Temple. Savitri was the goddess wife of Brahma until he married his second wife, Gayatri, in Savitri's absence. Naturally, Savitri was displeased and she pouted at the top of a high mountain, refusing to come down. Thus, the Savitri Temple stands high above the town, reachable only by a long winding stone staircase; in deference to the spurned goddess, it is always visited by pilgrims prior to any worship of Gayatri.

"Look up there," said Conway, pointing to the Savitri Temple looming in the distance. We stared at it for a while before he said, "Let's do it." He and I looked at each other and wordlessly set off through the twisting streets. Coming across a white couple walking in the other direction, we asked them if we were going the right way.

"Yeah," gasped the girl; they were pouring sweat and breathing heavily. "It's just through there. Bring water."

We carried on and found the start of the steps just around the corner: they curved and climbed up along the sharply rising hill, leading up to the old temple perched high above the city. Intimidating would be an understatement.

Conway decided to get a lead and began by sprinting up the first forty steps or so before collapsing and gagging for breath. The sun was hot and the air over the dry lake was strangely muggy. Within two minutes of beginning the climb we were roasting, and Connie took off his t-shirt, which is very much verboten for men in northern India.

"I'll slip it back on if we pass someone."

And so we climbed. And climbed. We tried telling jokes or making conversation to pass the time, but that only made us more winded. Then, while we hiked with our heads down, trying vainly to suck air, a young Indian family heading down passed us. We didn't see them approaching, and so Connie remained shirtless. The temple is, of course, primarily a religious site, and you could equate the look from the pilgrims to what you might receive if you walked into the Notre Dame Basilica without pants.

After what seemed like an eternity (but was probably closer to forty-five minutes) we reached the top and found a man at a kiosk selling bottled water at thrice the normal price, not that we cared what it cost at that moment. I quickly drank one and a bottle of Coke, which was pure salvation.

We ventured into the stone temple, which was drastically underwhelming. This is what we climbed for? Like most Hindu temples, it had the requisite small closet with the appropriate deific statue and neon light show. The remainder was empty space: no carvings on the walls, no intricate paints or designs; just stone. I suppose once you haul all your stone blocks up to the top, you probably don't feel very creative anymore.

The view salvaged the experience: everything was hazy from the heat and dusty desert air, but we could see a long way down the valley. A construction project was underway, a massive canal to bring water to the lake. The landscape seemed so very strange, foreign, slightly unreal: like a Hollywood interpretation of India. Perhaps it was just that so many of the stereotypes of the imagery of the country seemed true at that moment, high above the desert.

We found the journey down the hill to be far easier, of course. As we reached the bottom of the stairs we found two tourists about to begin the upward journey.

"Is it worth it?" asked one.

"Yeah," I said, "but bring some water."

*

We got a bit lost on the way back to the hotel. The alleyways all seemed the same and we couldn't figure out which way was north as we roamed the ancient town. Once we had our bearings, we were approached by an old Indian man who said he was a farmer and wanted to sell us whatever we wanted. That particular phrasing usually means things you're not supposed to sell or buy. I asked if he had hashish; indeed he did—on his person, in fact, which was handy.

Conway felt the pressing call of nature, so he went on ahead to the hotel while I followed the fellow into an alley. He produced the black substance, wrapped in plastic. I smelled it. I picked a piece off with a fingernail and tasted it. It seemed like hash to me.

The old man wanted a thousand rupees for what he claimed was ten grams but was clearly about five. That's about twenty dollars, and I was well into the bargaining culture by this point. I bartered hard and got him down to five hundred rupees. But when I opened my wallet I found only a one thousand note inside, so we had to walk until he found someone who could break it, which was a bit awkward. He gave me four hundred back and pleaded for a hundred rupee tip for himself.

"No way, a deal's a deal."

"But my farm is dying, I have no money."

"You agreed to the price my friend." He gave me the money. Charity is one thing; begging is another; but this was about business, and I wasn't about to let this man guilt me out of my money to go spend it on who-knows-what. You don't tip your dealer, especially when he tries to take it out of your pocket.

I stopped to buy rolling papers and more cigarettes before heading back to the hotel. Conway was getting out of the shower when I returned. I told him I was going to shower and that he should wait for me on the roof. I left him the ingredients—cigarettes, rolling papers and hashish—and told him to bake a cake.

When I had cleaned up and made my way upstairs he was smoking a cigarette and playing guitar in the shade. There were a few tourists off by themselves near the tents with their tabla drums. I sat down and grabbed the pack of cigarettes. As I pulled out a smoke, I saw the cake inside the pack.

"Well done," I said, taking both a cigarette and the joint. I passed the latter to Conway and he lit it. Just then the boy from the kitchen arrived with two large beers.

"Please, keep these on the floor," he said nervously. Given the number of tourists in this dry town I imagined that circumventing the rules had been a regular order of business for decades; then again, I wondered what the punishment or 'fine' would be. We promised to be discrete and he left.

Conway passed the joint to me. I pulled hard and held in the smoke, figuring that Indian hash would either be stupendous or a dud, though the option of poisonous also crossed my mind briefly. I couldn't tell what my accomplice was thinking, but given that he was also an enthusiastic user of substances he seemed bit hesitant; he must have been pondering the same thing.

We passed it back and forth, smoking our cigarettes when we didn't have the joint, then playing guitar when our cigarettes were finished.

"I don't feel anything."

"Me neither. Lousy bastard farmer."

"What did you pay for it?"

"Five hundred for about five grams."

"Shit!" He thought for a moment. "Well, I guess that's not that bad, really."

I nodded mindlessly and sipped my beer. The view from our couches on the shaded roof was quite scenic: low-rise buildings below us shining in the bright sun; the sounds from the street and the bazaar rising up to our level and mingling with the strumming of the guitar. Then, an idea.

"Hey," I said, grabbing the menu on the table, "what about those lassis?"

We had taken note the night before that the hotel had special lassis on their menu, 'special' being code for bhang. Bhang is basically pulverized marijuana, though there is often an extra hallucinogen added to the mixture. This herby pulp is legal in the state of

Rajasthan and sold in restaurants and government shops (though it's banned in Pushkar), and most often consumed in the form of bhang lassi: because who doesn't like drugs in their yoghurt-based drinks?

There was no explicit mention of bhang on the menu, of course, so I went down to the kitchen to make sure it wasn't just a fancy yoghurt shake. I wandered into the kitchen and asked the cook what was in a special lassi.

"Oh, very special," he said with a grin.

"Good. Two extra-special lassis to the roof. Thanks."

I went back up and had another cigarette with my beer as Connie played guitar. Fifteen minutes later, the boy brought our escapist beverages: two tall glasses with nuts and pomegranate seeds and yoghurt coloured with tiny green flecks. We toasted to Pushkar and tipped the glasses back. There were straws, but the chunky nature of the drinks subverted them.

It tasted like herbs. Not particularly like marijuana, just a vague flavour of something, like fresh oregano. It took some getting used to—herbs and fruit and yoghurt—but it didn't taste all that bad.

"Drink it slow," warned Conway, and I knew he was right. Put it down. Don't rush it. More will come.

We drank our beers and smoked our cigarettes while passing the guitar back and forth, ordering more beers, sipping the lassis. The mid-afternoon peak of sun was winding down and the city sounded far away as the drugs kicked in.

Not unlike ganja butter, I thought, noting the body high and the fullness of the effect in me. I felt saturated with excellence. This must be why the hippies come to India: it just feels good to get stoned in this ancient place.

Conway started playing a riff on the guitar. I couldn't tell if it was particularly good or not but he was really into it, playing it over and over with sincere gusto. Suddenly he stopped and shoved the guitar at me.

"Okay, that's the riff," he said with what seemed like horrifying enthusiasm. "Now play something on top of that."

"Huh?"

"On top of the riff. We're writing a song."

"We are?"

His frustration became apparent. "Yeah man, just... make something up."

"Fuck off. I'm stoned."

"Me too!" He laughed hysterically; maybe even menacingly.

°

A few hours later, the drugs seemed to have plateaued but were still strong with us.

"I'm going to piss."

I don't know if Connie heard me; he just kept playing with an intense and determined glaze over his face.

I went downstairs and used the toilet. When I popped into the kitchen to order more beers, I ran into one half of the Icelandic couple. She may or may not have picked up on my internal strangeness, but I felt awkward and wonderful, so I told her we were drinking the lassis. She seemed supportive but not very interested in carrying on the conversation; I don't suppose I can blame her.

I returned to the roof with the beers to find my partner engaged in conversation with two young beauties. And I mean young: high school, at best.

"Man, I don't want another beer."

Conway was sitting by himself on one couch, the two girls together on a loveseat. One was short with brown hair, a pretty-almost-cute face and lovely curves, not to mention her ample chest which threatened to topple her short body forward. The other was a long and lean blonde, a face like an attractive-but-unknown actress you immediately recognize because she's been in everything. The shorter one held a small guitar.

I introduced myself and they offered lovely smiles. Yikes. How old are they? And how much do I care?

The shorter well-endowed one was Eni, the tall blonde was Anja. I sat down next to Conway and put the beers on the table in front of us.

"Well, don't drink it then," I told him. "Perhaps one of you ladies would like a malty beverage?"

After an uncomfortable length of blank stares and silence I said the word 'beer' and they declined.

"Where are you from?" I asked as Eni and Connie mindlessly picked at their guitars.

"Austria."

I grabbed the pack of cigarettes and offered them one, but they declined. No drinking, no smoking, shy, very young, obviously inexperienced: next, please.

"Okay," said Conway with palpable impatience, "sing it." Eni smiled as she set her fingers on the frets and started strumming a very familiar tune that I couldn't place; not until Anja opened her mouth and let out her impossibly sweet, soft voice with the lyrics of Bitch…

> I'm a bitch, I'm a lover,
> I'm a child, I'm a mother,
> I'm a sinner, I'm a saint,
> I do not feel ashamed

Suddenly, I actually liked that song.

I stared at Anja a little dumbstruck. The drugs didn't help me hide my amazement. When they finished the song, Anja looked very bashful, even more so when we told them how fantastic that was and, please, play another.

They pulled out a songbook they had been compiling and we flipped through it to see what Conway and I could recognize: there were some American and British songs we knew, and even some Leonard Cohen that we jumped all over.

The four of us spent the rest of the night talking and playing music. Anja moved over to the couch with Conway and I sat next to Eni. More beer and smokes; some food, why not. The girls were both eighteen, indeed right out of high school, and yet I couldn't decide which one I found more attractive. At midnight we were told by the hotel staff to pack it in, and Conway and I began eyeing each other to see what the next move was.

"Which room are you guys in?"

"Oh, we're sleeping on the floor in the restaurant. They didn't have a room for us."

"Are you alone in there?"

"No, the cooks sleep there, too."

"Well, if you're not tired, 'cause we're not, you're welcome to come hang out in our room, if you like."

They looked at each other with small smiles; and declined.

We said it was nice to meet them, and we all walked downstairs together. How long are you staying? they ask. We booked our ticket onward to Bikaner for the day after tomorrow, we say. We're staying a few days longer than that, they tell us; just mentioning.

We made plans to meet in the afternoon and climb the smaller, closer mountain temple. I followed them into the kitchen and asked the cook for another beer. He obligingly crawled out of his bed on the floor to retrieve it for me and I felt slightly guilty and very white.

I bade the ladies good-night and headed back to the room. Conway had found a terrible movie on the English-language channel and we lounged on the bed and shared the beer.

"Oh God!" he said. "I can't stop thinking about her tits!" I passed him the beer. "Didn't you think she was hot?"

"Eni's too short for me," I said. "She is definitely cute. But I'd probably prefer Anja. Man, she can sing."

He passed the beer back as a vampire attacked someone on television.

✿

We didn't see the girls the next afternoon and our arranged time to meet and climb to the small temple came and went. Conway and I had wanted to go and watch the sun set from that vantage point, but we didn't want to go without the girls: our minds were running wild with imaginative designs that were less than virtuous.

As the clock ticked the day away, we eventually decided to go by ourselves, lest we miss the experience on our last full day in Pushkar. We left a note for the ladies and started walking.

The temple was close to our hotel, and we only had to climb for ten minutes before we found ourselves near the top. We stopped and sat on the steps, watching the ancient city darken below to the soft strumming of our guitar. Then an old man came to us from the dark temple up the steps. He spoke no English, not a word: he tried to communicate with gestures and select Hindi words, but it wasn't getting through. We thought he was telling us to leave.

Then he started singing; well, chanting... sort of. It was strangely hypnotic. He started enunciating the lyrics and encouraging us to sing along. Conway loved him. We came to a general agreement about what the old man was saying to us: judging by his appearance, he was a sadhu (holy man), possibly the caretaker of the temple, and he was trying to teach us something about something. Eventually he got pushy about whatever he was trying to say and we left.

Back to the hotel, where we found a note from the girls slipped under our door: they were sorry to have missed us; they were going out for dinner; they hoped they'd see us later. As we stood there reading the note, the Icelandic couple came down the stairs and asked if we'd like to join them for dinner.

The five of us, including their toddler son, headed out to a restaurant that they had been to a couple nights previous. It was down towards the non-lake, occupying the three upper floors of a concrete building. We opted for a rooftop table.

As we sat down and placed our orders, the lights went out everywhere except for another tourist restaurant in the building across the street, which must have had a generator, and which was made all the more conspicuous as the only source of electric light in the city.

"Look! The stars!" someone said.

I looked up and saw the beautiful star-spotted sky laid bare by the power outage. Practically the whole town was black, and the mountains surrounding us obstructed the lights from other settlements. The only place I had ever seen stars so clear and bright and unadulterated by electric lights was in rural Saskatchewan; as I sat there, revelling in the Indian night sky, I thought of Moose Jaw.

Just then, our fat, flirtatious, white hippie waitress came and told us that, because of the power outage, some of our food would be late. We settled in, ordered more vodka cocktails and waited for our grub in the dark.

Many drinks later, the food arrived and we ate, and drank some more, and then wandered back to our hotel together, four drunks and a child. The streets were completely empty, even though it was only eleven o'clock; this was normal, as most of India shutters its shops and stays at home once suppertime is over.

The door to the hotel was unlocked, but the girls of the family slept in the lobby with a guard dog who barked at everything, so we woke most of the building with our arrival. We scurried past the hound and startled sleepy women and climbed the stairs quickly. The Icelanders called it a night, but Conway and I stopped in the kitchen for beer. The cooks were lying on their mattresses watching a movie on television. The girls were nowhere to be seen. We took the beers and climbed up to the roof, where we heard giggling and guitars as we approached.

Anja and Eni were sitting on floor cushions. Their laughter went silent as they saw us.

"Hello, girls," I said.

Giggle.

We sat down with them and told them about the temple and how it was too bad we had missed them.

"Yes, sorry," said Eni with her lousy English and lovely accent. "We were having a lunch, and shopping then."

Drunk though we might have been, and Austrian though they might have been, there appeared to be something... off about the girls.

Suddenly Anja stood up; well, actually, she moved very slowly and carefully as she made her way to the swing bench and lay down upon it. Her new posture prompted her to let out a very dramatic sigh, which caused Eni to stop playing guitar and look over at her friend; this silent exchange set off another fit of hysterical giggling.

"You guys okay?" asked Conway.

They nodded and laughed and laughed and giggled and they couldn't stop but I wished they would because it was just too ridiculous for my drunk mind at that moment.

Eni sputtered as she began to get her laughter under control. She struggled to speak: "W-w-w-w-e drank, we drink the lassis!"

More giggling; and it made sense.

"When?"

"This afternoon. When we find your note."

"Wait, you each drank one?"

More giggling and the answer became apparent. Conway and I had each had one to ourselves and it launched us into the sky. These girls were not large men with a respectable amount of experience under their belts; they were kids, and they were gone-zo.

The conversation went nowhere: they were too whacked. Anja became very quiet and Eni kept giggling and then suddenly they apologized but they had to go to bed. They scampered downstairs and my watch said eleven-thirty.

"Come on," I said to Conway, "let's go watch TV."

"Man," he said, fighting gravity to get off the ground, "those tits…"

Strange Ukrainian in a train station

We changed our train tickets the next morning to give us more time with the girls. I had made up my mind to make a move on Anja before we left, but the day after they drank the bhang lassis she became quite sick and Eni spent her time taking care of her friend. So Conway and I spent the next two days by ourselves, getting stoned during the day and drunk at night, wandering the holy Hindu streets with enhanced minds.

Eventually, it became time to move on, and no one was happier than I: Pushkar is a place to unwind and relax, take things slowly, decompress from India. I wanted none of that. I loved the road, and all the chaotic trappings that came with it. Moose Jaw is a world away from Pushkar, but I began to feel the familiar sense of complacency creeping in; so we headed for Bikaner.

But first we had to stop for a few hours in Jaipur yet again, where we changed trains and wasted an afternoon around the station. I met a very odd Ukrainian fellow there: young, with a cast on his foot and hobbling on crutches, wearing absolute rags for clothes. He looked like shit; he looked like he had been living on the streets of India for years. In fact, he had just arrived from the Ukraine two days earlier. He was a musician—so he claimed—and was going to make money playing solo gigs of some kind around India. Indians love Western music, he said in very disjointed English. He had broken his foot a week ago, but didn't have the vocabulary to explain how. What sort of mind believes it a good idea to come to a developing country with no clothes, no money, poor language skills and a freshly broken appendage I have yet to understand.

We left the Uke at the station with our best wishes and headed for Bikaner. Our train pulled in at four o'clock in the morning and we grabbed a rickshaw from the sparse early-hour selection crowding around us and headed for the Camel Man.

The Camel Man was listed in our books, highly touted as the finest and most reliable trek operator in Bikaner. He also ran a guesthouse on the outskirts of town, and so we showed up there in the middle of the night with no reservation and banged on his door. A boy answered and let us in without a word as he rubbed sleep from his eyes. We were led into a nicely decorated den and left standing there, presumably to wait for something. Suddenly, the ornate double doors opened and a burly Indian man in a plush housecoat burst into the room with open arms and far too much energy and bellowed, "My friends!"

This was, evidently, the Camel Man.

BIKANER

A camel is like a big horse

For the record, Bikaner is dull and largely uninteresting, bordering on lousy. We were there for one reason, and that was camels. The day after we arrived, Conway and I found ourselves palpably excited at the thought of riding strange beasts into the desert on an overnight excursion. I'd never seen a camel before; my primary images of it were from playing the Sega Genesis version of Aladdin, and perhaps from a television documentary I once watched and forgot. What do you expect from an animal you've never met?

After breakfast, one of our guides showed up and ushered us into a jeep. We were driven even farther out of town to a small village that had started to become part of the outskirts of Bikaner. Children played cricket in the dirt road and women carried heavy things on their heads and these two white guys wanted to pay money to ride camels. So be it.

And there they were, tied to a big tree: two weird and foreign beasts who were to be our ungainly steads for the next twenty-four hours. They were huge, far taller than I was expecting. Conway and I, both about six-and-a-half feet in height, were dwarfed. How the hell do you get on these suckers?

As I was contemplating a running leap, one of the guides walked briskly over to the camel and shouted at it. It moaned or groaned or perhaps cursed at him and backed away. He grabbed its reins and shouted again, and the camel kneeled on the ground.

Having spent significant time growing up immersed in the farm life of rural Saskatchewan, I'm comfortable around animals of a domesticated sort. But I wasn't expecting this: the camel <u>kneeled</u> like a <u>cow</u>.

For those who have never had the privilege, cows and horses (and camels, apparently) lie down in two steps: first, the frontal knees bend forward to lower half of the animal, which is always done with awkwardness no matter how many times it has performed this action before; then, once kneeling, a smoother transition for the back end ensues and the animal is lying down.

I watched carefully as the guides brought over heavy blankets and threw them on the camels' backs. Upon these were placed wooden saddles, plus more blankets on top for human comfort. We were called to sit on them, and the guides placed our feet in the stirrups and told us to hang on.

"Lean back," one of them said to me, almost as an after-thought. I did so just as he clicked his tongue at the beast. The camel stood in the reverse order in which it sat, which is to say ass-first; it took all the leaning-back in the world just to keep from pitching forward.

A third camel was hitched to a large cart with supplies, and away we went. We followed the roads through the village; with the chil-dren laughing at us, until we were into the farmland.

Riding a camel, I discovered, is very much like riding a horse; a very tall, awkward horse. Apparently, they're pretty fast runners; but given their lumbering gait and general lankiness, I wouldn't want to be riding one when it decided to break into a gallop.

Conway's beast and mine walked side by side. The guides sat in the cart, one holding the reins for the lead camel, the other man loosely hanging onto the leashes for our beasts. The scenery was somewhat desert-like, but more barren-looking farms than anything else. Was that sand? Or just sand-coloured dirt? There were low shrubs and some cacti, as well as taller thistles and a few sparse trees. This was certainly not the Sahara treks of the silver screen, but then this wasn't the Sahara, either. It was, however, certainly authentic enough for a tourist, and it wasn't too hard to imagine oneself as a poor farmer or traveller crossing this harsh landscape in a bygone era.

Our camels walked adjacent to each other behind the cart, and they kept moving too close together, inconsiderately crushing our legs in the process. But the worst problem with riding (and one that required an immediate solution) was that camels have humps, which the rider must position himself behind in the saddle. This is not an ideal scenario for the male anatomy, particularly when one considers the constant jostling and lurching that comes from such a bizarre prototype animal. The first twenty minutes were spent rearranging things and trying out techniques and rhythms until I found a system of synchronized movements and lifts to keep myself in time with the camel and out of the way of nut-crushing danger.

"Let's name them," said Conway. "I'm calling mine Lucy."

"They're both guys."

"Who cares."

"Fine." I looked at my camel: this ugly and slovenly thing that caused me pain in my nether regions.

"I'll name mine Mxxxxx," I said, the namesake being a certain girl in Montreal who had recently run my heart through with her salty lance.

"You can't do that! That's terrible, you jackass."

"Goddamn it, it's my camel and I'll name it what I want!"

We rode for about two hours before the guides pulled our convoy into a shaded area a short distance from the dirt road for lunch. We dismounted (once the camels sat down, of course) and were told to go stretch our legs. A folding table with a ratty tablecloth was produced, with only two stools set in front of it. We asked if we could help the guides, but they insisted that the paying guests not dirty their hands. A blanket was laid on the ground near the supplies cart, and they sat on this as they prepared the food.

Conway and I wandered around, examining the desert around us. We stayed close to the trees and the small degree of comfort their shade provided; the sun must have heated the air to well over forty degrees.

The camels were allowed to roam as well: one of them started rolling around in the sand, a sight unimaginable until beheld. They wandered freely and slowly over a dune, with the guides seemingly unconcerned about them.

After about an hour, the food was ready and we were told to sit at the table; a guide brought the dishes and set them down and returned to his place on the blanket. We called for them to join us, but we were politely rebuffed: they would, naturally, eat only after we had taken our fill and left scraps for them.

And so the guides/cooks upon whom we were totally dependent sat on the ground ten metres away while we perched ourselves on the stools and dug into dal and cabbage and roti, all of which were delicious.

I said we should be careful to leave enough food for the three men, and Conway agreed. We ate until we were satisfied but not stuffed, and then rose to indicate we had finished. Chai was served, and we sat back down as the table was cleared. The men ate the leftover food on their blanket and I felt very colonial.

We resumed our trek once all had been packed up. Another several hours of wandering under the hot sun, chugging along on the backs of camels trotting down a dirt road far far away from any signs of civilization until, with the worst of the sun absorbed into the sand and our skin, we arrived at the campsite. Perched on a barren plat-eau was a two-storey concrete building, very plain and skinny and without any windows or doors; each of the four walls could not have been more than three metres wide. Nearby were three tents and a rough-looking shanty-like structure. We dismounted and the guides busied themselves unloading the supplies, transferring them from the cart to the concrete building, which held absolutely nothing else, existing only for the shelter of occasional travellers. There were stairs built along the side of this concrete hut, leading to the second storey, which was actually the roof with a low abutment around it. I climbed up to see what I could see: the desert stretched endlessly with no sign of Bikaner (or anything else) in the distance. All I could see was part of the road we had followed, which twisted and turned so much that I couldn't be sure in which direction the city lay. The sun gave me my bearings, but we appeared to be alone for miles around, and it occurred to me that we were lost without the guides; they, who could not speak a word of English, were our means for survival in this very harsh, foreign environment.

More food was prepared as the camels were loosed to wander. A young boy of about fourteen had appeared seemingly out of thin air to join us, and he helped the guides make supper. In the time it took us to walk over to our tent, dump our bags and walk back to the makeshift kitchen, the men had set up the dinner table. The Indians deferred to us once again, and we sat and the meal was served. This time, Conway decided to polish off one of the dishes entirely rather than leave some for the other men, for which I chastised him, to which he replied with derision and profanity. The meal was exactly the same as lunch, as necessitated by the limited ingredients and supplies carried on a trek.

As we ate, a shadowy figure emerged from the horizon: the various objects slung about his slender frame flopped and jangled as he appeared from nowhere, walking over a dune and into our seemingly isolated existence. The sun had started setting, and in the early dusk his appearance made him seem a genuine bedouin.

The young boy went to greet him and together they began building a campfire. Connie and I finished our meal and went over to join them while the guides ate the leftovers by themselves. The stranger set up what looked like some sort of accordion that sat on the ground in front of him. The boy had a drum, and they started playing together.

The accordion was actually an instrument called a harmonium, which sounds similar to bagpipes played very quickly. The rhythmic tabla drumming and the ancient melody of the harmonium with the man's well-practised voice floating over top completely immersed us in our landscape: the sand, the camels, the fire, the expanse of humanity. More than anything I felt peaceful, imagining this land hundreds or thousands of years ago, with myself there as well somehow.

They played for two hours, encouraging Conway and I to sing and dance, which we did, laughing with them as we flailed about and gave ourselves over to the music and the desert night.

Eventually the man packed up his harmonium and the boy took his drum into his tent. The guides had cleaned up the table by this point and they brought us cups of chai. Conway and I spoke in French about how we should have thought ahead and brought along beer. But the chai was good and scene-appropriate, and we bade the musician man farewell as he walked over the dune, disappearing into the darkness from whence he had come.

The guides hid the camels' food sacks in the concrete shack and went to bed without a word to us, leaving Conway and I alone by the campfire. The sky was impossibly clear and the moon lit up the spooky old landscape, making it look like a dark oil painting, or perhaps a scene from a movie about ancient Arabia; yet, strangely, unexpectedly, it reminded me of prairie nights spent on the family farm growing up, when we would camp outdoors completely bereft of electric lights and isolated from civilization. Even on a camel trek in the Rajasthani desert, having run halfway around the world from my home, I was still a Saskatchewan boy in my heart of hearts.

We waited for the fire to burn down to coals, then pissed on it and poured what water we found over any hot spots. Once it was out, we went to bed in our small tent with two cots and not nearly enough blankets: I wore every piece of clothing I had brought on the trek, plus a large heavy quilt and another blanket, and it was still not enough to keep me from shivering in the desert night.

We awoke early and ill-rested. The guides were already up feeding the camels and preparing our breakfast. We ate, then helped to load the cart (the first work we were allowed to contribute to). Our group was down to two camels, one guide having taken one back into town himself, so Connie and I agreed that he would ride in the cart and I on the camel, and we would switch after the first hour.

But we were far closer to our starting point than we thought, less than thirty minutes; our journey to camp must have been meandering so as to give us tourists our money's worth. Back in the village, I dismounted and we stood waiting for our jeep to arrive. When it came, it brought a group of Dutch tourists ready for their own trek, some of them showing the same great anticipation we had had the previous morning. They laughed and took pictures of the waiting camels (which were not the ones we had taken, but other, presumably more rested, animals). As one of them climbed onto his kneeling camel, I yelled to him: "Lean back!"

He turned his head to look at me as the camel rose up sharply, throwing him heels over head to the ground.

We got into the jeep and sped off before he could pick himself up.

❉

We ate a delicious dinner that night, cooked by the Camel Man's teenage sons, along with multiple Kingfishers before retiring to our room with more bottles in tow.

Conway and I had started talking about science and philosophy and other such nonsense over dinner. It began when he said that he never drank liquids during a meal ever since reading a nutrition book where the author listed reasons why humans were not designed to eat this way. I questioned the validity of these claims, which sparked an argument over the nature and infallibility of scientific research, and with the beer things were getting heated.

"Science is all we have," he said. "It's the only true thing we can rely on."

"But there's not one science, and there's not one interpretation of science."

"What the hell does that mean?"

"Well, lots of things," I said. "For example: you said you wouldn't drink water when you ate, because, according to the science in the book you read, it's unhealthy.

"Well, that's one interpretation. The guy had some data, maybe did some experiments, a bit of research and drew a conclusion. It doesn't mean he's right or wrong, it's just an argument."

He shook his head and told me I was an idiot.

"Some science is indisputable. Like gravity."

I waved my hand dismissively as I sipped my beer. "Nothing is absolute. We know about gravity because its here now. But we can't know, truly know, that it will be here tomorrow."

He stared at me blankly, perhaps trying to display his reaction to my comment in a visual manner. I continued: "We deduce gravity by experiments, like dropping a book, or the cycles of the moon. We assume that every time you let go of an object on earth it will fall, thus proving gravity. And we arrange our lives around this assumption, which is necessary.

"But what if, just once, you let go of the book and it stayed there?"

Conway tried to erupt at this, but could only sputter in wild exasperation.

"You— no— there's no way— you can't— That's not an argument!"

I continued provoking him and refused to let up, all because I thought it was stupid that he refused to drink liquids during a meal. The friendliness of the trek was part of a veneer masking the tension between our personalities. It went on and on like this for hours, both of us just arguing to try and prove the other wrong, trying to antagonize each other. (Gravity, it should be noted, did not fail at any point during this time.)

Standing barefoot with lucky rodents

The mornings were, by and large, free of animosity between us. Dreams and sleep, whether restful or not, seemed to provide us with enough separation to forget all but the occasional enduring conflicts for a few hours. And so Conway and I woke up the next day, ate breakfast together jovially, and went to go see lots of rats.

Thirty kilometres south of Bikaner is the pilgrimage town of Deshnok, home of a famous rat temple. Our guidebook described it as a mad scene with thousands of rats; naturally, being a temple, shoes were forbidden inside, and the scurrying of rodents about one's bare feet offered the chance for good fortune: if a rat runs over your foot, it's a good omen. But, really, we just wanted to go stand barefoot in a rat pit and see what happened.

The bus ride south seemed endless, and we were, as usual, compacted between Indians and cargo on metal seats. When we arrived and found the temple, it was a disappointment. Rather than the promised thousands of holy vermin, maybe one hundred greeted us, not counting the dead ones that lay strewn about. A large bowl of milk had been set on the floor by the worshippers and the rats crowded there. A man placed his infant daughter next to this rat-swamped bowl for a photo-op and, presumably, good luck.

We poked around long enough to justify the forty-minute bus ride and then headed back. But the rail crossing just outside the town delayed our bus by an hour as we waited for an approaching train. Yes, waited: there was no sight or sound of it in the distance, but we had to stop and sit as though it might appear suddenly out of thin air.

I saw no electronic rail controls in rural India. At busy crossings like this one, there was a man posted, charged with raising and lowering the road barriers and erecting/dismantling a large red signal flag on the tracks. Indian labour is so cheap that this is the most cost-effective method.

The train (carrying what appeared to be some sort of fine black coal in its open cars) came and went, and the barriers were raised. But, while waiting, the traffic on either side had naturally tried to gain a leg up by pushing into the wrong lanes, so as to zip ahead at the first chance. Now a two-lane highway had opposing traffic in both lanes, resulting in blaring horns and another lengthy wait while drivers sorted it out with their vehicles paused on the tracks, having just waited a full hour safely behind the rail line for a train that no one could see or hear: the perfect snapshot of the absurdity of India.

Is he okay to drive?

After a day spent poking around the drudgery of Bikaner, we were ready to depart the dull and dirty town. We had booked our train tickets to Jaisalmer through the Camel Man, who had very reasonable rates that included a ride to the railway station. And so, when night fell and our departure time approached, we went to the burly gregarious man and reminded him that we needed to go.

The Camel Man had been in a back room in his house with his wife and two friends knocking back Indian rum and Kingfishers for hours. His sons, meanwhile, served us dinner and relayed our reminders to the adults of the household until, eventually, the Camel

Man emerged, staggered to the jeep and commanded us to load our baggage in.

He was such a unique character, so conspicuous and wildly friendly, ludicrously magnanimous, that I almost imagined him to be the Indian version of a Southern redneck as he peeled out of his compound and onto the two-lane highway: 'You boys like Mex-ee-co? Whooo!'

(In fact, the photos in the home showed that he was a direct descendant of Rajasthani royalty, which perhaps made him more akin to an eccentric Western millionaire with too much time and popularity on his hands.)

He drove in a more-or-less responsible fashion until he took a turn we weren't expecting; but we didn't know the town that well, so we said nothing. The streets narrowed sharply in this area and his driving seemed all the more erratic in the tight corridors: the jeep swerved and zoomed as the Camel Man began to realize he was lost and now needed to make up time to get us to our train. Moving at wild speeds in the dark city, goats looked the same as children, and we couldn't tell what sort of sentient being we had just nearly missed.

We came to a dead end, and the Camel Man was clearly not pleased. He whipped the jeep around and furiously retraced our route at high speed until we pulled up at the train station, two minutes before our train departed. The Camel Man thanked us with drunken gratefulness as we clambered out in a rush and hurried with our bags to the platform.

JAISALMER

Listen, my friend, I'm a journalist...

Conway and I drank a half-bottle of whisky on the train before lying down on our respective bunks for the night. But we once again underestimated the desert: within a few hours, we were wide awake and shivering on the drafty train, dressed only in long pants and t-shirts. I pulled a sweater out of my backpack, but it wasn't enough. The Indians on board had brought blankets and scarves with them, and we were the only ones not dozing comfortably on the frozen overnight train.

Conway and I suffered through most of the long journey, which was extended due to common unexplained delays. Our train pulled in at five-thirty in the morning and, chilled and sleepless, we staggered out in search of accommodation. Once we'd dumped our bags in our multi-storey open-air hotel, we ventured out into the old city, site of the ancient walled fort.

Jaisalmer is known as the Gold City for the colour of its sandstone buildings and fort. The latter dominates the old section of the town and the myriad labyrinthine corridors inside its walls hold countless shops and rustic hotels, most of them now geared towards tourists. We wandered the streets en route to the fort, passing beggars and bhang shops (the latter had the word 'government' on them, implying, correctly or not, that these drug shops were state-operated; what a wonderful country).

Inside the fort—past the steep entryway and the impressive gate where a bird shat on my hat—we wandered aimlessly, examining book shops and leather goods before entering a textiles store at the insistence of a young man who shouted at us.

He showed us scarves, and I mentioned that I was interested in cheaper silk ones. Maraj—that was his name—took us to his brother's shop, simply abandoning his wide-open store in the mean-time. Raju (who was called both brother and cousin by Maraj) showed us many different things while Maraj disappeared. I purchased five silk-cotton scarves for three thousand three hundred fifty rupees (about seventy dollars). But I was short on cash, so Raju called Maraj back, who came and took me through the fort streets to some other friend/brother/cousin at some other shop who let Maraj borrow his motorcycle. I climbed on the back behind him and we tore through the tiny, narrow, crooked alleyways of the ancient fort, Maraj expertly-but-barely dodging children and animals while I tried to fold my knees in close to the bike.

We exited the fort and drove through town. Maraj, while not driving like a maniac, was certainly reckless by Canadian standards; of course, helmets were not even a consideration.

The nearest bank we tried was closed, so we went to another; the machine had no money, which was common on a Sunday. We tried a few more until we found one with a line-up. I stood in the queue, got the cash, and we zoomed over cowshit and cobblestones back to the fort where I paid for the scarves plus a thirty rupee tip for the taxi service.

I felt pleased with my purchase, that false sense of having mastered a foreign land in only a few weeks creeping over me; I felt like a local.

Conway and I continued to poke around the fort, browsing in shops here and there until we found ourselves at the rear wall and could go no farther.

For whatever reason, Maraj was there. I wondered why he wasn't minding his shop, but he took us up some steps to the top of the fort wall where there was a rampart with an old cannon overlooking the entire ancient city. The view was astonishing: we were looking west, and if you blocked the lowering sun with your hand you could see the desert that stretched to the Pakistani border just a few dozen kilometres away.

Maraj was a friendly fellow. He talked to us about his brahmin caste and what the string around his neck meant and what he had to do with it when he went to the toilet. He told us about his wife, who was expecting their first child in the next two weeks. He told us about the strict religious culture in India, which wasn't exactly news, but it was interesting to have an insider's perspective, particularly since his English was very good.

Maraj would soon prove to be less than trustworthy, but he was friendly and open with us in discussing these things; I doubt he would have bothered to lie.

The city shone with the golden sun kicking the dust and dirt and history off its roofs to set them ablaze in the eyes of two white boys, who sat alongside a cannon on a rampart and smoked American cigarettes.

We left Maraj and continued wandering through the massive fort, which covers five square kilometres of maze-like territory; it is impossible to tell if you've been down a particular pathway or not without some experience.

A scarf exactly like one I had just bought caught my eye as it hung on a rack outside a textiles shop. I asked the shop keeper how much it was; he told me it was silk-synthetic and cost eighty rupees.

The old man brought us down the steps to his shop and showed us how to test for cotton, silk, wool and synthetic fabric with a lighter by the scent and texture of the singed material, a technique which does not damage the item. I realized the bastards had conned me.

Telling Conway to stay put, I stormed back to Raju's shop, but he was gone for lunch. Maraj was nowhere to be found either. Roaming around in a fury, almost ready to give up on the matter, I happened to see Maraj on his scooter. I explained calmly but stiffly that I was unhappy and he took me to Raju's shop, where he called his friend/brother/cousin and told him to come. Maraj apologized and pointed out that he didn't know what I had purchased, only what I had paid; this did not particularly console me.

When Raju came, he was defensive. At the risk of recklessly generalizing, there is a quality in most Indian men and women that enables them to sell water to a well. It works less well when their target is experienced or stubborn—which includes most of their countrymen— but with tourists, it's a beautiful thing to watch.

However, I am a stubborn sumbitch, and I'd made it this far in the country without getting burned (so far as I knew) by not being afraid to argue.

Raju tried to tell me that the scarves were truly a silk-cotton blend, despite my lighter demonstration to the contrary (I later learned that, when buying textiles, the mention of a lighter will serve as an indication to the salesman that you are no dumb tourist and he will not be sending his kids to college on your back).

I demanded a refund; Raju tried to compromise and reason with me, but I was adamant. We went back and forth for a while, until I decided to fight bullshit with bullshit.

"Listen, my friend," I said with surly calmness, "I'm a journalist. Okay? I'm a writer, that's my job. And if I write about this bad experience, and if other tourists read about it, it would be very bad for your business. You understand."

I could hear Thompson in my head: *You can't do this to me, you scum-sucker! I'm a doctor of journalism!*

It seemed to have some effect, to my surprise: Maraj and Raju spoke in Hindi briefly, and Raju got on the horn and called up his boss. Everyone has a boss.

Maraj left and Raju and I waited silently for the boss. I chain-smoked until he turned the ceiling fan on; then I smoked some more. He was uncomfortable and fidgety. Occasionally he would break the silence abruptly with some petulant arguments about the nature of the business and the quality of the scarves. I was patient and quiet, saying few words in reply and feeling quite unintimidated. Raju became more uncomfortable with every cigarette I smoked, so I kept smoking them, trying to put him at ill-ease.

After about thirty minutes of this, Maraj brought the boss, Tony, on his scooter. Tony was older than them, perhaps thirty, dressed in a black shirt and black pants. The little English he spoke was in a raspy voice. They talked in Hindi, and I was told that a refund was not possible as they had already declared taxes on it. Since I had paid cash three hours earlier and it was Sunday, this seemed like the laziest type of lie.

But I never really expected to get any money back; it was more about making sure that they knew that I knew I had been screwed with my pants on, and not letting them entirely get away with it. They offered to give me higher quality pure silk scarves: an exchange. This seemed to be my best option at coming out of a foolishly rushed purchase with some tangible benefit.

I selected two and convinced them to let me take them to the other shopkeeper for a second opinion; I trusted him after our brief encounter. He was old and humble, lacking the sort of youthful brashness or desperation that would incline a man to boldface lie.

The old man said they were good quality scarves, and the two-ply one would sell for one thousand rupees in his shop. I went back to Raju's place and agreed to exchange the five silk-synthetic scarves (which they were still maintaining were silk-cotton) for four two-ply pure silk scarves. Raju complained bitterly, but I pressed the boss-man and he agreed.

"Because you exchange these scarves, I take a loss today," Raju said pointedly. I looked up from examining my new scarves only briefly before gathering my things, shaking Tony's hand and leaving, feeling slightly less fucked.

Meanwhile, Conway had spent this entire time with the old shop-keeper, discussing the industry and his business. When I returned, Conway told me some of the stories he had heard, prompting the old man to jump in and correct him politely at times.

Centralized factories are rare in India, solely the domain of wealthy men who can afford the large start-up costs. The old man owned many looms, about eighty, and these were placed in the homes of the workers. The workers either rent his machines for five hundred rupees per month, or rent-to-own with installments. They are given x-number of kilograms of material and an order for x-number of, say, scarves of specific weights and qualities. These will take varying times to produce, from a few hours to weeks. The old man knows how long is reasonable and will therefore deduce how many hours per day an employee works and what their commensurate pay should be, around two hundred rupees for a full day's work.

Conway and I asked to see more scarves, deciding we were still in the market. Since this man seemed friendly and genuine, we figured it might be a good idea to take advantage of that fact and get our money's worth.

"What would you like to see?" he asked, not really waiting for an answer as he started towards his rows of shelves. Conway said pash-mina, and suddenly dozens of scarves folded into flat squares and wrapped in cellophane were on the floor in front of us, falling as fast as the old man could grab them. Connie began to examine them, finding a pattern he liked.

"Do you have this in blue?"

And a dozen more came raining down like so many frogs in Egypt. I asked for silk-pashmina and received my request twenty-fold.

We spent hours talking with the old man as he showed us scarves and shawls. He told us how he would go to inspect fabric from a wholesaler: for days beforehand he would soak his fingertips in warm water, then sand them down until they bled, repeating the proced-ure each night until they were soft and tender and smooth; then he would inspect the cloth by touch.

It seems everyone in every Indian industry, from street vendors to property developers, is trying to get a jump; like the kid in the novel *White Tiger* said, India may not have clean water or infrastructure, but they've got thousands and thousands of entrepreneurs. So textile merchants will try and cheat by weaving synthetics or cotton into their fabric in alternating bands, with the outer edges made of the high-quality stuff so as to pass the lighter test. But the old man, with his tender fingertips and years of experience, can close his eyes and feel the fabric and determine whether or not he is being cheated.

He tells us these things with an aged man's calm as we sit, fascin-ated, examining scarves; we buy many, his apparently genuine manner fully winning our trust.

Back at the hotel, with the sunset beginning to smoulder, we order several Kingfishers and sit on the terrace and play cards and order food and let India fade into the background, like lovely atmo-spheric music that makes a moment particularly special, even though you're not paying it any mind.

*

The next day, we bring all our scarves—including the ones from Jaipur—back to the old shopkeeper and ask him to package them for shipment. Our backpacks were stuffed with clothes and books (and the occasional bottle), and since these silken things were largely gifts, they might as well head home before us.

First the scarves were carefully folded and wrapped in plastic. Then, with minimal measurement, he cut lengths of plain sturdy white cloth, some sort of heavy cotton, and sewed two perfectly-sized sacks; in went the scarves. His apprentice sewed them closed by hand and placed lumps of melted wax on the seams. This, the old man explained to us, was to ensure that postal workers' fingers wouldn't find their way inside. This service cost us one hundred rupees (about two dollars) for two parcels.

We took the parcels to the post office but were told that insurance for foreign shipments was not possible. We feared those postal workers' fingers, so we went to a courier service recommended by the shopkeeper. We shipped them with FedEx: ten days delivery, two kilograms, one thousand two hundred seventy rupees. (They arrived in Canada some weeks later, with the cloth-and-wax packaging replaced by a cardboard box; fortunately, the customs officials didn't have sticky fingers.)

Pleased with accomplishing our task for the day, we walked through the hot city towards the air-conditioned coolness of our hotel. Passing through a market district, I spied a barber shop. I told Conway I wanted to get a straight-razor shave, and he said he'd meet me back at the hotel.

The barber, a slim man of about forty, was pleasant, but all business: he sat me down and placed a small damp towel below my neck, then lathered my face with four different soaps and creams with what looked like a busted lather brush. I looked around the shop: four barber chairs, cramped in front of a short counter and facing a wall-width mirror; a poster of the Petronas Twin Towers in Kuala Lumpur dominated the back wall. The barber pulled out his straight, long razor blade and my full attention turned to my hairy,

71

soapy face in the mirror. He moved quickly and gently, with the skill of many years tempering his motions.

He shaved with the grain and paid special attention to my uniquely pointed chin. He asked if I wanted the moustache gone as well, and I said yes, thinking that only in India would that be a standard question when shaving a beard. He shaved everything except the moustache anyway, then lathered me up once more and gave it another run, this time attacking the caterpillar above my lip.

Next came something bizarre: he wiped my face clean and mumbled something about a massage. Suddenly he sprayed my face with water and began pulverizing it with his fingertips. Forehead and cheeks were given special attention as he worked with lightning speed. He then repeated the procedure with several creams. Next, the focus shifted to my hair, which was sprayed with water and vigorously, even violently, massaged. He would occasionally pause, align three fingers and strike me in the head, making an odd cracking sound as his knuckles collided.

I emerged from this quintessentially Indian form of semi-complicit abuse quite dazed, but oddly relaxed. I touched my face: it was the softest, most delicate thing I'd ever felt; ten minutes earlier it had been a scraggly forest of hair sprouting out of never-moisturized skin. It was incredible, and not a bit emasculating.

I paid the agreed price of thirty rupees for the shave, but the barber tried to get twenty extra for the massage. I refused, but was so relaxed that I gave him another ten; arguing would have just spoiled my mood.

＊

India has its quirks and distinctive peccadillos, but some things are the same as in Canada, such as the proliferation of cell phones. Everyone has at least one mobile, often two, and the youth (with the exception of the very poor) are constantly texting and calling each other. The rates are dirt cheap, even by Indian standards, which makes them the primary form of communication.

But there is one unique aspect of the Indian cell phone culture that I hadn't observed elsewhere: the ability to have it function as a ghetto blaster. There must be a shortage of earphones in India, because everyone will listen to their blaring cell phones, pumping Bollywood music out of its crummy speaker on trains, in shops, in the street, absolutely everywhere. But that night, as Conway and I played cards over beer and food at the hotel, we heard music approaching that came from much more powerful stereos.

There were fireworks in the street to announce the coming hordes: it was the wedding season, meaning everyone who was of a certain age was getting hitched, or so it seemed. One had to wonder how many of these couples were self-determined and how many were of the old and ancient arranged variety.

As the crowd pushed into the street, the music came as well, blasting from a half-dozen large speakers on a cart. There were camels and horses, and the bride rode on a white variety of the latter. We went down into the crowd, trying to blend in, as though six-and-a-half-foot white men could get lost in a crowd of Indians; we hoped they were at least drunk by now.

And some of them were. The overall mood was joyful and excited. We were ignored as we stood and watched the proceedings, standing in the thick of the audience to see the bride being showered with rupee notes as a good luck measure. There was dancing and hugging, though we partook in neither. The crowd slowly moved towards the end of the street, where there was a complex with a gate, perhaps a religious temple, or some sort of venue for hosting large parties. Either way, it was evident that we weren't supposed to move inside, and so we went back to beer and cards amid the sounds of a great party.

JODHPUR

Finnish masala omelettes

We spent the next day wandering around the town's old fort and marketplaces, then caught the train in the evening. Our destination was Jodhpur, the Blue City, and when we arrived at five-twenty in the morning we were exhausted, though I was getting used to the early-morning/late-night travels. We found a rickshaw and took a room and promptly passed out.

I woke up first and went to our ensuite bathroom to piss. The sun was shining behind the curtains and I peeked out the window; the sight I beheld nearly caused me to water my own feet.

Every city and town in Rajasthan has a fort, given the battle-filled history of the state. They are all old stone structures, usually on a bit of a hill, and I would compare them to the cathedrals of Europe: they are all beautiful, but eventually they just run together.

And then there was Jodhpur: the fort was in clear view of our window, looming huge above us like nothing I'd ever seen. It was high above the city, yet it still seemed so massive, like those alien spaceships in *Independence Day:* menacing but beautiful, impossibly huge.

We climbed our way up there later in the day, getting lost in the tight winding streets en route as we looked for a path to reach the hillside behind the buildings.

The heat was intense, even in the early dusk, and once we found the break in the line of houses, it was a straight-up hike on the dusty hillside. The fort was up high on rocky cliffs, and we had no hope of scaling those, but we wanted to go as high as possible.

I stopped after a while and turned around to see how far we'd come. I called to Conway, and he came to stand beside me. From our vantage point, we had a view of much of the city, and her buildings (painted for centuries with bug-repelling indigo) had turned a deep, rich hue in the fading sun. The colour saturated everything, deep and bright, and the bustle of activity amongst the concrete shadows made it real and human and alive.

As we stood there in awe, the evening call to prayer rose from a mosque somewhere in the city below, the muezzin's practised voice floating up. A remarkably beautiful scene thus became a painfully timeless one, and as we watched the sun set on the Blue City, it occurred to me that this was a moment that would make me smile on my deathbed.

✲

It was in Jodhpur, behind the clock tower in the bazaar, that I had the greatest omelette of my life.

It happened the following afternoon: Conway was hungry and we happened to be near several omelette stands, so we decided to pick one and try our luck. Some guy at our hotel had told us that the omelettes in Jodhpur were phenomenal, but we figured he was just some damn fool white boy who couldn't stomach his curries.

There was talk in the guidebook of some place called The Omelette Man, which would have sounded sad and very un-Indian, except that the writers insisted it was a quintessentially Jodhpur experience; even locals ate there.

It wasn't far from our hotel, just down the street under the big British-built clock tower. A huge sign proclaimed this tiny stall filled with stacks and stacks of eggs (at least fifty double-dozen paper crates) to be the original Man, citing reviews from every guidebook known to humanity. Meanwhile, a couple stalls in the immediate vicinity were also called Omelette Man or some variation, but my instincts said trust the old man with the big audience instead of the young guys looking at him grumpily.

Conway and I sat down upon enthusiastic invite from a young man who was a waiter of sorts. We were handed plastic menus and immediately advised to order the Spanish masala omelette; the vague description sounded fine, so we did, one each.

The order was shouted to the old man, who barely acknowledged it or paused in his routine: crack eggs, mix in a bowl, add whatever, fry it up, serve and repeat.

It didn't take long for our first omelette to arrive, folded and sandwiched between two slices of mayo-slathered white toast; not exactly the traditional serving, but we were game. It was cut in half and so we shared it.

Words to express the flavours of this meal, to convey the subtleties of texture and taste, fail me: somehow, at some point, this small old man in the middle of an Indian city most people wouldn't be able to spell had perfected the omelette. The eggs and mayonnaise sat in the sun all day, but that just seemed to add to the complexity of flavours. Before our second Spanish masala came, we ordered two more.

"Do you have any chai?" I asked, seeing it on the menu, but wondering where it could possibly be prepared, since the old man took up the entire makeshift kitchen with his slim frame.

"Chai? Yes, chai!" exclaimed the waiter. He called over a young boy standing nearby (perhaps the kid was waiting to be given an errand; perhaps not) and sent him running around the corner. Soon we had piping hot chai in glasses delivered to us for four rupees each, which was cheaper than even the chai-wallahs.

Two Spanish masala omelettes with chai chasers, and we felt great. Conway went to a corner shop nearby to buy batteries for his camera while I waited for our next omelette to appear.

Two blonde girls arrived and sat down next to me, and I struck up a conversation with them. What guy wouldn't: they were gorgeous and Finnish, and when my accomplice returned he was pleased to see what I had done. We all talked over omelettes for a while until we rose to go our separate ways. I threw out an invitation to join us for a drink later at our hotel. It wasn't my best effort, and I didn't have much hope; really, I just said it to say it.

◦

Conway and I hired a rickshaw to take us to the fort, but we wound up stuck in a traffic jam that slowed us to a snail's pace through the city.

We passed a group of women in brightly coloured saris, carrying various things on their heads as they walked on the side of the road. They looked at me and I looked at them. My eyes locked with one woman, who was either too curious or indifferent to avoid my gaze. I saw a world I will never know, so far away from anything approaching my own; and she must have seen the same; for I would guess that I knew more about India before arriving than she knows about Canada, or even the Western world in general. We likely would have been unable to communicate much verbally had we tried, but we both saw differences we could not grab hold of in the eyes of the other: she is poor and I am rich, in the grand scheme, but I don't think of myself in that way, and she may hold a different self-view as well; our cultures, history, beliefs, language, food, customs, politics, everything is different between this woman and I.

That is the eternal limitation of travel: as an outsider, I can look into the eyes, into the soul of a country, but I can never truly understand or reconcile what I see with what I am. Outside the borders we call home, we are forever foreign.

We made it up the long road to the fort and paid our driver. The entrance fee was something like three hundred rupees, which was a steal for a site of this size. Built between the fifteenth and seventeenth centuries, the Mehrangarh fort had never been successfully breached by an attacking army, an impressive feat considering the number of fierce tribal wars fought in this part of the world. Aside from being built on a high cliff, there were brilliant engineering features that added to the defence capabilities of the massive structure; such as the gate: the entrance is in something of a corner, about ten metres away from a facing stone wall, perpendicular to the large stone pathway leading to the fort. This small detail—a simple right-angle turn—prevented armies from taking a running start with men or beasts to bust open the gate doors. If that wasn't enough, the huge metal doors had conspicuous and ominous spikes about ten feet from the floor: approximately where a charging elephant's head would strike.

The self-guided audio tour was fascinating, and Conway and I wandered around for hours, using up the rest of the day and enjoying the sunset from the ramparts before heading home and getting drunk.

We were on the rooftop of our hotel drinking Indian vodka neat and playing cards when the Finnish girls arrived, much to our pleasant surprise. They joined us at our table and helped to polish off the vodka. It was still early, and now with four drinkers we needed another bottle. The hotel manager offered to take Conway by motorcycle to the wine shop, and so I continued chatting with the ladies.

The taller one was a television documentary journalist who was working in London. The shorter one was still studying psychology or something, I can't quite recall. Though both were lovely, I was enjoying trading stories of journalism with the taller one when Connie returned and the vodka consumption resumed.

After several drinks and games of cards, I didn't know for sure which girl I was more interested in, but I suspected that it didn't really matter: they were both beauties, soft pale Scandinavian skin and blonde hair, good Finnish senses of humour, though the taller of the two spoke much better English. At some point, the shorter one asked if she could use our ensuite bathroom; I volunteered to take her to it.

I let her in the room and closed the door behind us. I didn't know for sure what she had in mind, if she was going to jump me or if she really just had to pee. The mood of the evening felt as if it could go either way. I turned the lights on, but she wanted to look outside, so I turned them off and joined her at the window. I pointed out the stars high above the looming fort, shining as bright as Jodhpur was dark. We began talking about the fort, and I didn't

79

know what she wanted. Was this just casual conversation between two people who had only recently met, or a prelude to something more?

I put a hand on her back, believing this to be a good, warm move that lets a girl know what's on your mind but won't get you slapped. Not only did she not hit me, she did nothing. I moved along her spine: no reaction. I turned my head so I could see her expression, but she was looking at the city.

This was the time for action and my vodka brain was up to the task: no inhibitions, all courage. I grabbed her and kissed her. And how. And, Jesus, did she kiss back or what. And how. In a rapid series of movements that lasted roughly fifty seconds, we shed all of our clothes, locked the door, closed the curtains and entangled ourselves in each other on the bed.

Foreplay ensued. I produced a condom and put it on. She pushed me back on the bed and straddled me. She kissed me. She grabbed my treasured personal belonging and began to slide herself dow—

—KNOCKKNOCKKNOCK

"Hey, man! Open up!"

"Not the best time, Connie!" I yelled with raging bitterness.

"Dude, the manager is freaking out. He's drunk or paranoid or something. He's closing the rooftop and wants cash for everything right now and I have no money!"

"Deal with it! I'm in the middle of something."

Silence. The girl and I began kissing again.

—KNOCK KNOCK.

"Jesus Christ, you lousy bastard!"

"I need to get my wallet!"

She had gotten off of me by this time, having resigned herself to dealing with the situation. I found my wallet and shoved a five-hundred-rupee note under the door.

"There, take it, go away. I'll see you in the morning."

A pause. "Where am I supposed to stay?"

"You moron," I said through the door, "you fool. Go ask the other girl if you can stay with her."

He was drunk and obviously hadn't made a move; she was (apparently) standing beside him listening, so this amounted to me making the first move on his behalf; lucky bastard to have a friend such as I.

They left, and my girl and I resumed our activities, this time to satisfactory completion. Afterwards, we lay in bed, struggling with conversation because of the language barrier, nevertheless happily exhausted and drunk in each other's arms.

"Didn't you have to pee?"

"I lied."

Into the Indian kitchen,
and drunken patriotism in the night

T he next day, we (my Finn and I) woke up to the sound of text messages on her phone. She communicated with her friend and we made a plan with the other half of our new quartet.

Let's say her name was Ellen. Ellen and I took a while to get out of bed, by which I mean we found better things to do in the bed. Eventually, hunger drove us to get dressed and head out. We said good-morning to the hotel manager as we left, a sad creepy middle-aged man who longed for the flesh of white women (not unlike many of his countrymen; a comparable generalization, perhaps, to white males' supposed fondness for Asian women).

But none of that was on my mind as we walked out together into the sun, the bustle of the street somehow perfect like everything else. Nothing improves one's view of the world like getting laid.

Ellen and I moseyed over to the Finns' hotel, which was far bigger and plusher than ours, with the accompanying price tag. As we knocked on the room door, I looked down from the balcony at the swimming pool in the courtyard below and briefly thought that I had gotten the short end of the stick.

Conway was in rough shape, and as we walked he and his Finn (let's call her Nadia) relived for us their side of the night, which included the loss of footwear, an argument with the hotel doorman and more beer.

The four of us sat down on the colourful cheap plastic stools in front of the Omelette Man's stall—which had fast become the centre of our little Jodhpurian world—and I felt a sense of goodness. The day had started out well and it just seemed to be getting better: sitting in the sun with two lovely girls and eating omelettes is not a bad way to kill a late morning, even on plastic stools in the middle of an Indian road.

They spoke in Finnish, which was fine, since we assumed they were talking about us and what stallions we were. We couldn't hide our conversation with either English or French, since Nadia spoke both, so Conway and I contented ourselves with jokes and omelettes.

"What are you guys doing today?" asked Nadia.

As if we had plans.

"We're taking a cooking course right over there—" she pointed down the road "—this afternoon. The lady said it would be cheaper if we had more people." She smiled. "And it could be fun."

We replied hesitatingly, getting the details of when and where and casually saying we'd show up if the mood moved us; men can be idiots.

The four of us wandered through the bazaar for a while, taking photos and buying more vodka and wine for the evening. Eventually we split up, as the girls were off to do a quick tour of the fort, which had already been scratched off our list.

And so Conway and I slowly wandered back to our hotel (which was by unspoken convention no longer his hotel but merely the place of lodging for his belongings). The manager was gone, but the young waiters smiled at us with a wink in their eye.

"I need to get my wallet so last night doesn't happen again," said Conway as we climbed the stairs up to our top-floor room.

"Yeah, you owe me five hundred rupees."

"Why?"

"Because I gave it to you under the door. For the bill."

"I never got five hundred rupees."

"You shithead, I know you did. Pay up."

"No, really," his face looking more innocent either by design or genuineness, "I didn't get anything."

I stopped walking and turned back to the waiters in the kitchen, who were no longer looking at us.

"Those bastards," I muttered as I fished out the keys for the door.

✿

We spent the day napping and reading on the roof, heading back down to street-level now and then for chai and fried stuff from a wallah on the corner midway between our hotel and the clock tower. A giant vat of bubbling oil promised nourishment: strange dough was lumped into it and fried until it became a misshapen piece of heaven.

It was almost time to meet the girls, but right across from the chai-wallah was a barber, and Conway decided he wanted a shave to impress the ladies. He went first, and I followed; this time, there was no massage and my neck was scraped and nicked to the point of bleeding. Always consider age when choosing a barber: enough to make them experienced, not so much that they jitter and shake with the blade in their hand.

At the appointed hour we made a game-time decision to go join the girls for the cooking class. It was seven hundred rupees each, which was a good chunk of money, close to twenty bucks. But this was no time be stingy: we were following our little leaders.

The class was in a spice shop near the clock tower. Attached to the small streetfront with racks of spices was the home of the woman who ran it, along with her family. She was about thirty or so, heavy-set like many Indian women who run their household: the very poor are scrawny, the young girls are thin and fit, but the housewives of the country are big and pudgy and proud of it, not unlike old European babas. If you want a lesson in female body image and empowerment on a personal level, go spend a day with one of these remarkable ladies.

The home/shop was very modest: plain concrete walls enclosed two main floor rooms with dirt floors; small stairs led to the second storey. In the kitchen were gas burners and many well-worn pots and pans, and it was here in the family home that we would have our class. Our teacher had made an attempt to make it seem professional for her tourist customers, but it was still very much a working-class Indian home, and I felt honoured to be inside (even though I was paying for the privilege).

It was just the four of us in the class, but it was fairly cramped. On the menu were seven items: masala chai, pakora, mixed vegetable curry, coriander chutney, raita, dal fry and chapati.

Chai was first and simple and delicious. I was amazed at how such a wonderful thing with complex flavours is not much more difficult to make than a sandwich, provided you have the freshest spices. (This would prove to be the overarching theme of Indian cuisine: simple preparation of quality ingredients.) Pakora are vegetables of any kind battered with chickpea flour and fried in oil, also quite simple to make. The veg curry was slightly more work, but not much: cabbage, potato, tomato and coriander were chopped up and fried with cumin, red chili powder, tumeric and other spices. This along with the chapati was a solid meal. Chapati is an Indian flatbread, distinct from naan in that it has no yeast whatsoever. Ridiculously simple to make, a staple of Indian home cooking, it is at its best when brushed with ghee (akin to clarified butter). Dal fry is simply lentils cooked with spices in a pressure cooker and then fried with more spices and oil.

The four of us and our teacher worked as a team to cook enough for all of us to eat. We took turns chopping, battering, frying and forming dough into chapatis. Our teacher had written out several pages of recipes in elegant handwriting so we could follow along instead of writing down notes.

The cooking lessons had been added to the original spice shop business when, some years ago, an Italian fellow bought a large amount of spices but said he didn't know how to cook; he was the woman's first student, receiving a six-hour lesson on the spot. She spoke (in quite fine English, the result of attending Catholic school in her youth) of great dreams for her modest business, of reaching thousands of people with her lessons. As she stood saying these things in her concrete-walled dirt-floor home, I couldn't help but love her and whatever world spawned the likes of her.

We cooked and ate and laughed, and five hours later we were stuffed and exhausted. Our host's husband came home near the end of our stay, and as we paid (plus a generous tip) he told us how he wanted to come to Canada and serve chai and sandwiches in a small shop. The way his eyes lit up as he talked about it, you would have thought he was talking about becoming an astronaut; for these modest and simple people—still fairly poor, if not quite hand-to-mouth—this seemingly basic idea was as far away as anything, merely a fantasy, not something to be realistic about.

Conway immediately began making his own plans to open a sidewalk chai stand in downtown Montreal (which seems feasible and would probably be successful, though maybe not in the dead of winter). I tried to think back to the Indian food I had eaten in Canada, attempting to place names and flavours to those faraway meals.

We left the shop with the promise that we would accept our hosts' invitation to return early the next morning for chai with the family.

The four of us went back to our hotel (that is, my and Conway's hotel, which was now my and Ellen's hotel) and took up residence at our now-usual table on the rooftop terrace with a deck of cards and bottles of liquor. We drank and laughed for a few hours, but once it reached midnight, the girls informed us that it was now Finnish Independence Day and national pride must take precedence over the sleeping locals' desire for silence.

They stood and proudly belted out the Finnish national anthem in full voice, which we applauded and followed with more vodka, wine, brandy and beer. I brought our guitar out of the room and the evening carried on until the wee hours when, exhausted and patriotic, we called it a night. Conway and Nadia exited the premises, and Ellen and I went to explore our room once more.

*

Early-morning text messages in Finnish once again determined our plan for the morning. Conway and I had a train to catch in the afternoon, but first our quartet assembled at the spice shop for chai with our teacher, who seemed surprised that we had actually come.

We wolfed down the chai and said thank-you and headed to the Omelette Man, where we had all met forty-eight hours previously. Planting ourselves on the stools, we consumed eight Spanish masala delights between us, plus many cups of chai brought by an eager little boy. It seemed like a fair excuse to splurge: the girls had been good fun and good company, and we were all a little sad to be split-ting up.

After a few photos with the Omelette Man, we said our good-byes in the street: embraces turned to passionate kissing, which lasted quite a while before I recalled that public affection is severely frowned upon, and we might as well have been fucking in the road. When we separated, there were many people staring at us, especially men. Ellen and I looked at each other and kissed again just for the hell of it. I hugged Nadia, and Ellen hugged Connie, and we said farewell in front of the Omelette Man's little plot of heaven.

From there, Conway and I plunged into hell as we headed to the train station.

The Indian concept of a queue is a frustrating one from a West-ern perspective. At the front of a queue is the person being served; behind him are people waiting in line; on either side of him are line-jumpers: people who simply walk past the queue (regardless of the length, or perhaps directly due to it) and try to push their way into being served next or immediately. At a railway ticket office, this tactic usually involves shoving forms at the clerk's window in the middle of another person's transaction, usually accompanied by a flurry of words from everyone involved save for the clerk, who couldn't care less whom he serves next.

These jumpers will continuously appear. Often they are rebuffed by those waiting patiently or by other jumpers. Some will argue their case in the local language along with various hand gestures. The one exception to these rules are women, of any colour, who are allowed to jump to the front of a queue without question or comment.

All these things were becoming part of our everyday lives and expectations, but they took great patience, particularly on this day as we spent ninety minutes fighting to reach the ticket window. Eventually, we booked our train and headed out of Jodhpur.

En route, I met a girl named Babita who spoke English quite well. She was twenty years old and travelling with her family, and she helped translate some questions that her family and other passengers had for me. Conway was on the top bunk with his earphones in and a book in front of him, but I was on the lower seat being approached by Indian men who wanted to know everything about me: where I was going; what my good name was; what my profession was; whether I was married; whether I liked India; where I came from.

Eventually, Babita and I started speaking more freely together, not relying on questions from the crowd, who listened intently and waited for her to translate. She was quite attractive, and all the more so for her fearlessness in speaking openly with me, something I had not seen before in Indian girls.

Conway joined us after a while, curious of the crowd I had attracted. Babita offered us some food, and I refused only so long as to be polite. She produced a tiffin box (metal food container) of puri and green chili chutney: very simple food, but incredibly delicious, one of the best meals I had eaten in the country.

We reached our destination shortly thereafter and, amid the flurry of farewells from everyone in the train car, it felt sad to say good-bye.

UDAIPUR

**Do not jump off this building, no matter
what the eight-pussied woman tells you**

U daipur is widely renowned as the most romantic city in
India. Having just gotten laid in our previous city, which
held no such title, my expectations were quite high. But
there were no pretty and willing Finnish girls around; just Conway.

We tried a few hotels that our rickshaw driver suggested (one was
vetoed by Conway because the sit-toilet didn't have a seat) and chose
one on the quieter side of the river.

Udaipur's fame rests on three primary things, all of which are
more or less related. First, there is the floating palace, which is
neither floating nor any longer a palace, but does look quite regal on
its island in the centre of the bay that the city overlooks; the Indo-
European architecture fronting the water, coupled with the seclu-
sion of an island, only add to the romantic appeal of the outrageously
expensive hotel.

The second part of Udaipur's celebrity is simply its claim, oft-
repeated in guidebooks, as the most romantic city in India, which
stems directly from the concept of having a romantic evening on the
island hotel.

And, thirdly, these two previous things no doubt contributed to
the decision to set the classic 1983 James Bond film *Octopussy* here,
in romantically exotic surroundings.

However, aside from the fact that we had no female companionship in this town, the romantic ideal of the city was undercut by a few things. First of all, Udaipur itself is exactly like any other Indian city: dirty, noisy, crowded; it seems no more of a natural honeymoon destination than Jaisalmer. Secondly, goats; as in, the bleating humourless bastards who had wandered down to the marshes left by the receding water of the bay (which also revealed a great deal of trash beneath it) to feed and run and, most entertainingly, fight. A swampy goat-battle arena does not a romantic city make, and even those who shell out the six hundred dollars per night to stay at the floating palace still must endure the clash of goats in the distance.

We wandered around the city, stopping to see the Jagdish temple, which would have been more impressive had we not been exhausted. We found the market, strolled through the bazaar, observed all the action; but after a few hours, we needed to sit down.

I bought a pack of tobacco from a shop near our hotel and we found a table on the waterfront terrace of a mid-scale tourist restaurant (and by waterfront, I mean goat-occupied marshfront).

I rolled two cigarettes for us and we ordered beers and pakora and the sun slipped away faster and faster. We played cards until we couldn't be bothered and we kept ordering beers like we owned the place. Conway pulled out his guidebook to see what was on offer for cultural nightlife. He flipped through it and tossed it to me. A show caught my eye in the listings: just across the water, not far from here, there was an exhibition of traditional Rajasthani dance and music starting soon.

"Sounds good to me," said Conway, and we settled up our bill and headed across the short stone-arch bridge.

Inside the open-air theatre a crowd sat on the floor and a few benches: mostly Westerners, especially with young families, but also a large number of Indians; I supposed they were also likely tourists rather than locals.

The show began with an old lady playing the harmonium and a fellow beating on a drum. The music built a background for the first scene: a battle between a devil character in an elaborate black costume with colourful flaps like the petals of an evil flower, and a goddess in a resplendent angelic outfit (they were both played by men). The devil held his sword sideways in front of him and spun four times before the goddess entered the scene on the back of a giant cat (also played by a man) to start the war. I didn't understand all the symbolism, but it was surreal and ancient, and mesmerizing to watch. There was undoubtedly something universal in the story being told—though I hadn't a clue what.

The devil yelped repeatedly like a crow, and this was the only sound uttered by the odd characters. A stage hand brought hot coals onstage and the goddess moved them to a tray with a spoon held in his/her mouth. They clashed and danced and I think the goddess won in the end.

The second act was two women dancing with fire: one older and experienced, the other young and uncertain but capable. The older one gave the audience a toothy smile throughout her performance, a seasoned veteran, and they both spun and twirled and danced while swinging the flaming implements with great concentration.

Next appeared a woman of about thirty who sat on the floor with small cymbals attached to her body, including six or seven on her leg and foot. She wielded a long string with small stones on each end, with which she would expertly swing and strike the cymbals to achieve different tones, creating music. She moved progressively faster, deftly striking her tiny targets with perfect precision.

The rest of the acts were impressive—dancers and puppeteers and whatnot—but they were easily forgotten after the final performer.

A heavy-set woman of about fifty appeared onstage with a clay pot about thirty centimetres tall perched on her head. She danced gracefully with it before adding another on top. More dancing ensued as the pots barely wobbled. Then an assistant came, removed the pots, placed a cushion on her head, replaced the two and added a third, bringing the total height of the pots balanced on this woman's skull to one metre. Watching the pots being lifted, I would guess that the largest of them easily weighed twenty pounds.

The woman sat down without touching the three pots (impressive on its own) and leaned to her right towards a flower vase covered by a silk scarf, which was sitting on the floor. Her head was cocked to keep the pots vertical as her body was stretched out sideways on the floor. She grabbed the scarf with her teeth—gently, delicately lifting it off of the flower without so much as a quiver from the vase—before straightening up and rising to her feet, all while the pots barely wobbled.

Cheers and wild applause followed, but she wasn't done.

Three more pots were added by the assistant to the stack, which now numbered six and rose to about one-and-two-thirds of a metre —taller than the woman standing beneath them. A metal bowl was placed on the floor and she balanced with her feet on the edges of it, slapping one side down repeatedly to spin in a circle, rocking it back and forth to walk forward. Did I mention she had six pots on her head?

I almost felt bad for the woman when the assistant appeared with three more pots. The total was now nine, which easily cleared two metres above her short frame and made me both curious and afraid of what she might do next.

Standing still without toppling her cargo was impressive enough; but then thick broken glass was spread out on the floor, and she effortlessly walked barefoot across it, slightly grazing a tree near the open-air stage with the highest pots as she moved.

She smiled and sang along with the music while her muscles made minute adjustments to her posture, tiny recalibrations that were invisible to the audience but were necessary to keep the pots atop her head. The lifetime of practice that this woman had endured simply to amuse on a stage was staggering. The show ended, and I joined the crowd of people who rushed up to offer the woman a tip for her incredible performance.

Conway and I were walking home through the dark streets, still in awe, when we were approached by a man.

"Excuse me sir, you want marijuana? You want hashish, I have for you, good price."

"Not now, pal," I said as we brushed past him. I wanted to get home and write down everything I could remember from the show. Maybe I could turn it into a story, a magazine article of some kind. I was debating whether to go back and see if I could get a translator and an interview tomorrow with the woman, or perhaps I should hurry home to my notebook to empty my brain before it all slipped away.

"Marijuana, hashish, opium, you like?"

"Not now, man!"

I was now well ahead of Conway, speed-walking over the bridge and into the hotel.

✿

The next morning was spent lounging about in the Internet café, trying to book train tickets and writing emails home. We had break-fast at our marshfront resto, which actually had very good food (goats notwithstanding), and in the afternoon we wandered into the city.

A travel agent was the first item on the to-do list, since we couldn't find what we needed on the web. We booked a bus to Ahmedabad for the following day, where we would catch a train to the south of Gujarat, home state of Gandhi and the jumping-off point for a little island paradise called Diu.

It was late in the afternoon, and we stopped at an extremely touristy German bakery for danishes and espresso, which struck an unexpected chord within me: I had not yet been homesick, nor was I about to become so, but I couldn't deny that good coffee and European baked goods were wonderful to rediscover.

I left Conway and retraced our path from the night before, trying to find the guy who had offered us drugs. I was specifically inter-ested in one thing he had mentioned.

Was this him here? Maybe.

I approached him and nodded and he nodded back, speaking in low tones once I got close.

"You want to buy today? Marijuana? Hashish?"

"Nah. How much for opium?"

"No-no sir, no opium." He shook his head.

"Last night you said you had opium."

More head shaking.

Opium is a deep and historic part of Rajasthani tradition, offered to house guests and honoured travellers. We'd leave Rajasthan (where it was illegal but supposedly widely tolerated) after Udaipur, so I thought I'd try my luck.

"Fine, nothing then." I began walking away.

"Okay, okay, sir." I came back to him. "I can get, okay? For you, I can get."

"How much?"

"One thousand rupees per gram."

"What?! That's ridiculous!"

He said nothing.

"Listen, my friend," I said. "I will pay you one thousand to take me to your house and smoke with me. You understand? I want to smoke with you."

This was a practical plan on my part: first of all, I had no idea what to do with opium, nor how much I would need to buy. It would be easier to overpay for the product and get a tutor along with it. After all, one thousand rupees was about twenty bucks: not bad for a once-in-a-lifetime experience.

Also, if I'm smoking with the guy I'm buying from, it's harder for him to rip me off. If I get a dud product, I'm not paying: try before you buy was my motto. As well, I had heard of a scam whereby drug dealers tip off the police, who wait nearby until a foreigner buys the product, then shake him down for a bribe on the spot. The dealer gets the money from the sale and a cut of the 'fine' as well. I was interested in protecting myself: after all, you can't be too careful when buying illegal street drugs in a foreign country.

"No, no, no," he said. "One thousand, one gram. You smoke. You take."

I insisted, but he wasn't interested, and that was the end of it. I headed back to the hotel to find Conway, who had gone on ahead of me.

◦

Perhaps the most distinctive aspect of Udaipur is the strange cult of *Octopussy*. Predictably, the success of the movie gave hotel and café owners a chance to boost their business by cashing in on Bondmania. Every single tourist-related establishment in the city has a sign proclaiming that they show Octopussy daily, often repeatedly, and at least one place had non-stop showings.

Since we were already bored with Udaipur, I suggested that bhang lassis and a flick were a fine way to pass some time.

I had found one hotel with a resto that was showing the film on the scenic rooftop at seven o'clock that evening. It was perfect: a television and rows of plastic chairs surrounded by a lovely view of the city during daylight hours. We went for dinner at the marshfront joint; but as we ordered food and drinks, Connie said that he wasn't in the mood for bhang: I was on my own. The service was slow and we were running late for the show, so I had to gulp it down quickly as we headed out.

We were the only ones on the hotel rooftop when the waiter came up and turned on the film, no doubt well-accustomed to turning on the same film for the same-looking white kids every night.

As the movie began, I started feeling the effects of the bhang settling over me. It was stronger than the previous lassis in its come-ons, in its foreplay; and I remember thinking: *You bastard, that was too quick. This will come back on you...*

I'd seen *Octopussy* before, but not for many years. The drugs came down hard on me and I couldn't follow the dialogue on the screen. Two girls came up to the roof and sat a few rows ahead of us on the white plastic lawn chairs set out with expectations of an audience, but I didn't notice them until a few minutes later when they seemed to appear out of nowhere, causing me to gasp so loudly that they turned back to glance at the noise, frightening me further.

The sounds of the night superceded the film: rickshaws raced around on the screen while rickshaws honked in the city streets below. Which was real? Which was really happening?

Oh, you've done it now, boy. You broke your mind. And now it will break you.

Did someone move the TV? Or was it always that far away? Maybe they moved my chair when I wasn't looking.

The noise overwhelmed me, even though no one was talking and the television volume was reasonable. Everything blurred and everything amplified and nothing was stable enough to hold on to. I needed a rock, something sturdy, something to grab and hold until I could ride this out.

...Impossible to walk in this muck. No footing at all. Order some golf shoes. We'll never get out of here alive...

...Thompson's dead, goddamn it. This is your problem. He can't help you...

"Where are you going?"

I was sitting on the concrete, and the movie was over. No, wait... I can hear it. I looked behind me and saw the television stand, which fully obscured me from Conway and the rest of the audience as I sat behind it, near the edge of the rooftop. How long had I been here? I couldn't see over the two-foot concrete abutment that ran along the edge, but I knew we were six storeys in the air.

The night felt cooler over here. Sitting lower to the ground seemed to help steady my head. I felt more in control, aside from a powerful curiosity about jumping off the building.

...Maybe I should just go take a peek. See the view...

Fortunately, I was glued to the floor, unable to rise. My body took no physical instructions or commands as my mind locked itself in.

...It's coming into view. Your world is not ending. There's no need to jump. Go find Conway...

I zoned in and out of conscious thinking, unaware of the passage of time.

...Why would I jump? I don't want to jump. That's ridiculous...

"Hey, man." I jumped at the sound of his voice beside me. "You all right back here?"

"Uh." I looked around and reassessed my surroundings. "Yeah, I'm cool," I said, nodding very enthusiastically to reassure him. He stared at me.

"Go ahead, I'm fine. Back with you in a minute."

He nodded and went back to his chair, and I took a few minutes to collect myself, still zoning in and out of focus. I then stood with great care and style and walked in front of the television.

There were many more people in the audience now, which I wasn't prepared for. All those eyes on me, the fucked-up guy in front of the screen. Get out of the way! Down in front! Why don't you go jump off a building!

...All in my head. Sit down. Sit the fuck down. There's Connie. Put your ass in the chair...

"Here's your beer."

"What's this?"

"You ordered us beers before you left. Hurry up and drink it."

...Take the beer. It will steady you. Grip it tightly, don't drop it...

The movie was easier to follow now, and I lost myself in it as I sipped my beer. Something exploded and Bond kissed a woman—and then the credits rolled.

"What, that's it?" I asked incredulously.

I took my beer with me as we left the hotel, with Conway leading the charge into the night. The city streets were dark: it was around nine-thirty, and there were few people besides locals still milling about.

We headed back to our side of the river, unsure of our next move. Back at the hotel, we ran into one of the young boys, about fifteen or so, who ran errands for the manager and whom Conway had been asking about buying pot. Now the kid told us that we should go talk to this guy who worked in another hotel just down the road, which was either part of our hotel or had some kind of business connection with it. We headed straight there, where we asked for the fellow by name, and then told him what we wanted.

When I say we did all this, I mean Conway: I was busy inspecting the colour of the concrete walls with strange and paranoid interest. I let my accomplice sort out the details.

"Please, go upstairs."

"Upstairs?"

"Yes, my friend. Go, sit in restaurant. Maybe have a beer? I will come back and bring to you, okay?"

And so we went up to the fourth-floor resto, where we took up residence in a long, low booth at the back. I recall being very confused by the layout of the place: there was a large desk right in the middle of the restaurant seating, and the rest of the tables were organized with sheer randomness.

The place was empty: no customers, no waiters. Music played, nevertheless, through a stereo system, and Conway and I talked about the relevance of *Octopussy* to modern India—or something.

I had finished my beer by this time and would have liked another, but with no wait staff I was out of luck. I pulled out my tobacco and rolled two cigarettes, and we lounged in the booth with great casual style, like two bigwigs smoking in a booth at the back of an empty restaurant while waiting for their drugs to arrive.

"Hey man!" Conway shouted across the restaurant at a young waiter crossing the floor. "Can we order some beers?"

He looked to his right and shouted something in Hindi. Someone shouted something back and he turned to us and nodded, "Okay, okay," and ran off.

"Does that mean we're getting beer or not?" I asked.

"Fuck if I know. This country has terrible service."

"I guess that's the hidden downside to child labour."

We waited for what seemed like dry eternity, but our other man did come back. Conway checked the ganja and made a big show about being concerned it was too dry or something, but paid for it in the end anyway.

"Can we smoke here?"

Our friend looked nervously around; there was no one else there, and we were far to the back in the open-air resto.

"Okay, smoke here."

"We ordered beers, too. Can we have two beers?"

"Oh, yes, sir," he said, pleased to take legitimate orders. "Two beers. Anything else?"

"Nah, that's it."

He scuttled off and I revelled in the sensation of sending your dealer to fetch drinks.

Connie rolled a joint, and the beers came, and we smoked the joint and drank the beers and all was well. Conway then announced he was going to the bathroom; there was a television across from our booth, and while he was gone I waved over the waiter.

My partner returned and sat down.

"Ah, shit no! *Octopussy* again?!"

"It's a classic," I said. "I feel I might have missed some of the subtleties the first time around."

I recall staying for quite a while, with the movie playing in the background, but eventually (and I don't remember leaving) we ended up back at the marshfront resto, where I ordered malai kofta and tried to get another beer, which they refused to sell me.

There were actually quite a few tourists on the restaurant patio at that late hour, and we smoked and observed them smoking until the kofta came and blew my mind. It was the greatest thing I had ever eaten, the single most glorious concoction to ever take up residence in my mouth. I do like malai kofta, which are vegetable balls in a cream sauce, but not to the point of ecstasy, so I had to give due credit to the drugs.

Wet boys in a dry state

I woke up in bed the following morning well-rested with a good feeling inside me, despite the galaxy of chaos my brain had endured the night before. We checked out, had breakfast and hit the road, taking a bus to Ahmedabad: the capital of Gujarat state, and our final departure from Rajasthan.

We had been on the road now for a month and a half. Udaipur had not helped our relationship, despite its romantic reputation. Conway was getting on my nerves, and it had built up to the point that I saw him as a near-constant irritant to me, deservedly so or not. It wasn't all bad all the time, but our moments of conflict had surpassed our times of good humour in prominence and frequency. I held my tongue and relied on my patience, but I could only listen to so many rants about the lazy nature of Indians, or a bombastic lesson on the virtues of capitalism and Ayn Rand, or watch him flagrantly disregard local customs and act as though he was on a wild weekend in Montreal. (I spared myself from that last category; though I did have my moments, I tried to keep a modicum of respect and dignity, and had gone out of my way to not harass or upset the locals since the Mango Lassi incident.)

The bus ride was long and bumpy and took up much of the day.

We arrived in Ahmedabad in the early evening and, to get to the train station, we had to scramble and argue for a reasonable rickshaw price at the 'bus station' (read: random street) where we were let out. As in Canada, taxi drivers stake out bus and train stations; but in India they have the advantage of being able to haggle with impunity, free from the burden of metres and regulation.

But we were not shy and not afraid to argue, and that saved us from getting gouged most of the time. We found the train station, where we took up residence, staking out a corner of floor for ourselves, only somewhat removed from the crowd.

I bought some fried delights and packaged nuts for the journey, along with a bottle of ginger ale. Conway busied himself surreptitiously digging the bottle of whisky out of his bag.

Gujarat has been a dry state since 1961 as an homage to its most famous son, Mahatma Gandhi. Diu, a tiny island two kilometres off its southern coast, is soaked in booze. But rather than endure a day travelling without alcohol, we planned ahead and picked up a bottle before we left Udaipur. Conway and I quickly drank a third of the ginger ale and covertly filled the rest of the bottle with whisky, passing the concoction back and forth as we waited for our train.

o

"Get up, you bastard."

I opened my eyes and realized it was daylight. The train had stopped and the car was empty; only Conway and I remained, and he was pulling on his shoes in the lower bunk.

I climbed down and did the same and we collected our backpacks and squeezed through the narrow corridor of the train, exiting onto the platform in the bright early-morning sun.

The signs said Veraval, which meant that we had indeed reached our destination, though not our ultimate one. There were people walking towards the exit at one end of the platform, but the train cars were empty. I wondered how long ago we had arrived; fortunately it didn't matter, since Veraval is the end of the line, the farthest south one can travel by train in Gujarat.

We were still a few hundred kilometres from Diu, and we now had to catch a ride to the bus station, where it took some serious cross-cultural communication skills to find the bus that would take us in the correct direction. The name Diu (sounds like d'yoo) apparently requires a very precise accent to pronounce properly. If you're off by even a hair, it's incomprehensible to locals; either that or the guys at the station were screwing with us.

The first bus was a far cry from the decently comfortable coach we had ridden to Ahmedabad: this was a metal sardine can with hard benches, straight out of the 1950s and with questionable longevity regarding the immediate future. Passengers were already on board, but there were a handful of cramped spaces to be had. The top of the vehicle had a large luggage rack where a young boy was tying bags down. The driver was standing nearby smoking a beedi.

"Can I ride up there?" I asked, pointing to the roof.

He looked up at the boy and back at me.

"Up there?" He chuckled to himself. "No, no, no."

Everyone knows the iconic images of Indian trains packed to the gills, with passengers crowding the metal roofs of cars, wind blowing through their hair. That practice has been illegal (in the enforced sense) since the 1970s, but riding on the roofs on buses supposedly still occurs in rural areas. Anyway, it's India, and rules are meant to be broken: that's what bribes are for.

"How much to ride up there?"

"No, no, no," said the driver, still smiling. "Why you want to ride up there?"

How to explain it so he'd understand?

"I want to smoke," I said, holding up my tobacco. He laughed heartily at this.

"My friend, you may smoke on the bus. Of course."

And with that, he walked away laughing and got into the cab as I joined Conway, who had found us two very cramped seats at the front.

DIU

**Paradise found,
hearts broken,
prices paid**

T hree bus rides later (all of which I failed to procure a
rooftop seat for) over endlessly terrible roads, we arrived in
Diu Town, the de facto capital of the island. Completely
disoriented, we nevertheless found the bus station on the map in our
guidebook and judged by the sun which way was east. Conway and I
set off on foot and proceeded to get very lost in the alleys of the
charmingly quiet town.

Diu is not like any other part of India. On its forty square kilometres it has Latin architecture and elaborate whitewashed Catholic
churches, along with countless other cultural relics stemming from
its lengthy history as a colony: Portugal held control of Diu from the
early sixteenth century to 19 December 1961, when the Indian military was sent in to annex the territory (along with its more celebrated
sister state Goa) after asking nicely a few times first.

We had picked out a handful of decent-sounding hotels in the
guidebook to inspect, with one in particular at the top of my list: Sao
Tome Reitiro, set in St. Thomas' church and featuring an all-you-
can-eat barbecue every other night. We found the church by acci-
dent, though it was hardly inconspicuous: high spires and immaculate white walls broadcast its location from a slight hill.

We were greeted there by a lady, who told us she had only one room available. I went up to check it out: the small, simple room was high up above the main part of the church, accessible via a ladder and a precarious walk along the roof. The view was lovely, but I worried about us falling off drunk at night. It didn't matter, since Conway refused to have a place without an attached bathroom; he was cranky and in need of a bit of pampering after the arduous journey.

The lady was very kind when we told her no; she said we might try Herança Goesa, another family-run hotel just around the bend.

Herança Goesa was in the book as well, but under the restaurant section. The building was classical and well-maintained, with the owner's family living in the main house and the hotel's thirteen rooms in adjacent buildings on the small grounds. The trees and greenery shrouded everything in lushness; we opened the large iron gate and stepped into a quaint oasis.

The owner was an Indian of mixed Portuguese descent, and he and his son and wife all spoke Portuguese to each other, as well as a strange-but-wonderful Latin/Indian-inflected English. He showed us the room: spacious, two beds, very clean, with an ensuite bathroom. It was seven-fifty a night: I balked but Conway was sold, and he managed to convince me to splurge since I was exhausted and didn't want to walk around in the heat anymore.

One can justify almost any expense in India by counting it in dollars (seven hundred fifty is about thirteen bucks), but that is a dangerous habit when living for as long as possible on limited funds. Everything can always be gotten for cheaper. I knew this, I had seen it, and it was in danger of becoming my religion in this place.

We went with the owner to sign the usual ledgers and such, and gave him our passports.

"Would you gentlemen like anything? Food? Beer?"

"Beer," Conway replied instantly, "two of 'em."

"Yes, sir. Thank you."

Thus began a wasted afternoon drinking beer in the hot sun next to our room on the back patio of the hotel. We played cards and smoked cigarettes and recuperated from what had been a stressful and trying journey to this island paradise.

At about seven o'clock, we headed back to Sao Tome Reitiro

for the barbecue. We were early, the first ones there, and a man told us to take a seat on the large concrete bench that wrapped around a fire pit. Conway and I were soon joined by a host of other travellers: a young English couple; three brothers—one Kazakh and two Latvians—who now lived in Israel; a lone middle-aged Portuguese man; and an Irishman in his sixties, who said he was a former restauranteur. There was also a couple whom we had briefly met in Jodhpur and a few other places, which was not unusual: a lot of young tourists start in Delhi and work their way south along the coast via Rajasthan, so the same faces tend to crop up along the road.

The food was phenomenal: tuna and shark steaks, cooked over the fire in foil, served with pasta, salad, rice, vegetables and fresh buns. We ate and drank and smoked and told stories of the road, and the atmosphere was very open and relaxed.

The Irishman had been travelling to India regularly for thirty five years. He had also been to Sri Lanka, and he told the story of how he helped a family he had befriended there by building them a proper house to replace their endlessly-broken mud hut; the year after he did this, they died in the tsunami.

The three brothers of mixed nationality (who called themselves Russians in any case) were all former soldiers and private security types, though none were particularly large. They had been in Sikkim and Nepal and elsewhere (as tourists, not soldiers) and the youngest of them, who was twenty-three) told stories of the various strains of ganja there with great enthusiasm.

The British couple were an interesting pair: the girl said almost nothing over the course of several hours, but her man grew fiercer and louder in his often-angry and rather hateful views as the night went on, especially concerning Indians. After a few drinks, Conway began enthusiastically venting along with him; I stayed out of it.

Stuffed full of food and beer, the Russians then brought out a chillum for us to pass around. A chillum is how they smoke their ganja in Sikkim, Tibet and Nepal: it's a simple device, merely a straight stone pipe, but it does the job.

More beer and cigarettes and stories, and we called it a night, heading home to our palatial abode around the bend. I remember thinking that Diu was going to be great.

°

Herança Goesa is primarily known on the island for its breakfasts: when we awoke and stumbled out into the daylight of the front terrace, there were already many full tables of tourists from other hotels.

We sat and I ordered some sort of spicy scrambled egg dish and a masala chai, and Conway said the same, and I rolled a cigarette and he pulled one out of his pack. Palm trees notwithstanding, we might as well have been people-watching outside some café in Montreal: sipping our hot drinks, smoking our cigarettes, nursing our hangovers as the sun soaked through our skin.

Our food came and it was great. In no rush to move on, we ordered coffees after. Diu slows you down: no matter how much you tell yourself you want to get out there and see the sights, the pace of local life simply won't allow for hustle.

What should we do today? Who cares.

Let's do something. Let's roam.

So we asked our hotel owner and he said he could arrange motorbikes for us. After breakfast, we drove towards the western part of the island along its southern coastline with the Arabian Sea.

The wind blew through my hair and cooled me from the raging sun above. The scenery was beyond beautiful, unlike anything I had ever seen: we drove past endless expanses of perfect, empty beaches, looking out over soft blue waters from under palm trees. We stopped and I took off my shoes and stood in the sea for a while, thinking too many thoughts at once to gauge my state of mind. I felt strangely serene and, though I couldn't say why that would be strange in such a place, I couldn't shake the feeling.

We kept driving and ended up in a small fishing port on the westernmost tip of the island called Vanakbara (Diu Town is on the eastern point; the island is only twelve kilometres long). We parked the bikes on the docks and found dozens of fishing boats, some still unloading their catch at that early afternoon hour.

Most of the fish we couldn't identify, including a huge creature about two metres long, spread out on the dock, that looked like a cross between a shark and a manta ray; it appeared to be a bottom feeder of some sort, but, of course, none of the fishermen or boys nearby could speak enough English to enlighten us.

Great blocks of ice were brought in by trucks and hacked into manageable pieces by the boys, who were all about twelve to sixteen years old. The ice was then fed into a chipper and the resulting shards were used to pack the fish for transport to other parts of the island and beyond.

Nearby, just off the docks, was a ship-building yard where around fifty people—men, women and children—worked to build old-style wooden fishing boats by hand, all of them at least two storeys tall (the boats, not the workers).

The women and children worked on the wood pile: chopping, sorting, removing bark; whatever their strength would allow. The men laboured at the nearby band saw and on the boats themselves. It took six men to lift one log and carry it to the saw, where it was cut into pieces to be used as planks in the hulls.

The people paid us no mind as we watched them. They worked hard under the hot sun with the same sunny determination we saw in the faces of the fishermen. It's a quality that seemed to be in abundance in India; I thought about my own country, and the differences between my generation and my grandparents'.

"Look at them," I said. "They work because they have to, and they do it without complaining. They're a very resilient people."

Conway had been calling Indians, in general, lazy and greedy and a nation of beggars, mostly based on the touts and drivers and hotel managers who tried to rip us off and get something for nothing. He wasn't shy about it, and as we put more road behind us, he became both more weary of those things and more emboldened to speak his mind, regardless of who was listening. That, and that alone, was grinding me down and straining our friendship.

Now he was silent, saying nothing in reply to me, worn out from the sun, perhaps even a little bored and restless. But this shipyard and these people, were exactly what I wanted to see, exactly why I left Moose Jaw.

We drove around a while longer, exploring the island and the tiny villages that dotted the two-lane highways. This was the perfect place in India for driving: the roads were immaculate, likely paved within the past year, and almost entirely empty. Even in Diu Town, the traffic was leisurely and not threatening to ride up your ass if you didn't get out of the way fast enough.

After a nap back at the hotel and, why not, a beer as well, we went to a nearby restaurant that came highly recommended by both the book and other Diu travellers. It was called O'Coquiero, the Portuguese word for coconut.

Looking over the menu, we became lost among the great many fish dishes to choose from, all of which were tempting, most from Portuguese or Portuguese-Indian or Coan cuisines. Unwilling to limit ourselves, we settled on the fish platter, which had just about everything they could haul out of the Arabian Sea for four hundred rupees; we ordered one each.

It was one of the best meals of my life, and Conway said the same: the tuna, kingfish, shark, calamari and prawns were all perfectly cooked and served in great portions; there was no question it was fresh, caught that very day said the owner, who was also the waiter. We might have even watched it being unloaded that morning. It was almost too good to eat, all for seven dollars. I began to question whether I would ever leave this island.

The meal inspired us: we inquired at the hotel and they told us that the first catches of the day in Vanakbara usually come in around seven in the morning; by nine, it's all being taken out of the sun.

We woke up early the next day and tooled out of town around sunrise, heading for fishy paradise.

Conway and I had a plan: we had acquired some aluminum foil and a sharp kitchen knife in order to have ourselves a fish fry on the beach. We arrived at the market after half an hour of driving and parked the bikes and walked towards the crowd at the end of the docks.

And what a crowd: entirely women, easily a hundred of them, with thousands of fish piled on the concrete dock. One immediately noticed the colours of all these women in their saris which were, as usual, clean and bright despite the fact that they were all working poor and handling fish on a dock.

The men unloaded what was left on the boats, or sat and smoked beedis and drank cups of chai, having finished their work for the morning. Their wives and daughters (most of the women selling were middle-aged) were in charge of running the point of sale in the marketplace, and the women yelped out prices and other foreign words beyond our comprehension.

The haggling was fascinating to watch, even though we couldn't follow a word of it. Indians are a passionate people and, like Italians, they speak with their hands quite a bit. In Rajasthan, the women we met and saw were mostly quiet in public, though I had read that they are often the dominant ones in the privacy of the home. But in the fish market they took charge, arguing and shouting, animating the docks with a sense of fire and timelessness; perhaps it is the fire itself that is timeless.

Conway and I wandered through the market, trying to stay out of the way and not step on the piles of fish underfoot while also inspecting the catches and soaking in the chaos that surrounded us. Most of the women paid us no mind, unless we were looking at their stock and they had no other customers; then they would speak and gesture to us, though it quickly became apparent that none of them spoke the slightest word of English. It also dawned on us that we had no idea what many of these species were and had no way of asking.

We wound up going the safe route, picking two things we could readily recognize: tuna and squid. We haggled with number-fingers, but not too hard, and were satisfied with our fat tuna and eight baby squid for about a dollar-fifty in total; the women likely laughed afterwards at how we overpaid.

I put the plastic bag containing our quarry by my feet on the scooter and we headed back to the highway, stopping at a market to buy a lemon before driving to a beach just west of Diu Town.

Conway and I collected what we could find for dry wood and started a small fire. He prepared the squid while I gutted and filleted the tuna. We cooked each separately with the lemon and sat on the beach eating it with our hands as the tide rolled up and a salt wind stole in to ruffle our hair and cool our shirtless bodies in the tropical sun.

Things fall apart

L ater that same day, we went to a cyber café to check emails. Conway was silent at his computer until he started a video chat with someone, apparently his girl Mel back in Montreal.

I could only hear one side of the conversation: it was brief but emotional, and he was asking for reasons and second chances, so I knew it wasn't good.

I went downstairs to wait for him. When he came, he confirmed what I had surmised.

"She broke up with me," he said without emotion. Staring blankly into the street, he paused. "Fine. So be it."

Fine, so be it.

The vibrations he was emitting were changed after that: sadder, of a different frequency altogether maybe. Regardless, I did what any good friend would and should do: I immediately took him to a bar and got him drunk.

Bars in Diu don't serve drinks per se. You can't go in and ask for a whisky sour or even a shot of anything. Basically, a Diu bar is a bottle shop with chairs and glasses, and it's how all bars should be forever and ever amen.

We bought a bottle of vodka and sat down at a table with our cigarettes and deck of cards and played and drank and smoked and I talked to him about anything, anything at all, whatever I could think of to distract him from his thoughts. If the lion remembered the thorn stuck in his paw, well, I didn't care to imagine what he might do to extract it.

There were a few other men in the joint; women were by convention not allowed. The bar (which was really just a retail counter) was on one side, and five or six booths were opposite it. There was a old television playing some Indian dramatic film and a few liquor advertisement posters on the wall. That was it: extraordinarily plain. Perhaps a dozen men sat in groups drinking Kingfisher or, if they were manly, a mickey of whisky that they mixed with cola. We were drinking the vodka straight, and they noticed this and murmured amongst themselves as Conway and I played cards.

We left the fourth dimension behind and time became irrelevant, measurable only by the level of liquid in our bottle. We ran out of cigarettes in what seemed to be an impossibly short amount of time, since we were chain-smoking heavily and ignoring everything outside of our booth.

I went across the street to the tobacco stall and bought two more packs. When I returned, Connie's expression had changed: it was darker, glum, dismally broken-hearted. I threw a pack at his chest.

"Wake up, you bastard. Your mother says smoke these beautiful cigarettes."

He grumbled something and opened the pack. I sipped some vodka; he was slipping into darkness. I waved the barman over to our booth.

"Yes, sir?"

"We," I said, "would like to buy a round for the house."

He blinked. "Sir?"

I took some slight umbrage at having to walk him through this concept; but I was drunk, so I let it slide.

"I want to buy a bottle—" I tapped the lid with my palm for emphasis "—and I want you to give some to everyone in the bar." I gestured with my finger at every man present.

The barman looked horrified and apologetic as he understood.

"No, no, no, sir." He smiled uncomfortably. "Please, sir—" He stopped short, lacking the words, and ran back to the bar and spoke to another man while gesturing towards us. They both came over and the barman's new mouthpiece spoke to us.

"Sir, these men do not drink like you. They cannot drink this—" he gestured to the vodka as the group of teenage boys in the next booth began snapping photos of us, nothing unusual "—this... It is not in their character. Look," he turned and gestured to the men with their beers, "they only drink beer."

"I understand that, but one shot of vodka won't kill them. Come on, I'm paying for it."

"Yeah, it's just a shot," piped in Conway, holding up thumb and forefinger to emphasize just how small an amount we were talking about.

"No, sir, no." He smiled and chuckled but he was pleading now.

We gave up, but told him to put another bottle in the freezer for us, since we were almost done the first one. He looked frightened and a bit reverential as he walked away.

I got up to go take a piss in the back—literally, as the bathroom was simply a doorway leading to a soiled wall in an alley—and when I returned, Conway had made friends with the boys in the next booth. They were all around eighteen years old and we asked if they wanted to play cards with us.

White folk are celebrities in most parts of India, especially amongst the youth. In this case, the boys were fascinated not only by our skin but by the apparently unfathomable idea that we high-class rich sahibs would venture into a dirty, miserable bar intended for dark-skinned commoners. In any case, we taught them how to play crazy eights and they declined our vodka and snapped photos of us while we smoked. They were good kids.

Eventually they wandered off and we cracked our second bottle and kept going. God knows how long we were in that place.

"Fuck!"

Conway was going downhill. The booze had grabbed hold of both of us a long time ago, but it was turning his mind and heart black.

"I need to go check my email," he said with his face in his palm.

"No, you don't." He started to stand and I grabbed him and pulled him back down. "Listen, man. There's nothing you can go do or say or read right now that will make anything better. You under-stand?" I stared straight into his miserable cloudy brown eyes. "You can only make things worse."

He processed this, or gave semblance of doing so, before standing with wobbly gusto.

"I gotta go."

"You're not driving, are you?"

"No."

"Do you have your scooter keys on you?"

"No."

I held out my hand; he searched all the pockets on his shorts and came up empty.

"All right. I'll meet you back at the hotel and we'll go for dinner."

He left and I had another cigarette and a drink and then did the same, carrying the half-full second bottle of vodka with me as I staggered home, my legs not obeying their master in the slightest.

India is quite surreal while drunk, but Diu was not really India as I knew it: the streets were quiet and peaceful, fairly well-maintained, and there were bits and pieces of Portugal scattered everywhere, lost memories and gifted fragments of colonialism.

It was late and the sun was just about down. We were in that bar for musta-been six hours. I ambled slowly, not in any particular rush: Conway would likely be a while at the computer café.

I wandered around town, looking at the houses and shacks, the parked motorbikes and, eventually, the black starry sky. Thoughts of Moose Jaw and Montreal and Canada fumbled through my mind: the towns, the people I had known in those places, how far away everything was. And how far away I was; the breadth and scope and context of the distance I had created. There, on a tropical island I had never heard of when I left Moose Jaw, I was as far away from my world as I could be; and it felt good, like a bespoke suit that fit me better than anything I had ever worn.

I arrived back at the hotel some while later, just in time to see Conway roar up to the gate on his scooter. He parked it and dismounted with shaky drunken style, swerving wildly in his gait as his legs tried to steady themselves.

"You asshole. What the fuck is wrong with you?"

He said nothing as he lurched past me, opening the gate and staggering around to the back of the building where our room was; I followed him.

He tried to open our door, but it was locked. I had the key and, with trial and error, I opened it and Conway burst in noisily, turning on every light in the place and sitting down on his bed.

"Okay, let's go for dinner."

"You cockhead! Are you out of your skull? You can't even stand. Stand! And you're driving? You fucking lied to me, you fucker, you cheap shitknife."

I paused, drunk and unsteady myself, running out of things to yell at him.

"You can go eat your fucking dinner alone."

He said nothing, but got up with great energy and began tearing his bag apart, looking for god-knows-what and maybe he didn't either. Madness… I thought he might have had a gun in there to shoot me with, or a bow and arrow set to play William Tell with an apple in my goddamn teeth.

Whatever his search was for, he abandoned it and stormed out wordlessly. I followed him and watched him climb on his scooter.

"Connie, man, don't be a fucking asshole."

I have no problem with fatalism: if he wanted self-destruction of a more dramatic flavour, that was his choice (which is to say, I would have tried to talk him out of it, but I wouldn't have been as furious as I was); but he was selfishly reckless in riding completely plastered in the middle of the night through the narrow crooked streets of the town, where he could easily take out a child, a beggar and a goat in one fell mechanical swoop.

He fired up the engine and looked at me.

"You only live once, my friend!" With that, he swerved off into the night, an asshole with wheels.

I went back to the room and lit a cigarette, weighing the situation.

God, I was drunk; really very drunk. And he was equally so, which was frightening to think about. The room spun about me and my thoughts slopped and sloshed up against each other like a fish tank on the back of a monster truck; no way in hell I'd have considered driving in that state.

I looked around the room: the contents of our two bags were strewn about the place. I thought about throwing his stuff into the street, but I doubted whether he'd pick up on the message.

As I smoked I thought about the past six weeks of travel with this man, this beast, this friend of mine I was only now beginning to understand. He was the personification of the expression 'a little knowledge is a dangerous thing'. He had read some and thought he knew all. His ego dwarfed even mine. He was pompous and crass and generally a pain to be endured outside of raucous drinking nights. I thought back to Agra and our first fight, my escape plan formulated but never executed. Since then, there had been count-less fights and arguments, and there would surely have been more if not for my attempts at patience. I make no claim to sainthood; but nor do I rashly apply my admittedly narrow worldview to an entire race of people on the basis of having eaten Ayn Rand and read some Indian food once in a while.

God, I was drunk; really very drunk. I needed food.

I smoked yet another cigarette as I shuffled down the poorly lit road to O'Coquiero. The lights and noisy conversation spilled out of the premises and into the street, and as usual a number of motorbikes were parked out front; one of them looked like Conway's scooter. As I approached the entrance, he sauntered out of it with a styrofoam food container.

"Hey man, I got you a sandwich."

"Take it and fuck yourself with it," I hissed, brushing him aside and walking past.

There were a few people at a few tables. I took a seat at an empty one and the owner/waiter brought me a menu and I glanced it over while thinking about Conway. The more I rolled it over in my head, the more sense it made to split up. This had been building for some time; the night's events had made me angry, but were certainly not enough on their own to break up a wonderfully hideous and dynamic partnership such as ours.

But the partnership was no longer dynamic: it was more a test of my patience, forcing myself into passive silence when my friend went too far or grated on my nerves, which was at least daily, often more. I was tired of travelling with him. Sitting at that table, I made up my mind that the end had come.

Conway came back a few minutes later, having forgotten that I had the only room key. He was brusk, but I had regained my (drunken) composure and politely asked him to sit down with me so we could talk. He wanted none of it; just the room key, which he asked for with rudeness and anger, and which I threw at him as demeaningly as I could manage without getting kicked out of the restaurant. He left, and I spotted Jack and Gary at another table, and they invited me to join them.

Jugglin' Jack was from Bristol, and was indeed a juggler who had come to India with some sort of charity group, entertaining kids or teaching them how to juggle or something like that; very odd young fellow, pure itinerant sort, not to be trusted but amusing company.

Arizona Gary was a sixty-something American with a Southwestern accent and a mysterious past: he claimed that last year he sold everything he owned in the States, tied up all his "loose ends," and moved to Darjeeling, a few hundred kilometres north of Calcutta. He didn't seem at all the type for a soul-searching journey, so there appeared to be something else at play. For all I knew, he was on the lam after murdering his entire family with a nine-iron. Friendly, though. He was staying in the room next to us at Herança Goesa.

As we sat and ate and drank and smoked (Gary abstained from the latter two for some non-specific reason; Jack certainly did not), they asked me about Conway and I let go of a few things. Gary told me he didn't want to interfere and he didn't know either of us from Betty Ford, but his observations since we had arrived made him believe Connie was very immature and possibly even dangerous. This meant a lot to me at the time, something of an outside validation, even from a weird, old, potentially homicidal Yank.

We stayed until the restaurant closed and then headed home: Jack to his hotel, Gary and I to ours. The old man went into his room and we bade each other good-night and I knocked on my locked door.

No answer. No sounds of movement.

The windows were black and it was late, so I assumed he had gone to bed or passed out, since his scooter was out front.

I knocked again, louder. No answer.

Sigh. The bastard.

Perhaps he'd walked somewhere; I had nothing to do but wait. I lit a cigarette and looked at the stars around the faintly glowing whitewashed church in the distance, beautiful and strange, like a mosque in Moose Jaw.

After a while I got restless. I walked around to the front and double-checked that his scooter was there. The curtains in the windows of the room were drawn shut, so I couldn't see inside; but the bottom section of the glass slid open, and I was able to wiggle it from the outside and pull the curtain aside. There under the window was Conway, in his bed, asleep.

"Hey!" I yelled as quietly as I could. "Open the door, you fuck-case!"

He licked his lips and ignored me.

"Conway, you bastard, let me in."

He appeared to be sleeping, or fake sleeping; I couldn't tell for certain (as you'll recall, I was drunk; really very drunk) and I couldn't reach him through the bars on the window. Finding a length of discarded plastic tubing on the ground, I hit him on the face: at first lightly tapping and then progressing to hard whips; no response.

I whispered and shouted and abused him, but he wouldn't budge, though, in my drunken and emotional state, I refused to be convinced he was unconscious. I took the tubing and poked him in the eye quite hard, as hard as I dared without blinding him. He grimaced and moved his head away and continued snoring.

"You fish cock. I'll kill you for this."

I dropped the tubing onto his head and walked back to examine the door of the room. There was no way in: I was stuck outside.

Gary's light was still on, and that seemed like a slightly more hospitable option than the concrete. I knocked and he answered with his fat white belly hanging over his once-white-now-grey briefs. His room had two beds and he let me stay the night. I passed out while he continued reading his Stephen Hawking book and scratching his belly in bed.

o

In the morning, Gary and I went to the front terrace for breakfast. It was early and I knew Conway wouldn't be up yet. I ordered my usual spicy scrambled eggs and black coffee, and I smoked while Gary talked about something uninteresting.

While we were lingering over coffee, Conway appeared.

"Morning, sunshine!" I bellowed. He looked rough, like a man who'd just fought off an octopus at the bottom of the ocean.

"Mornin'," he mumbled, shuffling past our table.

"You heading out?"

"Yeah," he stopped unwillingly, "Internet café."

"Well, you don't mind if I borrow the room key, do you?" It was my intention to be as facetious as possible, but he may have been missing too many brain cells to pick up on it.

"Sure." He dug it out of his pocket and handed it to me. "See you in a bit."

Gary and I watched him get on his scooter and ride away with his droopy eyes in front and the stench of a bad hangover trailing behind.

"Know any cheap hotels in town?" I asked.

✿

I used the time that Conway was out to pack up all my things and move across town into a dive hotel. It had a faulty shower and a squat toilet and a television and a balcony, all for two hundred rupees a night, almost half my share of the room at Herança Goesa.

This was the split: the decision, the action that changed everything.

I left the room key with the owner at Herança Goesa and stayed away for a few hours, long enough to be certain Conway had returned and seen that I'd moved out.

I found him sitting at a table with Gary, who quickly muttered something about seeing how Jack was doing and scuttled off.

I sat down with Conway. He was upset: he challenged the wisdom of what I was doing; he questioned whether it was necessary; he accused me, his pleas bordered on begging. For once, I was in control; for once, he had no choice but to listen. I'd be lying if I said I didn't enjoy that at least a little bit.

"Did it ever occur to you that I might need a friend right now?" he said. In truth, I felt lousy about the timing, and I told him so; but this was something inevitable, and which he had first predicted long ago, which I also pointed out, and it seemed a natural point to break at.

I was resolved not to relent and eventually he had to give up. We had train tickets to Bombay in two days: I would not be going.

We talked awkwardly and at intervals for a while before Jack came over (oblivious to our conversation) and invited us to come along with him and Gary to a treehouse restaurant called Bon Apetit. I said sure; Conway agreed more reluctantly.

We spent a tense day together at the restaurant before the group drove back into town and split up, with Conway and I going to our respective hotels.

Somewhere around this time, I discovered that Kristi and Jenny —two girls we had met a few times at the St. Thomas barbecues— were staying in my new hotel. We had a few drinks together and talked and I went along with them to the barbecue that night, where we found Conway, who was rigid and withdrawn even in a friendly and familiar group setting. He went home early, back to his solitary room and thoughts, and I stayed and chatted with the girls.

Our final day together was much improved, once we'd both had a chance to sleep on things. We took another drive to the treehouse restaurant and ate grandly; then beers and a swim in the ocean. Connie had little gas left in his bike so he left it outside of town and hopped on mine.

He and I bantered and laughed and talked about the good times, and a few of the bad. The dynamic was thicker than it once was, still coated with the bad blood and the knowledge we'd be parting in a few hours, but it had loosened up enough to flex. I'm glad we had that day; it meant a great deal to me to laugh our way towards the exit, arms over shoulders.

I dropped him off at his bike afterwards. We had one last cigarette together on the side of the road, talking about our immediate futures: he was off to Bombay by train, meeting up there with friends from back home who, though some work connections, had scored a free room at a well-known five-star hotel over Christmas; he was carrying on with our plans without me. I, the instigator of the split and disrupter of plans, suddenly had my options wide open. I elected to stay in Diu for the time being; at least for Christmas. We had been there a week already, and between Jack and Gary and Kristi and Jenny, I had built up a good group that seemed to offer some promising times ahead.

We finished our smokes and crushed them on the pavement next to the beach. The formal pretense of a handshake was not needed; we simply hugged and wished the other well. Conway got on his bike and tore off down the highway towards town, where he'd go pack up his things and catch his bus.

I stood there a while longer on the beach and lit another cigarette. The sun was getting late-day heavy over the water. Conway was gone; that chapter was finished. It finally stuck me that I was alone, and that the remainder of the trip was now completely without definition; it rested upon me alone to define it.

I drove back to the hotel, where I ran into the girls. Jenny was a very good looking blonde girl from Bristol. Her accent was more refined than Jack's, and she seemed to come from money and education and perhaps a bit of snobbery. Jenny was doing her master's in psychology and something about her struck me as strange, unusual, indefinable, all in the good and attractive sense.

Kristi was fairly short but very cute. Jenny and I were in our mid-twenties, but Kristi was thirty-something, though she certainly didn't look like it. She was Estonian and quite proud of the fact that Skype was invented there. Her accent was somewhere between generic eastern European and a bad impression of BBC announcers. The girls said they were having dinner at O'Coquiero; would I like to join them?

A brave new world

The hotel that the girls and I were staying at was on the other side of town from O'Coquiero, so we drove there on our scooters; Devang was already waiting when we arrived.

Devang was a middle-aged Gujarati man who'd left India many years ago to live, study and work in London. He was a psychologist of some sort, and Jenny talked to him at length about concepts and technical mind-things that made them both sound a little condescending at times. His English accent was strong and very proper, his clothes were Western and sharp; he looked like he had walked out of a Burberry ad and back into India. The girls had met him at one of the barbecues, and they had all become fast friends.

We sat and ate and talked, sharing experiences and stories of our respective homelands and current travels. We talked about Conway and our split, though I did my best to keep my guard up on that subject.

Jenny was quickly winning me over: very lovely and animated with an easy laugh that I didn't tire of hearing; and we were staying in the same hotel, where I now had my own room. Oh yes: my targets were set that night.

I told the group about the early-morning fish market out on the western tip of the island, and together we resolved to go out in the morning and find something tasty.

We paid our bill and said our good-nights and the two girls and I went back to our hotel (Devang was staying elsewhere in town). As we climbed the stairs to our rooms, I asked if either of them would like a nightcap. Kristi said no; Jenny thought about it long enough to get my hopes up before declining. Good-night, off to bed.

Bright and early the next morning: up we get and off we go, down the highway along the coast. While Conway and I had always pushed the gutless little scooters to their top speed of 50 km/h, the girls and Devang were much more cautious, and I soon found myself far ahead of them. No matter: the sun was out and the salty sea air was smacking my face and ruffling my hair and I happily slowed down to re-join the pack.

We made it to Vanakbara sometime around eight o'clock and threw ourselves into the fish market. I was the lone veteran among us, but Devang spoke Gujarati, which made a big difference. He didn't know fish names in his mother tongue, but we could at least barter properly and talk to the women.

Two plump tunas, one eel and a big bag of prawns, all for a couple of bucks, purchased a few dozen metres away from the hand-built boat that caught them that morning.

We elected to drive back to Bon Apetit to have a non-fish break-fast in the treehouse. By this point, we were all friends with the proprietor, so he didn't mind putting our fishy wares in his fridge for a few hours. We ate breakfast, then spent the morning lounging around on the beach before we got hungry again and reclaimed the fish. Devang and the girls had found this great little dive restaurant on the north part of the island; they'd probably cook it up for us, he said. So we started off, and within fifteen minutes we'd managed to stumble upon the place.

They charged us four hundred rupees to prepare everything, including side dishes. We gave them the bag of fish along with our marching orders: one tuna biryani (a spicy fried rice dish, borrowed from Persia); eel fried in butter and spices; prepare the prawns in a tomato-coconut curry; and stuff the second tuna with spices and bake it in the tandoor oven.

We sat and waited and ordered beer on the terrace, talking and joking as Bollywood music played from speakers to set the scene under the palm trees. These three new friends of mine were decent people: overly cautious, perhaps, and a bit fearful of their own humanity, but determined to be pleasant company for as long as possible. I liked them, and they seemed to like me.

Devang ordered us one cup of some sort of local liquor distilled from palm flowers: it tasted absolutely horrid; we each had a sip and then gave it to some kid on the street, who seemed confused as to why we were giving away perfectly good booze.

The food arrived and the feast began: it was sublime, wonderfully fresh and flavourful and cooked to perfection, and we spent more than four hours sitting on that terrace talking and eating; it was after dark when we left and went back to the town.

Diu is an addictive lifestyle: something simple like a morning trip to the fish market easily turns into a day-long affair with unexpected new friendships and India soaking into your skin. The beaches and roads are mostly empty; the food is dirt cheap and glorious, as is the liquor. Life is lived slow in Diu by everyone. There are no touts, zero. Just good honest simple people who are more interested in having a beer with you than in trying to rip you off. (In fact, I feel more than a little guilty writing about such an unspoiled, unheard-of corner of India; better to keep it off the tourist trail for as long as possible.)

The next day, Kristi, Devang, Jenny and I regrouped and spent another day together, wandering around town, swimming at the beach, exploring the old Portuguese fort. In the evening, we all went for ice cream, which led to a group decision to have gin and tonics.

So we headed to the bar, where women do not go, not so much by law as convention. I think it would have been worse had Devang not been there: not only visibly Indian, he was also able to speak the language and tell us what was being said by the old drunk men about the girls, who were not exactly modestly dressed.

We sat in a booth, and it wasn't long before a strange old man sitting behind Devang was chattering Gujarati in his ear. Devang seemed to ignore him at first; then his expression changed. We asked what was said.

Devang looked at Kristi. "He said you have a good energy in you. He likes your face." Devang paused. "I think he's some sort of a fortune teller or spiritual guide."

Kristi's demeanour and visage changed permanently after that translation. Devang continued as interpreter for the man, who was egged on by a somewhat nervous Kristi.

"He says you have a very open and honest face, and he likes your soul, but you are uneasy inside."

This carried on for a while, until Devang, while listening to the old man, suddenly went as pale as an Englishman.

After some prodding, Devang told us that the man had said that he (Devang) was unhappy with his relationships (he was divorced and had recently broke up with his girlfriend), and that, for various and unexplained reasons, Devang would never be happy. A blunt fortune, to be sure, but a vague enough one to apply to most anyone. Still, Devang and Kristi were deeply affected by this man's nonsense; Jenny and I listened and drank our drinks in silence.

Eventually, at Devang's insistence, we left and went for masala dosas; it was his favourite Indian food and he probably wanted to distract himself from his destiny of doomed love.

We found a seaside place that served them on a terrace. My God, they were fantastic. I'd never had anything so wonderful in my life. The masala dosa is a South Indian rice pancake: thin, big, crispy and filled with potato and spices. I wanted to shovel it into my greedy face.

During this evening, it occurred to me that it was nearly impossible to get closer to Jenny with the other two around. Her and I had started to develop a bit of a rapport, a private secondary

123

layer to the dynamic of our group, with inside jokes and glances. But she kept refusing my offers of a nightcap or any other attempts for some one-on-one time.

Devang bade us farewell around midnight and the girls and I drove back to our hotel. Once again, I offered a nightcap (in my room, of course, since the bars were closed). Kristi declined with her usual promptness (I think she was clueing in to my deeper appreciation of Jenny's charms). Jenny again thought about it, but said no: she was looking forward to going for an early morning walk on the beach; would I like to come? Why, certainly. Nothing more alone than that.

She knocked on my door at eight-thirty in the morning and we drove to a secluded beach way out past Bon Apetit and walked for about an hour. There was not a soul in sight in the five kilometre view of the shoreline. Her and I talked about ourselves and our lives and all the usual things, which we had only touched upon before. The situation seemed to be full of romantic potential, and after an hour spent together I was tempted to make a move right then and there: what better place than alone on a beach in paradise? But the vibe was friendship, and ours had grown stronger, and that was progress enough for one morning.

Jenny and I wound up spending much of the day alone together: walking, driving, eating, talking; Kristi and Devang joined us later, and we had fresh pineapple and oranges on the beach and swam in the sea. More friends arrived and joined us until, after a while, everyone decided to head back—except Jenny and I. Oh, look, another walk on the beach with romantic undertones, this time at sunset with the horizon set ablaze.

I wrestled internally as we walked, fighting with the idea of making a move. I flirted constantly, trying to gauge her interest, but she was too hard to read (perhaps, in retrospect, I was too hesitant; but I imagine our story would have been the same regardless). I reluctantly decided to play the long game: we still had several days together before I would leave and head to Bombay.

The date was 24 December, and O'Coquiero was hosting a Christmas barbecue banquet. It was an outstanding party with all the Western tourists on the island: Jack, Gary, all the regulars from the St. Thomas barbecues, the many expats and travellers I had met through friends of friends in the same loose circle of familiarity. It felt like a huge family gathering.

The food was on a completely different level: mind-blowingly, mouth-wateringly incredible tastebud pornography; even for the high flavourful standards of Diu, this was impressive. The buffet had just about every type of fish available in the Arabian Sea, prepared in every possible traditional way, plus Portuguese influences with chorizo dishes and Latin accents. And it was all-you-could-eat for about ten dollars. The beer was cheap and flowing, and Jack and I got smashed early on.

Jenny and I sat across from each other and discussed our plans for moving on from Diu: we were both heading to Bombay next; she had a train ticket booked from Ahmedabad in three days. Maybe I should join her? What a great idea. Should be fun. And so it was resolved.

After several hours of gorging ourselves on food and drink, our group decided to go to midnight mass, which was being held at a Catholic church nearby. Jenny, Kristi, Devang and I wandered down the dark streets, trying to find the place. We followed some bad directions before coming upon it by chance: this huge, immaculate white cathedral, looking so perfect and lovely and out of place in India that I had to keep reminding myself of where I was.

The place was packed with Indians in the pews, all of them dressed sharply Western: the men in suits, the women in tasteful dresses but without hats. We stood at the back and waited for them to finish the hymn they were singing.

The priest stepped forward and began his Christmas sermon. He spoke in heavily-accented English about Jesus and such things. I spied the old British restauranteur in the congregation; he didn't look happy. The priest continued, switching to a history lesson as he told us how the Lord saved India from the wicked British; I'm not sure I remember that story from Sunday school. It went on and on like this, a long litany of British wrongs righted by Christ, and eventually the old Brit just jumped up and scurried out past us. I followed him and called his name to see what he had to say.

"I've never heard a sermon like that in my entire life!" he spat, looking past me back into the church with a dark scowl on his face. "These fucking people," and he walked away.

I turned and looked at the church from the outside in the night: the exterior was dark and cold, but the interior was brightly lit up, and with the happy crowd singing inside on Christmas it seemed a familiar and welcome comfort, even to a non-believer.

I lit a cigarette and wandered around the side of the church. I had wisely brought my flask with me, and I took a little shot for our ol' lord and saviour. There was a door on the side where I could peer in at the congregation. India or not, I certainly couldn't smoke in the church, so I kept a respectful distance where no one inside could see me standing in the darkness.

The family who owned Herança Goesa was there, dressed resplendently. From this vantage point, I could look to the back of the church where Jenny was standing. She looked beautiful as she listened to the sermon; I regretted not kissing her on the beach when I'd had the chance.

I turned away and walked to the road that ran along the side of the church. It was dark and quiet. The Christians were in church, the Hindus were in bed and I was drunk.

I took a piss on the road and cranked my head to the sky, losing myself in the fiery stars above as I evacuated onto the earth. The city was quite dark and the dots in the sky burned bright and hot.

As I walked back to the church, I saw Devang, who had come out of the church as well. I offered him a cigarette and a drink and we looked at the stars and left the praying for our souls to those wiser than we.

Eventually, Jenny and Kristi emerged, bored by the service, and we headed back to O'Coquiero where the party was down to the diehards but still strong in spirit. Jack was at one of the tables holding court with a bunch of people, some of whom I recognized. At another table were strangers with a few familiar faces peppered in, and one old, brown, dishevelled man looking like an Indian bum that had wandered up and joined the party.

Our quartet sat down with Jack, and I ordered what turned out to be the last beer in the house. Fortunately there were drugs to be had, thanks to Jugglin' Jack's endless rolling of joints.

The old brown man started calling over to our table in a North American accent, mostly at Jenny and Kristi, and it was becoming more and more crude. I started barking back at him, encouraging him to shut up. He was obviously pretty goddamn gone, and Jenny and Kristi were wincing with his suggestions that they should join him at his table, then in his hotel room, then obliquely hinting at what he might like to do to them.

I stood up and walked over. Some in his group looked appalled, others bemused. I calmly told him to shut the fuck up and chill out. He drunkenly apologized and I went to go smoke a joint with Jack in the road.

The girls came but declined to smoke. Devang soon appeared, and he and Kristi announced they were going home to their respective quarters. The old brown drunk and his group came out as well, and he came over to apologized to us all again.

"Where are you from?" he asked me.

"Canada."

"No shit! Me too! Where?"

"Saskatchewan."

"No shit! Me too!" He was starting to remind me of Tommy Chong, only browner and shiftier. I wasn't sure if I could believe anything he said, so I tried beating him to the punch.

"Where in Saskatchewan?" I asked.

"Moose Jaw, man."

"Fuck off."

"You know Moose Jaw?"

I worked for the newspaper there." I thought for a moment. "Where'd you go to high school?"

"Central, man. Go Cyclones."

With Kristi and Devang now gone, I saw my opening with Jenny. She wasn't drinking much, but that didn't matter: there was no more booze to satisfy the rest of the seething crowd. A decision was made to go do mushrooms on the beach, but Jenny said she'd rather go back to the hotel instead. As much as I wanted to hallucinate on an Indian beach, I also wanted to make it with Jenny. We bade the crowd farewell and I quietly told Jack I might meet up with them later.

Jenny and I wandered the dark, silent streets back to our hotel. It was about one-thirty in the morning and she said she was quite tired, which didn't bode well for me; but my liquored-up optimism was driving me now and I let it steer me back to the hotel.

The gate in the entryway was locked, with a teenage boy sleeping on the floor just inside it. We woke him up and he looked for the key, but couldn't find it. He let us in a side entrance instead, and I knew as I watched the kid lock the door and go back to sleep on the floor that my backup plan of drugs on the beach was gone.

We climbed the stairs. My room was one floor below hers, so when we reached it that meant it was time to say good-night. I offered her a nightcap, knowing she'd refuse. She did; and I kissed her. And she kissed back. And when we separated, she giggled nervously and said good-night, as I suspected she would. I watched her climb the stairs with a smile, and she watched me watch her climb the stairs with a smile, and when she was out of sight I walked down the hall to my room and walked out onto the balcony and sat down lit a cigarette took a drink and felt truly fucking righteous on this the night of the birth of our lord and saviour. Amen. Cheers.

○

My final two days on the island were spent soaking up Diu as much as possible: on the beaches, on motorbikes, in the treehouse resto. Food and drink flowed freely as I tried to swallow the island whole, to somehow take it with me.

As my time in Diu neared its end, I was confronted with the scope of influence the place had exerted on my life and my immediate future. The list, after two weeks in paradise: split with Connie, thereby altering my voyage entirely; met, befriended and kissed a pretty girl and made plans to travel at least briefly with her; formed absurd and remarkable friendships; and perhaps even gained a new perspective on myself and my adventure.

I think of the island, above all, as a simple place: days lived slow, yet gone all too fast. As Devang prepared to go back to Ahmedabad and thence on to England, he mused over his masala omelette that it was better to leave a place before you want to rather than once you're sick of it; there is at least some wisdom in that, I think.

For the final party before Jenny and I left for Bombay, the gang gathered one last time at Bon Apetit. Jack and Gary were there, and Kristi of course, as well as Eli, a loud brash burly young American who had joined our pack of rats in the preceding week and had very much endeared himself to everyone. We ate a feast in the treehouse and shot pool and had some drinks, and then it was time to go. Jack and I hugged good-bye at the end, and I realized with surprise that I would miss him.

Jenny and Kristi and I left together, driving back in the dark on the two-lane highway for the final time. When Conway left, I was deeply sad and felt like a part of me was lost, but there was an equal sense of freedom; leaving Diu myself, I felt only loss. That time and place with those characters and situations could never be recreated. Such is the traveller's lifestyle, and the wanderer's burden: the whole point is to not be tied down; but nothing is free.

When we returned to the hotel, Jenny agreed to a nightcap on the rooftop patio. It turned out to be a surreal determination of our 'relationship', if you could give it a name like that after one kiss.

Over the course of an hour and a half, and several neat gins, we discussed everything from our non-future together, how we felt about each other, the possibility of sex (!), emotional risk versus gain, and so on. To summarize our summit: she liked me and wasn't opposed to sexual congress (I'm paraphrasing), but she was fearful of risking her emotional stability on something short-term; I liked her and was very much in favour of a boink (I'm paraphrasing), and the fact that we both knew it would be a short-term thing meant that we could throw caution (and our underwear) to the wind.

Actually having a conversation of this tone, topic and tenor with a girl I had known less than two weeks and kissed once was not exactly business as usual. I finished my glass of gin; the more she talked, the more I liked her.

°

Very early the next morning, Jenny and I grabbed our bags and headed to the bus station. It was still dark enough that we had to walk with care and hesitation, cautiously squinting ahead for broken pavement. Once arrived, I parked my bag with her and left to find a chai-wallah; I returned fifteen minutes later with two cups and a plastic bag in danger of melting from its piping-hot contents.

I managed to carefully pour two cups and we toasted. I lit a cigarette for breakfast and watched the sun rise into the sky, slowly lighting us. Diu was India-but-not-India. Now after two weeks I was throwing myself back into the madness and chaos. I wondered how I would cope.

My plans were much rougher than Jenny's: we were catching a bus to Ahmedabad; she had a second-class train ticket booked from there to Bombay for that evening, arriving the following morning; then, in the evening of that same day, she would catch another train to the southern state of Kerala to meet her mother for a brief vacation.

I had a bus ticket to Ahmedabad as well. That was it. Have your way with me, fate.

Railway bouncers, the frosty smell of urine, and the confusion in us

The bus ride was surprisingly enjoyable: the roads in Gujarat were awful, and the bus seats were hard and cramped, but Jenny and I talked and played cards and genuinely had fun. It seemed impossible to believe afterwards: an eight hour uncomfortable bus ride on horrible roads in sweltering heat? Snap. Just like that.

It was dusk by the time we arrived in Ahmedabad. We took a rickshaw to the train station, and I was briefly struck by the realization that the last time I was there I was stealthily drinking a bottle of whisky with Conway on the floor.

But there was no time for reminiscing: I needed a ticket on Jenny's train. I waited impatiently in line for ten minutes only to shove my way to the front and be told that I was in the wrong line. I waited in the correct queue and was told by the clerk that the foreign tourist quota (a number of seats on each train reserved for non-Indians) was exhausted. I insisted; I insisted with cash in my outstretched hand: there was nothing to be done. Jenny was defeated, but I said I'd try to talk some bullshit to the station master.

I found him in his office on the phone. He made me wait several minutes before gruffly asking what I wanted.

"Sir," I began, "I need your help." (Always prostrate yourself in the opening.) "My fiancée has a ticket on the nine o'clock train to Bombay, and they've just told me it's sold out. Please, sir, I must get on that train! Please help me!"

He examined me over his wire-frame spectacles. "What class is she travelling in?"

"Second, sir," I said quickly, "but I'll travel wherever there's a seat."

When begging for help, it's best to speak the local language. Since I couldn't manage Gujarati, the next-best choice was Indian English. It's based on outdated British English with unique manner-isms, cadences and slang. The head bob is helpful, but must not be exaggerated or overused lest it be seen as mockery. Without a doubt, speaking Indian English in a calm and dignified manner will always work better than simply approaching someone and speaking in your own voice; I learned this while travelling with Conway.

"I cannot help you."

"Please sir. I'll pay a… penalty, if you like."

He looked at me and sighed.

"I don't need a berth, I'll share one with my fiancée." He considered this.

"Go to the ticket counter," he said, putting his hand on my shoulder and walking me to the door of his office on the platform. "Buy a basic fare ticket, the cheapest one. Board the train, and give that to the ticket inspector when he comes round. He will charge you the difference in the fare, and you will have to share the berth."

I hesitated. "That's it?"

"Yes." I thanked him profusely and went to buy the ticket and tell Jenny.

We drank some chai and ate some fried stuff and then it was time to go. We climbed on board the second-class carriage and found Jenny's berth.

Second class might sound lousy, but not in the context of an Indian train. First class is air conditioned with private rooms and starched sheets. Second class has a curtain rather than a door for the compartment, but is otherwise more or less the same. I usually travelled sleeper class, which is jam-packed with people (seats are often loosely assigned) and has hard platforms for beds, no sheets, plenty of rats and bugs and rowdiness, and a very loose no-smoking policy.

A middle-aged Indian couple were sitting on the convertible beds, which were in their daytime sitting mode. We sat down and they chatted with us in high-brow polite English. Jenny was wearing long pants and looked fine, but I was in grubby shorts and a t-shirt with shit-covered shoes and three days' growth on my face.

"Does anyone know if they sell cigarettes on the platform?" I asked, standing up. The couple stared at me blankly for a moment before the man answered that he didn't think so because, he added pointedly, you can't smoke on the train.

We had twenty minutes to kill and I didn't feel like sitting and talking, so I ventured out to have myself proven wrong. I walked the range of the platform, revelling in the colourful, chaotic lives of the station's inhabitants, both short- and long term. I returned to the compartment as the train was about to leave and found Jenny still yakking.

The couple asked if we were, presumably, occupying the top two bunks; Jenny replied no, we only had the one to share. The couple tried to seem at ease with this idea, but it was clear that we were disrupting their idea of high society: a blue-collar gentleman such as myself with purchasing power equal to theirs must have seemed a nightmare come true.

Soon we all agreed to set up the beds, a task normally left to the passengers themselves in the lower classes. But the woman called a porter (porter?) to come and lower the beds, bring pillows (pillows?) and neatly make up the four places with clean starched sheets and blankets (!).

The other upper bunk in the compartment, opposite from Jenny's, was not occupied, but I knew the train was sold out, which meant someone with a reservation would get on sooner or later. For now, I sat on it while Jenny made herself comfortable sitting cross-legged on hers.

The train had been rolling for about half an hour when the ticket inspector appeared, making his rounds through the cars. He checked the couple's tickets with no problems, followed by Jenny's. He held out his hand for mine and I handed him my cheap, supposedly-upgradable ticket: he looked at it in confused disbelief, as though I had just put a dead fish in his hand.

"This is not a ticket," he said sternly, though it clearly was; it was not, however, a ticket for this train or class.

I proceeded to quickly but calmly explain the situation to him him, mentioning the station master as much as possible and stating with wallet in hand that I was prepared to pay for the difference in price (and bribe him if necessary, though I kept that to myself for the time being).

He shook his head. "No no no no no no no no." He handed my ticket back to me and walked away.

"Did you just get away with it?" asked Jenny.

"I truly doubt it."

Twenty minutes later, the ticket inspector returned with a very large, burly man, apparently the train bouncer.

"This one," said the inspector, gesturing to me. "Throw him off."

"Hey, wait a minute," I said. "I was told by the station master that this would be acceptable."

I went through the whole scenario once again while the inspector shook his head and said no repeatedly over my speech. The boun-cer, however, perked his ears up when I mentioned the station master, and that I would be willing to pay the difference in fare.

The collector was yelling at me again, but the bouncer grabbed him (instead of me, which was a relief) and spoke in a foreign language. They conversed for a minute, and it seemed like the bouncer was suddenly in charge; he turned to me: "You pay?"

"Yes, yes, I'll pay."

"You must pay the fare, and you must also pay a fee."

"Uh-huh. Sure." They pulled out a chart of some sort and determined my penalty, which turned out to be one hundred rupees, a number they threw at me in an attempt to scare me. Considering the price of a real ticket was around seven hundred rupees (twelve dollars), two bucks on top of that as a fee/bribe wasn't so bad. They scolded me as they left, and reminded me to stay off of the empty bunk.

The remainder of the journey was not a pleasant experience. Jenny went to sleep, with me perched at the end of her bunk. The beds were really too small for two Western-sized people, even if we had been a romantic couple. I sat up the whole night, first on her bunk, then chivalrously letting her stretch out while I sat on a small seat by the bathroom between cars, which was slightly less uncomfortable but very cold and smelly. Thirteen hours later, we arrived at the heart of the subcontinent.

MUMBAI

**Falafels and gin,
Strange affairs of the heart,
Move along, sir**

J enny and I arrived in Bombay at seven in the morning. We collected our things and moseyed to a cab, whose driver I argued with to get a better price; it took several minutes, and Jenny was completely bewildered, having consistently taken the non-confrontational route on her trip.

The first order of business was finding a hotel room for me. I had scanned the guidebook and picked out an establishment in Colaba district that seemed cheap and promising. When we arrived, the doors were shuttered and a sign said it was closed for renovations; but there was another hotel on a different floor of the same building, which turned out to be freshly renovated, spic and span, and dirt cheap for a closet of a room. I took it, and Jenny and I dumped our bags and went out to spend our one day in the city together.

The streets bustled with morning activity as the sun began to hint at its uncomfortable potential. Colaba district is built on reclaimed land in the far south of the city (which officially changed its name, with some controversy, to Mumbai in 1995 with the argument that 'Bombay' was a remnant of Portuguese colonialism, though this claim is disputed; in any case, a great many Indians, including Mumbikars/Bombayites, still use the former moniker that served the city for hundreds of years). Colaba is nicer than other parts of town in some ways, which is to say the drug addicts approach you outside Levi's and Chanel stores instead of slums. The main drag, Colaba Causeway, with Western shops and Western fast food and Western clothing, felt cheap and hollow and uninteresting.

We were starving, so we went to a falafel place: overpriced and Westernized and familiar and tasty. Coffee was important for those of us who had sat up all night by a train toilet, so we found a café and killed some time.

Our day in the city wasn't filled with excitement or adventure: we wandered around and checked our email and had a drink at a pub. What mattered more was that we were spending time together, and we both felt very happy about that for some reason. We flirted and held hands and bonded. At one point, things were going so well that I not-so-subtly suggested that we still had time to get back to my hotel room, if you know what I mean. She did; and she ignored me. There was to be no copulating between us, so I resigned myself to that fact and simply enjoyed our chemistry for the little time we had left together.

When nightfall came, we left the bar we were in and wandered along the waterfront between my hotel and the Gateway of India. Across the street was the famous Taj Mahal Hotel, site of major terrorist attacks the previous year and now sporting a heavy military presence. But despite the soldiers and weaponry outside, it was a beautiful and majestic building, and we decided to have one last drink together in the seat of opulence.

As usual, she was dressed nicer than I, though we both fell short of the occasion. Being white makes a palpable difference in these situations: they don't care much what we're wearing because they know we have dollars or euros or pounds in our pockets and, being on holiday, are likely to spend them freely.

We were shown to a private booth with a window and handed wine and spirit lists. Jenny ordered some sort of a fancy cocktail; I settled for Chivas 18 when they said they were out of Johnnie Blue.

The joint was elegant, to say the least. The snobbery of the place was such that I caught the curtains turning their noses up at us when we weren't looking. There were sculptures of things I didn't comprehend, dim orange lighting, very courteous and well-spoken wait staff fluent in multiple languages, and exorbitant prices: the scotch flowed at six hundred rupees per ounce. But as Jenny and I talked about Diu in Bombay, I felt good. We talked about everything, except the situation at hand.

I couldn't really figure out what was going on between Jenny and I. At the start, I was just trying to start sparks because I thought she was cute. But, forced into the group situation in Diu, we became friends (though I still thought she was hot). Once alone in Mumbai, I had made another move and been rejected, but still we were friends who held hands, still I enjoyed the company.

Suddenly, we were late: she had a train to catch to Kerala, and we had to hurry. I paid the bill and we left, walking briskly down the dark waterfront street, hand in hand.

She found a cab outside the hotel and began negotiating a fare while I ran upstairs to retrieve her bags from my room. I came back down, threw them into the trunk and followed her around to the rear passenger door.

"Sorry for not saying a proper good-bye," she said.

Jenny moved quickly and surely, no doubt having made up her mind before this moment: she grabbed me and kissed me. I kissed back, but was caught entirely off-guard and stumbled slightly into her, charming fellow that I am. After a few moments, she got into the cab. I leaned in to say something that I can't recall and may never have really known and she kissed me again. I wished her a safe trip and closed the door.

She was gone already, behind glass and steel, sitting right in front of me. She waved as the cab started and sped away, gone around the corner towards the Gateway of India in an instant. The precise moment she was out of sight (and you could measure this with astronaut precision) I sank into the road.

I looked up and down the dark street and sat on the curb to smoke. My feelings were surprising: more than missing Jenny, I realized that for the first and deepest time ever in my life I was utterly alone. I had conspired with time and geography to isolate myself: my family was on the other side of the world; the one real friend I had here I had pushed away; and now Jenny was gone. I sat and smoked and fell into a daze of confused emotion.

I couldn't follow the pace of time, but twenty minutes or so had passed when two khaki-clad cops approached and began to interrogate me sternly.

"Why are you here?"

I mumbled something.

"Are you drunk?"

"No."

"What is your business? Are you waiting for someone?"

"My girl just left me," I said, tapping my heart for emphasis. (I realized it was over-the-top, but I just wanted them away from me.)

The cops seemed to understand and maybe even sympathize; but they said I couldn't sit there on the curb. They gathered me up and walked me ten metres to the door of my hotel.

"Sit there," one of them commanded with a practised strict tone. I sat in the old abandoned office chair on the sidewalk that he pointed at. They smiled and tried to convey something in poor English, then walked away to continue their rounds. A wooden lever cart piled with sacks of something stood in front of me, parked on the street with a young boy sitting on the sacks; a man stood and smoked in front of it. The street was dark and quiet, and I crawled inside my brain and went to sleep.

New eyes with which to digest opulence

P rior to my split with Conway, my parents had arranged to send a package to me for Christmas. Connie had already used his friend's connections to get us booked with them into a swanky suite in a five-star swinging establishment in Bombay; this was how I was to spend my Christmas in India before I cut myself out of the picture.

But the package had already been sent to the hotel in my name well before that night in Diu, and so I now had to go there and retrieve it.

First, I called ahead so as to make sure they knew I was coming, and to ensure that a non-guest could receive a package from a foreign country without police attention or gunfire. To be safe, I lied and said I would also be checking in, and they reassured me that all was fine.

I walked to the train station near the Oval Maiden, a huge grassy field in the middle of the bustle of the city where cricketers both skilled and not play in the shadows of Raj-era buildings. I took a train north to Santa Cruz station and, with a rough idea of where I was going, began walking east. This was a much less touristic area than Colaba, far closer to the India I knew; ordinary lives were lived here, away from the Levi's stores and expensive Scotch. I asked for directions once, but I was surprisingly close to my target.

Turning down a side street that ran along the edge of the hotel complex, which loomed into view like some space shuttle housing, I saw the slum that surrounded the five-star palace: like every other such place I had seen in the country, there were old and young on the ground, in the street, under sheet metal shanties with small fires in pits. The road was paved, and behind the shanties were public housing projects: huge apartment complexes with poor faces crammed against the windows. I walked past all of this and was thoroughly ignored, even by the few children who noticed me.

I rounded the corner to the front of the fenced hotel grounds and found more fences, these ones much more stylish, though still imposing: wrought iron with spikes rather than chain-link and barbed wire. They were guarded by uniformed men: men in hotel porters costumes who spoke to me and were quite friendly; and men nearby in commando garb with assault rifles and sunglasses who said nothing as they stared me down.

I explained my business, and was screened with a metal detector. Once in the clear, the gates opened and I walked up the brick drive to the front door, which another porter opened for me with a smile.

The interior was staggering: opulence had been thrown everywhere, scattered, splattered like creamed corn sprayed from a fire-hose wielded by epileptic children. The word 'posh' leapt to mind and was rejected as understatement. The lobby was less a lobby than an open two-storey spectacle of gold trim Persian rugs fake waterfalls spiral staircases glass diamonds marble soft music soft armchairs perfect lighting bronze statues and sculptures of the finest order, all of it very expensive and heavily air conditioned.

My family background notwithstanding, I can (or like to think I can) put on airs and blend in with the snootiest of snooty. I can be entitled. I can act like I belong anywhere. Picking my jaw up off the floor and raising my nose precisely nine-and-a-half degrees (international standard for poshness), I sauntered up the massively-wide carpeted staircase to the mezzanine in my shit-covered sneakers, dirty shorts and sweat-soaked polo shirt.

I headed for the concierge desk, where a well-groomed Indian man and an equally dashing woman stood. He seemed to be in charge but was on the phone as I approached. She peeked around him at me and asked if she could help.

"Ah, yes, ahem," I said, reapplying my airs to ensure they were indeed put on, "I believe you have a package for me."

She asked my name and I gave her only my last one, as rich people who expect you to know their family do. The young woman looked under the desk but found nothing. The man ended his phone call and looked at her as if to offer assistance; she told him my last name, nothing more, and he instantly opened a drawer and produced a large envelope with my name on it.

"Thank you, sir," he said. Canadians apologize when you bump into them, but I don't think we say thank-you when we do someone a service.

I sat down in a plush armchair to open my package: a nice note from my family; a t-shirt for the Vancouver Olympics, which would begin soon; two Cuban cigars; German chocolates, squashed but tasty; beef jerky; a copy of The Hockey News; individual letters from my mother, father and sister. It was almost a week after Christmas, but as I sat in that gorgeous armchair surrounded by artificially cold air, I missed home for the first time.

o

That night I went back to the same bar in which Jenny and I had spent much of the latter part of our day together drinking two-for-one gin and tonics during happy hour. It had been a long day and I was melancholy, still wondering what it meant to be alone in India, the wide open road before my uncertain feet with no one to hold me back or influence my chosen path or keep me company. The joint was very stylish and swanky, full of neo-hip urbanites, all of them locals, nearly all of them young. I sat at the bar. Already seven drinks into my night and steadily developing my personal rapport with the bartender, I left my glass at the bar and went outside for a cigarette.

The night was cool but comfortable. The street was fairly animated with couples walking and groups moving from one bar to the next. I wasn't on the street corner for more than a couple minutes when a stocky middle-aged Indian man approached me.

"What are you doing tomorrow?" he asked. Before I could tell him that I was flattered but he wasn't really my type, he continued: "Want to be in a Bollywood television series?"

Without letting me answer, he told me he would pay one thousand rupees (around twenty dollars) for one full day of work. I had nothing to do, and it sounded interesting; I readily agreed.

The man smiled and handed me his card. His name was Imran and he was a talent agent for foreign tourists, which must be a very niche market in any country.

Imran asked to see my hair and I took off my fedora. He gazed at the thick messy pile of brown stands and nodded neither approvingly nor disapprovingly.

"You'll be playing a British officer," he said, speaking as Charlie to one of his Angels. "And you may have to say a few lines in English. Is that all right?"

I said it was and agreed to be outside the Salvation Army across the street from the bar at eight o'clock the following morning for my pick-up.

"It will be a full day, but we'll have you back at your hotel by eleven, maybe eleven-thirty tomorrow night." That was the last I ever saw of Imran.

Dream sequences,
battle scenes,
and the trash heap of the Indian film industry

I woke up bright and early the next day, threw on some clothes and headed out the door. I made it to the Salvation Army on time, but Imran was nowhere to be found. There was a young kid, maybe eighteen years old, standing on the sidewalk with his spiky hair and Nike jacket, trying very hard to look like he wasn't trying to look cool.

We were the only ones around, and he approached me: "You go to Bollywood?" I nodded. He led me to the curb, pointed at a Yamaha motorcycle and said with a smirk, "I ride a bike. Okay?"

Despite my hopes of sleeping off my newfound hangover in the comfort of a car, I had little choice and climbed on behind him, hanging onto the seat as The Kid's perfectly spiked hair stood motionless in the wind.

We drove north through downtown Mumbai, then rocketed on elevated expressways into the suburbs. The towers of glass and steel and concrete from various decades gave way rather suddenly to shabbier apartment blocks and slums.

Traffic at that morning hour was surprisingly light and we made good time. But after an hour of driving, The Kid admitted that he didn't know where he was going. He had a text message with direc-tions to somewhere, but they were in English and he couldn't read them. I read them to him, but they were just names of roads and buildings, little help in the thick and disorderly jungle of an Indian city. We asked rickshaw drivers for help, and they pointed us in vari-ous directions. Finally we found the building: a dilapidated office tower that would only house squatters and dubious businesses if it existed in an occidental city.

I was brought into the office and told that, despite being over an hour late based on the time we had been given, we were actually two hours early. And so I sat in the reception area while The Kid went to procure some breakfast for him and I. A few other people appeared and sat down as I waited, including a young white guy who spoke Hindi to everyone. He introduced himself as Tyler and spoke American-accented English to me; he explained that he was an Australian who had spent much of his childhood in India and California; he called me 'dude' far too often.

A large man arrived around noon, appearing to be flustered. He spoke only in Hindi and pointed at a few people, who replied in Hindi. He looked at me for a while. Then he turned and walked back down the stairs, with everyone following him. The Kid told me to come along. We all got into a jeep and I realized that we were finally making our way to the set. We stopped twice along the way to pick up a couple more people, and with our car full we began the two-and-a-half hour drive to the promised land of Bollywood.

The highways were fine, and the scenery was quite nice at times, but the washed-out lumpy road leading us up to the production lot was an omen, a small sample of things to come. The series was being filmed on an expansive lot with several indoor and outdoor sets. On the south side of this was a chain fence which separated us from stagnant pools of water and piles of garbage: whereas Hollywood is often accused of being filled with trash, Bollywood is actually directly next to large amounts of it.

Our group exited the jeep and followed our driver, walking through the gates and past the security guards who didn't look all that secure. Suddenly, I was in nineteenth century colonial India, in the middle of a town with people in period dress smoking beedis and drinking chai. Some squatted on the ground as they ate from metal thali plates. I had no idea what I was doing or where I was supposed to go, so I followed Tyler to one of the dressing rooms and dropped off my bag. He said we had nothing to do for the time being, so I decided to wander around.

The production seemed to be fairly professional—at least enough so as to impress a greenhorn like myself. The cameras and sound equipment seemed modern and expensive, and the crew operating them appeared to know what they were doing. The sets were not made out of cardboard but wood. People hustled about doing various jobs in various places. All conversations were in Hindi or Marathi, so I had no idea what was going on. A scene was being shot in what appeared to be some sort of Indian regal setting, perhaps with a prince character. I walked along the perimeter of the set, watching on a monitor as the camera zoomed in on a frightening-looking fellow with a ridiculous moustache. He looked outraged, then stood and whispered something, then began shouting dramatically, all with the typical Bollywood flair that is usually interpreted in the West as overacting. He repeated this scene several times, responding to whatever the director was saying to him between takes. This was my first look at the man in charge: tall, stocky, disinterested. Most of his directions came in short, soft-spoken sentences, which would then be amplified by the shorter, louder man sitting, next to him: this fellow was the director's pit bull, barking orders in harsh sounding language to anyone and everyone.

The scene ended and I went back outside. There were different scenes being shot on various parts of the lot, and so the crew was eating in shifts. A new bunch had come and grabbed their thali plates, scarfing down the greasy food as quickly as possible so as to get more before it all disappeared. I spied the chai and headed straight for it.

Re-energized by several cups of the sugary fuel, I looked at my watch and realized I'd been there nearly two hours and had lost track of Tyler, the one person I knew who could speak fluent English. I headed back to the dressing room, but he wasn't there. I wandered around the buildings and sets all over the lot: he was gone. Just then, the Pit Bull and his lackey approached me.

"You are Alex?" asked the Pit Bull. I said I wasn't and introduced myself. He said he was the production manager, or stage manager, or something like that; his English was fairly good, but he spoke very quickly and was hard to understand.

"Do you know what part you are playing?"

I told them that I believed I was playing a British officer, to which their nodded in understanding and flipped a few pages in the script.

"So," he continued, "you can read a few lines as well?"

I replied that I could. He tore out two pages from a script, circled some things and handed them to me. The text was all in Hindi; I turned the page over as if it were a menu, with English on the back: no such luck.

"I don't speak Hindi," I said, and for the first time since arriving in India, that statement elicited shock from Indians as it escaped my lips.

"You don't speak Hindi?" they cried.

"I don't speak Hindi."

Secure in this fact, they then spoke about me in Hindi, looking very concerned. "If we write these lines in English, will you read them?" asked the Pit Bull.

I said that I would be happy to read any English lines they might give me. With that, the Pit Bull went and sat down on a step, scribbling furiously on the script and consulting others around him for translations of specific words and phrases. In the meantime, I went and had another chai.

Twenty minutes later, the Pit Bull sauntered up to me and waved some papers in my face. "Read this," he demanded. I grabbed the script and looked at it: he had written the lines using the Latin alphabet, but the words were still in Hindi.

"This is still Hindi!" I cried.

"But it's in English. You can read it."

"This is not English," I said. "This is Hindi. I don't speak Hindi. I have never spoken Hindi."

"You must read these lines," said the Pit Bull, tapping the papers I held. I examined my first line, written out in ballpoint pen:

OFFICER: SIR! MANIKARNIKA KA
KARVAN BITTUR SE KANPUR
HOTE HUE KALPI MEIN PAHLA
CAMP DELGA

There was a page and a half of this mumbo-jumbo. I said there was no way I could memorize everything. I argued that I had only agreed to read lines in English. I argued that I had never spoken more Hindi than to say Hello or order chai. He asked me to try reading the lines aloud. I did: it was awkward and terrible, and I had no clue where to put emphasis or pauses, but he pretended it had promise. I pressed him further and argued to do the lines in English. He agreed to re-write a small part of the dialogue in my mother tongue, but the majority had to remain in Hindi as the substance of it was crucial to the plotline and the audience needed to understand it. I assured him I would be terrible; he said he had confidence. I reluctantly agreed to try.

"How long do I have?"

"Lots of time to practise," he assured me. "One hour."

I swore at him in French and walked away to find a quiet place. I wandered the lot, reading the lines over and over again, repeating them to myself. The great thing about a production lot is that you can talk to yourself as loudly and dramatically as you like and no one cares.

One hour passed: nothing happened. No one came to get me; I certainly wasn't going to go looking. Actually, I was beginning to feel surprisingly confident in my chances of pulling this off with any success. Another half hour passed and my mastery of the lines grew stronger.

I went back to the dressing room and found Tyler, wearing a ridiculous puffy shirt with britches, getting his makeup done and reciting his lines with great passion into the mirror. His lines sounded very familiar, and a quick glance at my script confirmed that he was playing Simon Fraser, the British leader to my officer, and the person I would be speaking my lines to.

I told him this as the makeup guy glued on his fake moustache, and he offered to give our scene a practice reading.

My confidence was shattered: I forgot words, mixed up others, stumbled through the pronunciation like, well, like someone who can't speak the language worth a damn. Tyler's Hindi was perfect, the result of a childhood spent in India, but he spoke it with an intentionally bad accent by order of the director ("After all," said Tyler, "the British couldn't speak it properly, right?").

He encouraged me and tried to pick up my spirits for a while before going back to staring himself down in the mirror. I glumly picked up my script again with a sense of impending doom.

The door opened and a small Indian man asked for the officer. He took me down twisted hallways to the back of the building where the costuming department was. He flipped through his collection of British military clothing and selected a white dress jacket with those frilly gold shoulder pads that you see in old-time movies when the soldiers dress up. A black pair of slacks and a black belt with a holster completed the outfit. I lumbered back to the dressing, room to change into it; miraculously, it all more or less fit my six-foot-five frame. I saw myself in the mirror: I looked ridiculous; fortunately, so did all the other actors in their period get-ups, which meant no one would be laughing at me.

I went back to sulking alone with my lines for a while until the Pit Bull came in. He spoke to Tyler (who had now fully transformed into Simon Fraser and would not relinquish the character's manner-isms or accent for several hours) in Hindi and they sat down together. The Pit Bull watched closely as Fraser gathered himself and began reciting his lines with the same gusto that he had used with the mirror. A few times the Pit Bull stepped in to correct or advise Fraser in English: say it like this, put a pause after that.

After Fraser finished, the Pit Bull pointed straight at me and ordered: "Sit." I sat. "Read your scene together," he told us.

My lines were first, and I tried to look like I was reaching deep for inspiration so as to buy some time to remember the still-strange words.

I stumbled almost immediately after the opening "Sir!" The Pit Bull was patient, calming, reassuring. "Take your time, try again, it's easy." I breathed deep and began again. This time I made it through the first line, and Fraser gave his smug reply. Now came my second bit, and I butchered it entirely. It consisted of four sentences, only the first of which I could remember. The Pit Bull was less forgiving the time and reprimanded me. I tried and failed again, and he shook his head, becoming more indignant.

"These are simple words!" he said, not bothering to hide his frus-tration. "Why can't you read them? What's wrong with you?"

"I don't speak Hindi, goddamn it!" I yelled at him. He didn't flinch.

"You're just not trying hard enough!" he barked. "If you tried—"

"I don't speak Hindi!" I hollered over top of him. "I've never spoken it!"

"It's a matter of memorizing a few simple words."

"It's simple for you because you speak Hindi!" I said. "My brain doesn't recognize these words, and I can't remember them after only a couple hours of practice." We were no longer yelling, but merely speaking angrily. I tried to reason with him: "What if I gave you lines in French or Italian to memorize in one hour?"

"I could do it," he said solemnly, "because I have the right atti-tude."

As I contemplated either smacking him or storming out or both, Fraser spoke to him in Hindi; I could tell that he was attempting to defend me. But the Pit Bull would have none of it: he wanted the lines right, and fast; yet he seemed to read that he had pushed me too far and he suddenly became conciliatory.

"Okay, okay," he said in a softer voice. "I know you are trying."

I had nothing invested in the production. I could care less if it failed or had to cancel shooting for the day if I walked out. I was there for the experience, and for a story to write. I was angry and provoked and had nothing to lose. But the cunning little Pit Bull said the one thing that resonated with me.

"You've already spent many hours here. You've come all this way. You've already gotten into costume. You might as well give it a shot."

I was mollified. I agreed to keep practising the lines for another half hour, but I repeated again that I could not promise that I would be any good in such a short time, and the Pit Bull accepted that condition.

He left, and it was time for makeup. A prepubescent boy gave me a straight razor shave (apparently nineteenth century British soldiers didn't have two days' growth and a soul patch) and then the makeup man spread various powders and cosmetics on my face. All the while, I kept repeating the lines in my head, avoiding peeking at the script. (I never bothered to read the English lines in the other scene; I knew the Hindi scene would be shot first, and I had enough confidence in my memory to do the English scene on the spot.) The pièce de résistance was a thick brown moustache glued in place.

A few minutes later, Fraser and I were beckoned. Showtime. We were led to the set, which was Fraser's office: an imposing imperial room with portraits of Queen Victoria on the dark wooden walls and a huge desk in the centre. There were around twenty crew members milling about, preparing the many cameras and lights for our big performance. Everyone in the room was fluent in the language I was about to speak, except for me. The lights and the uniform made me sweat even more than the nerves alone. A crew member put a heavy wooden pistol in my holster. I was ready.

✢

The director apparently had a bad case of mouth sores for which he had to hold some sort of medicine in his mouth, leaving him unable to speak during shooting. His vague gestures and head movements were interpreted by the Pit Bull and barked into verbal language.

Fraser was to stand facing a side wall, while I was positioned in front of his desk. I was only able to get a vague idea of the scene: an officer (me) comes to Fraser with news that a caravan of Indians has reached a camp and mentions some of the people travelling; Fraser jumps on the name of a seemingly unimportant servant and, believing him to be a great threat, changes his military strategy.

As Fraser and I gathered around the desk, the Pit Bull instructed us as to what he wanted from his actors: I would begin speaking to Fraser, who would whirl around and face me at the news I was delivering, then walk to his desk where I would demonstrate something to him on the map that lay upon it.

What's this? A map? This was news to me: I had enough trouble convincingly recalling the Hindi lines as it was; now I had to gesture on a map at the same time. This is much more difficult than it sounds, far beyond rubbing your belly while patting your head. I tried to readjust on the spot, reciting the lines in my head as I pointed randomly to the different camps on the large map.

But the time for practice and rehearsals had passed. Apparently we were behind schedule, so the Pit Bull yelped and barked until everyone was in position. A few straggling voices were shut up by the calls for "Silence!" which passed through the set. "Rolling," said the Pit Bull flatly, which was apparently a command and not a question, for he waited for the videographer around the corner to reply: "Rolling, sir!"

"Action!"

I gave sufficient pause before speaking, steadying myself.

"Sir!" I began confidently. "Manikarnika ka karvan." At this, Fraser turned and walked to meet me at his desk with great flair, and I began gesturing to the map. But as soon as I diverged from my rigid colonial posture to point at the map, I was lost. The words were there, sort of, but they were scrambled like a messy dal fry; they became nearly as meaningless for Hindi speakers as they were for me.

"Cut!" yelped the Pit Bull when I couldn't finish the scene. He walked over and joined Fraser in reassuring me. I ignored both of them and pulled my lines out of my pocket to give them another quick read.

"Take your time," said the Pit Bull, holding up his palms to me as though I might hit him.

I read. I read again. I looked at the Pit Bull and shrugged. He took this as a sign that I was ready for another take.

Somehow I managed to escape that second try unscathed; if my Hindi was mangled, at least I got through it. The Pit Bull, on the director's behalf, nevertheless called for a reshoot while congratulating me on me "strong delivery."

The opportunity for third and fourth takes didn't mean my Hindi improved; I suspect it was at least slightly rushed on my part, since I just wanted to get the damn thing over with. I think we did about eight or nine takes of that scene, and it was hard to tell whether they were just tinkering with things in general or whether they were hoping I would suddenly impress them.

Next up was a scene that didn't involve Fraser or I, so we went outside for chai. A short while later, we were called back for our next scene, where I had my actual English lines to speak. I still had not even glanced at them; I pulled them out of my pocket and quickly read them to myself as the Pit Bull shouted at crew members to stand here or there. He asked if I was ready and I said yes, slipping the script back into my pocket. I nailed it on the first try, and both the Pit Bull and the silent director did a poor job of hiding their surprise. I wonder if they realized, even then, that it was the language barrier and time constraints imposed on me, not my 'attitude', that made me such a painfully lousy actor.

After a few takes of that scene, I had read all my lines. But Fraser had warned me that the close-up shots would be done later, individually, so I knew I wasn't finished. In the meantime, I hung around the set. Thalis were provided, much the same as lunch: a few different curry dishes along with puris and samosas; plus the inexhaustible and all-important chai supply, which kept flowing as the day grew longer. The crew were obviously tiring by the time I was called for my close-ups several hours later, around eight o'clock.

First up was the English scene, which I performed flawlessly once again. But then came the horrible Hindi: I had foolishly not spent my time rehearsing and had not read the lines for several hours. Tired and with a camera a foot away from my face, I struggled and stumbled through the lines painfully, far worse than before. I felt bad for the crew, who had to stay until we were finished and were likely cursing this foreign moron under their breath. The Pit Bull was also getting crankier, and he started harping on me once again, asking why I couldn't read the lines anymore. I tried to ignore him and focus on re-reading the lines in between screwed-up takes (around twenty in all for that one scene). Finally, the director said it was good enough (actually, he couldn't say anything; his vague gesture to the Pit Bull could have been more along the lines of "Just move on, he'll never get it").

I asked to leave at this point, but I still had yet to film my hand shots, which were needed for when my character pointed on the map. These at least were silent, but they took some time, and it was ten o'clock by the time we finished. Even then, the Pit Bull had me stand around for another hour before he turned to me and said, "That's a day for you." I shook his hand and the director's and walked off the set; but before I got far, the makeup fellow caught me and confiscated my moustache, ruining my plans of stealing it.

In the dressing room I found The Kid, passed out on a mattress on the floor: the poor guy had been working until six in the morning the night before, then picked me up at eight. I changed quickly and gave my ridiculous costume to a crew member and nudged The Kid until he woke up. Just then, Simon Fraser (who had been filming his own close-ups) burst into the room and, with exhilarated loudness and profanity, suggested we leave. The Kid got up to find us a ride back to Mumbai while Fraser changed his clothes and personality back to Tyler.

There were several large jeeps to shuttle everyone back to the city, and Tyler felt that we as actors ought to be ahead of the crew; he declared this loudly to the tired crowd waiting in the dark, and no one challenged him, so I climbed into the first car with him. After several detours, a stop for gas and an uncomfortable two-hour ride, we arrived back at the office in Bombay at three in the morning. Everyone had private transportation or lived within walking distance except me: my hotel was in Colaba, still another hour's ride south. The Kid was responsible for getting me there.

And so we rode on his motorcycle, both sleep-deprived and helmetless, through sleeping Mumbai in the middle of the surprisingly cold night. I was still wearing short and a t-shirt, and my teeth were chattering by the time he dropped me off at four o'clock. The Kid's eyes were barely open. He paid me my thousand rupees from Imran and I gave him three hundred for a tip, which seemed to surprise him.

I woke up the boy in the hotel to open the front door and fell into my bed, vowing to never again set foot in Bollywood in any capacity. When I watched the episode online the following week, my entire presence had been reduced to a silent four seconds during a montage, with an Indian peasant character giving the news to Fraser instead.

Just as well, I suppose: I don't think I'm cut out for television.

Ruby Thursday,
and how the other half lives

After two months on the road, I began to believe I had India under my thumb, figured out better than the rest of the tourists who come to slag off and drink cheap cocktails by the beach. In my heart of hearts I knew this not to be true, but it didn't matter; it is the natural creep of overconfidence, of compla-cency, of the young soul that wants to have accomplished something, anything, more than it has.

I had heard of a slum tour from someone or somewhere, but find-ing the company's office was no simple matter: through a conveni-ence store, up a stairway hidden behind the shelves and through an unmarked steel door. Once I tracked it down, I bought a ticket for the next day's tour.

The rest of the early afternoon was spent drinking rum, investig-ating restaurant options, booking my train ticket onward; once I ran out of things to accomplish (and rum), I began to get bored. I tried several bars with terrible service full of white ex-pats and tourists, mostly Brits and Aussies and a few Yanks, judging by accents. None of it interested me, and all the people seemed phony for some reason. Finally, as night settled on Colaba, I moseyed to the bar above Leopold's.

Leo's is a lousy restaurant in a very heavily touristed area, just down the street from McDonald's. The food, no matter what you order, is pitiful and wildly overpriced; yet it is popular, primarily because people, of any race or background, are often drawn to estab-lishments popular with their own kind; and, secondly, because Leo's was featured in a certain work of literature which I have heard endless reviews about but have not yet bothered to read because it is the size of a goddamn phone book.

The bar upstairs was very different from the T.G.I. Friday's-esque vibe below: fairly trendy with acid jazz playing over the low lighting and red ambient glows. I sat at the bar and ordered a Kingfisher, which was overpriced. The crowd was sparse, entirely middle-class Indian. The air conditioner was cranked up too high for nighttime. I felt out of place; it wasn't my speed. I drank quickly and asked for the bill just as two bodacious brown beauties sauntered into the joint and sat down right next to me at the bar.

The bartender brought me the cheque, and I awkwardly ordered another beer. The girls ordered something or other, speaking to the bartender and each other in a mix of their native language and English words thrown in for trendiness. They were probably in their early twenties and definitely drop-dead gorgeous, dressed to the nines. The one sitting next to me kept tossing glances my way, and I'd catch her and we'd smile at each other.

"Good evening, ladies."

They smiled bashfully at me, but said nothing and turned back to their own conversation. I sipped my beer patiently for a minute before trying again.

"Are you from Bombay?"

"Yes, we are." It was the one next to me who spoke, and she did so with intentional disinterest. She also pointedly did not ask me the logical and highly common return enquiry.

And so I ignored them as they ignored me. I kept glancing sideways to try and catch her peeking my way, but she seemed to be avoiding it. So be it: I quickly finished my beer and called for the cheque. But, apparently, this was a game of chicken, and by giving up I had actually won: as soon as I signalled to the bartender, she spoke.

"So, where are you from?"

"Canada."

"Canada. That's nice. Is Canada nice?"

And thus began my introduction to Ruby Matthews, a stewardess on (what else?) Kingfisher Airlines. Her friend, a stewardess on Qatar Airways, was less interested in including me in the conversation; fortunately, she also seemed the submissive type, so Ruby got her way.

"You guys are dressed up tonight," I observed, shrewdly combining conversation with compliments while also fishing for details. "What are you up to after this?"

"Oh, we have a party to go to," said Ruby, who spoke too fast in her thick accent. She turned and said something to her friend, then asked me in a coy voice, "Are you leaving?"

"No, I think I'll stay for one more."

I ordered another beer and we chatted about, well, her, mostly. Ruby loved to talk and she loved to talk about herself. She also talked about things she clearly knew nothing about, like history and world politics. She spoke with passion and conviction, masking the fact that a great deal of her statements were flawed, faulty or just plain nuts. But she was entertaining, not unlike a female Conway, though infinitely more pleasing to the eye.

Ruby offered to buy me a drink, anything I wanted, and I mentioned the bottle of Jack Daniels that had caught my eye. Bona fide brand-name Western liquor is very pricey, but she thought nothing of ordering me a triple, and Jack and cokes for her and her friend.

I was happy to humour her rantings, drink her drinks, and flirt shamelessly with eye contact and a few innuendos, which were well-received. Then Ruby escalated things by touching my leg; this was not unwelcome and she was casual about it, and I returned the friendly signal. She took my hand and held it, running her fingers along the inside of mine softly. All this went on around the lower half of the bar while the three of us carried on conversation above.

Suddenly, Ruby put her leg on top of mine. This was a huge jump ahead of clandestine flirting, especially considering the shortness of her skirt. I wasn't sure what to do: I remembered Jodhpur, making out with the Finnish girls in the street and the stares of disapproval from the locals. I glanced around the dark bar and found no one looking at us; I decided that if she didn't care what her fellow Mumbikars thought, neither did I.

Ruby was drunk now. I was several drinks in, but still well within my range. She was ignoring her friend more and more and talking to me with both words and secret hands.

"Where are you staying?" she asked in a low voice.

"Two blocks from here. Why don't you come over?"

"I can't," she said with a tone of sadness. "I have to go to my friend's party."

"Just come for a while, and then go."

"What about my friend?" she whispered, motioning to the all-but-forgotten girl beside her at the bar (who could almost certainly hear our conversation, and who was very clearly bored with our shenanigans and her third-wheel status).

"Bring her along." I didn't really care, and I wasn't even sure I'd be allowed to sneak a girl or two past the front desk: the hotel was tiny, the partitions of the rooms didn't reach the ceiling, and my room was directly next to the reception desk.

The bigger trouble was letting this opportunity slip away: Indian women (especially young women) are as a general rule very shy around Western men, and there seemed to be no hope of ever meeting one on more than a strictly superficial level, such as buying cigarettes from a shop girl. If I was ever going to get down with a local girl, this was probably my one chance; that much I knew. (Although, truth be told, when a beautiful girl is buying one drinks and feeling one up at the bar, one doesn't much care where she is from.)

"Come on, let's just run back to my place for a little bit. I'll leave some money for your friend's drink and we'll come back and meet her in thirty minutes."

But Ruby wouldn't go: she hummed and hawed and after twenty more minutes of heavy petting and American whisky she decided to head to the party with her friend; I was never invited.

I walked them downstairs and we had a cigarette. She flagged a cab down and, to my surprise, the driver waited patiently while we smoked.

"Wait, give me a piece of paper."

I fished out a hotel business card from my pocket. She threw away her cigarette and scrawled her name and email address on it. Then Ruby kissed me passionately and said good-bye and got into the cab and sped away. That seems to happen a lot in Bombay; maybe it's just me.

✿

Mumbai is Bombay, Bombay is Mumbai.

The city is something of a reflection of the world on a smaller scale, and, of course, in Indian terms. Fifty-five percent of its twelve million souls live in slums; multitudes more of the greater city's twenty million suffer slightly lesser degrees of poverty. At the same time, there is incredible wealth and progress that defies your belief that you are indeed still in India. Colaba and other parts of downtown could have been transplanted from any of a number of major Western cities, the Indian flavour explained as the result of immigrants. McDonald's, Nike, Levi's, Sony, LaSenza, Dominos—oh, my.

But the beggars come there, too, after those rich pockets laden with guilt. They tug at your heartstrings: the ragged women with their skinny children; the legless man in the hand-powered tricycle; the drug dealers who open conversations like degenerate Willie Nelsons ("Hello, hash?"). Maybe I had too small of a time frame to read much into it, but I never saw anyone in Mumbai give alms.

Outside the downtown core, where the poor are the majority, life is very different. Just like the greater planetary picture, the city has vast wealth held by a small number of people; this does not appear to help the vast majority of Mumbikars, particularly with the corruption that still plagues Indian politics at all levels. If anything, the condos, hotels and boutiques that spring up around their slums and public housing can only serve to remind them of how badly off they are. And the swanky areas are invariably next to a slum: there are simply so many poor people that the developers have no choice but to build in their midst and hope the neighbourhood will get better. Gentrification doesn't work in shantytowns.

Every city has its rich and poor, its middle class and the adjacent extremes. Sometimes, in some places, these disparate parts are close enough in proximity to see the juxtaposition in a glance. But the gap in Bombay is so wide and so pervasive, so glaringly and heart-droppingly obvious nearly everywhere you look, that the chasm between the groups becomes staggeringly clear. If you believe the world is slowly getting better, if you think that India is growing stronger and will soon be on a par with the West, Mumbai will both confirm and dispel that idea.

As I make my way from my hotel to, say, Churchgate train station, I have to cross through Colaba district any number of ways. As I do, I will be hounded along Arthur Bunder Road by the dealers: the same seven or eight young men with glazed or crazed or amazed eyes who lie in wait. I'm not sure exactly what their criteria is for determining the most likely potential customers for their products (in their scarcely-changing order: hash, marijuana, cocaine, brown sugar and sometimes ecstasy); maybe it's simply young and white; maybe they don't have criteria. In any case, they either have short-term memory troubles or are boundlessly hopeful. In the course of one day I will be approached by the same men at least twice, often more, depending on my route.

One fellow in a blue shirt who looked like he could have been the bassist in a pop-punk band took the top prize for absurdity: he offered me hash, and I said no, reminding him that he asks me every day and I always say no. I walked a short distance down the road and sat down on a bench. Within five minutes he walked down the same way, saw me sitting, crossed the street in a hurry and offered me hash. I stared at him incredulously, wondering if I was Bill Murray in *Groundhog Day* with more drugs and darker skin tones, until he realized who I was and laughed at himself. "India," he said as he shrugged and walked away; I couldn't have phrased it better.

❖

I woke up in my closet of a hotel room late the next morning, covered my hangover with the cleanest clothes I had, and hustled to Churchgate station, the meeting point for my slum tour. Our guides collected the paying tourists, split us up into groups and brought us by train to the money-making hellhole of Dharavi.

Dharavi is the heart of Bombay, or so the tour guides like to say: it's roughly in the middle between the Western and Central Railways, which somewhat parallel each other as they run down either side of the city. But the heart of Bombay is about more than just geography. Dharavi has made something out of nothing: in fact, the nearly one-million residents of the slum have become professional something-from-nothing manufacturers through their recycling businesses. The people are trampled on, caught in the cycle of poverty that swallows generation after generation, and yet they produce; they work; they create; they fight for the lives they know on a regular basis, and they do so against all odds with precious little ground to stand on. In this way, more than any other, Dharavi is the heart and soul of Mumbai.

We began by entering a fairly basic Indian street scene: dirty, busy, crowded, bustling with business and traffic and noise. The eight of us—the guide and his friend (both former children of the slum), four Australians, one American, one Canadian—walked for some length down this road, and it seemed to be nothing out of the ordinary, nothing we hadn't seen before. There was great poverty, but there was also work, shops, people in clean clothes, people with purpose and dignity: this was India, after all.

Turning a corner into the industrial and manufacturing district of Dharavi, we found huge piles of sacks stuffed with empty plastic drink bottles stacked in and around a makeshift warehouse. I had seen the women who roam the city with these sacks on their backs, collecting bottles from the road, but I'd always wondered where they took them. The bottles are crushed and left on the roof to dry out; then they are crushed again to produce plastic chips, which are melted, coloured, pressed into long thin strings, cooled, and chopped into small pellets. All of this happens in Dharavi, using machinery built right on site by the people who live there. The entire operation takes place in a scattered division-of-labour fashion throughout the manufacturing district, with each labourer devoted to his step in the process. The pellets are then sold to larger compan-ies, who may turn them into anything from earrings to sunglasses to who-knows-what.

In much the same way, aluminum is taken from the city streets and reclaimed for profit by Dharavi workers. Cans and such are shredded into fine spiralled scrapings; these are then melted down over a fire and cast into components for food processors and the like, which are then sold on the domestic and international markets.

Recycling isn't the only thriving industry in Dharavi. Garments such as men's shirts are produced elsewhere in the slum, and we visited such a workshop. The workers busied themselves sewing on the floor; every completed item earns them twenty-five rupees, and each worker may make ten to fifteen garments per day. There also exists a dyeing business where finished garments and raw textiles are coloured in large vats by workers. The chemicals used are noxious and dangerous, but the hands, feet and clothes of the men and boys were soaked in it. They stirred the vats to evenly soak the clothes, spilling blue liquid on themselves as they did, and they laughed with us and showed us their blue hands with a grin.

Our group was then led through a narrow corridor that cut

through the buildings of the slum. It was never more than a metre wide and often less, and the metal roofing panels and overhead wires lowered the head clearance to six feet at most. The heavy air was damp and putrid, though it was difficult to determine exactly what had produced the odour; urine and compost were certainly present, but gasoline, chemicals and the vague smell of burnt-something stung the nostrils as we walked single-file behind the guide. The corridor was dark and the ground broken and uneven with open sewers, but the crowds of people who walked with and against us were sure in their footing.

This was a residential area, and we glanced inside many homes as we walked: on average, the residents have only a couple square metres of living space. Families are grouped together in tiny, cramped shanties. The children who stood in the doorways or ran between us were energetic, boisterous, friendly, dirty, unwashed. Their clothes were ragged and most of them ran barefoot on the dirt and concrete. They ran ahead of us and lined the corridor with their friends, standing and waving at us, calling "Hello!" as we passed. We returned their eager greetings but with heavy hearts that they were too young to understand; for while the adults and older children must surely be aware of their station in life, the youngest residents of the slum do not know how poor they are, and how different their lives are from ours. But in their eyes, in their infectious smiles and youthful energy, we saw our common humanity, and the smiles we returned to them were genuine.

The corridor opened onto a large courtyard where the public toilets were housed. Our guide said the cleaning was the responsibility of the government, but it was never done, and thus the conditions were atrocious since an average of twelve people share one Dharavi toilet. In the mornings the commodes see huge lineups, which explains why many people—men, women and children—simply choose to use the ground as a toilet, either in open areas or in open sewers. Like many other parts of life in the slums, health concerns are not part of the equation, sometimes due to ignorance, more often sidelined by a lack of options. Yet, given the apparent sense of community in Dharavi, it was somewhat surprising that the people themselves would not rally together and find a solution in the absence of government.

Not far away was the area's communal garbage pile, which dwarfed the endless smaller piles throughout the streets of Dharavi. All garbage that could burn was burned, and children ran and played barefoot in the black smoke.

Children were everywhere in the little city-within-a-city. We were brought to a school, poking our heads into a class as our guide told us that government-run schools, like all endeavours of the state, are highly mistrusted. The school we were in was partially funded by the companies that use labour in Dharavi. Most children go to school, said the guide as the class of forty waved to us politely.

The slum also hosts the second-largest leather production plant in India, churning out ten million pelts annually. Sheep, buffalo and goat hides are brought in from a slaughterhouse ten miles away to be sheared, treated and dried before shipped onward. (It should be noted that the Indian leather industry is notorious for its horrific treatment of animals; our guide claimed innocence, but watching the thin labourers working needle-and-thread in and out of the pelts, I wondered how much strife and suffering was needed to make a profit for the owners of this and other Dharavi businesses, none of whom live in the slum themselves.)

Like every industry in Dharavi, the workers are motivated by commission, the key to a living wage for everyone in the slum. A potter, for instance, makes one thousand clay pots each day, not because it's easy, but because she needs to feed her family.

The land Dharavi sits on is owned by the government, which means none of the structures belong to the people who live in them. The government has had a long-standing, often-delayed plan to redevelop Dharavi's five hundred thirty-five acres, under which occupants of structures built prior to the new millennium will be entitled to small apartments. But where do the people go while the project is being built on their demolished homes?

The gross domestic product of Dharavi has been estimated as high as one billion dollars annually. Though the profits don't stay in the slum; though the slum itself may disappear; though, with an estimated head count of between six hundred thousand and one million souls, it is merely the fifth-largest slum in Bombay; Dharavi represents the old and new, Bombay and Mumbai, poverty and profit, the heart and soul of the city.

We finish the tour and I leave Dharavi deeply moved. As I sit in a train station waiting to go back to Colaba, young men take pictures of me and I yell at them so loudly that they quickly turn and walk away in fear, and I wonder if India might be getting to me for the first time.

HAMPI

**The Desperados ride strong in the land
of drugs, cards and monkey-gods**

After a miserable few days in Goa—highlighted by an extended stint of intestinal troubles that put me on a short leash
from the toilet, and a strange friendship with a sex-addicted
middle-aged German motorcycle stunt rider named Tomas who gave
me my new nickname of Pineapple Slim to go with my new favourite
drink of rum and brandy mixed with fresh pineapple juice—I set out
by sleeper bus to Hampi, hallowed battlefield of the gods.

Hampi is a small town in the eastern part of the state of
Karnataka, well inland and most famous for its landscape. The odd
piles of boulders that stretch for miles around give the impression
that someone has blown up a mountain; or, perhaps, picked it apart.

The legend goes that giant monkey-gods tore apart the hills and
mountains that once stood, throwing chunks of the stones at each
other until everything was destroyed. Looking around at the endless
bizarre rubble, no logical or intuitive scientific explanation comes to
mind. I much prefer the legend, in any case; this is the sort of landscape that makes myth and religion seductive.

I met a handful of people on the bus, most notably Tom the
Chemical Expert. There was hardly a substance on the planet that
he hadn't inhaled, insufflated, swallowed, injected, popped, cut, or
otherwise consumed; he listed endless chemical compounds with
enormous names, discussing their pros and cons, their highs and

163

lows. Most people who make such claims are lying, especially when they are only thirty years old. But Tom was such a laid back Aussie, such an earnest, naturally likeable fellow without any pretenses, that it didn't matter if it was true because you liked him, and therefore you believed him; if it was a lie, it was a well-told one, and I respect that at least as much as the truth.

The town of Hampi is situated on a river. The bulk of the settlement (which isn't much) is on the same side as the bus station: dirty and crummy and largely generic India save for a few temples and ruins. But the other side of the river, accessible only by ferry boat (ever since the bridge, which had severely cut into the profits of the ferrymen, mysteriously fell down the previous year), sported a long row of rustic hostels, all very low-key and laid back with picturesque views. It was a little touristy, but it was cheaper than the rest of the town, and after my bathroom tour of Goa I was ready for some familiar and unadventurous cuisine.

But before Chemical Tom and I could head there, we had to deal with the touts, who were clambering at the sides of our early-morning bus before it even stopped. Some foolish passengers— young, British girls mostly—were making deals with them through the windows ("And you promise you'll take us straight to the hotel? And it's cheap and nice? Well, okay…"). Tom and I ignored all of this and barrelled our way through to the door, through the crowd of shouting touts, on down towards the ferry, which I had located on a map in my guidebook and which was the only destination I would accept. Just as doctors are empowered by knowledge and jargon, so too are the touts by the ignorant unpreparedness of most tourists, whom they are happy to eat alive.

The ferry was a small boat that safely held twenty but here carried forty-five or so, which was good because the line was huge. Chemical Tom and I eventually made it across and started down the row of hippie hotels. We stuck together, going into each one and enquiring about the rates. The biggest obstacle seemed to be finding a vacancy at any place within our budget.

The crowd from the bus was following behind us at a bit of a distance, slowly catching up. Tom decided to spend the money and take a private cabin at a mid-scale place, while I kept hunting and found something for half the price: a tiny one-room hut at a crummy little joint set five hundred metres off the road into the bush, complete with mosquitoes and crawling things.

I wandered back to Tom's hotel and joined him for breakfast and, why not, beer and cigarettes. We had arrived early, but that first day was a write-off from the start. Tom had taken diazepam for the bus ride, but I'd gotten no sleep on the sleeper, having been wedged into a top bunk far too short for my frame at the back of the bus behind the wheels, which meant any bump launched me into the air to be swatted back down to the hard mattress by the ceiling.

And so our day cheerfully slipped away from us: a nap was followed by more beer and food and smoking until the evening came and we added some more newcomers to our crew.

There was Bhavesh, a Londoner of Indian background; Matt, another Brit and a writer whose dry sarcasm endeared him to the group; Uri, an Israeli of small stature who was friendly enough, but gave off the impression that he could engage in international drug smuggling at any moment; and Brian, a British fellow in his sixties whom Tom just happened to run into after first meeting him at a mad drug-fuelled rave in Goa the previous year.

We all sat around a round stone table in the courtyard restaurant of the hotel where nearly all but I were staying, ordering drinks, smoking joints openly and playing cards. We swapped stories and bullshit and discussed what there was to do in Hampi for the next day. Someone, I forget who, suggested renting motorcycles and driving around; thus were the Desperados born.

I suggested the name and it stuck, and the next day Uri took charge (as he liked to do) of renting the bikes, which were more like scooters and mopeds than beasts on wheels, but fine enough for the job.

Uri wore a ridiculously large leather Indiana Jones hat and sunglasses and quietly designated himself leader of the gang. I had my suspicions about that guy, but I chalked it up to the standard mandatory Israeli army service.

The first day was spent just driving to get lost, heading first to a vague destination where there might have been a waterfall or some other attraction; but we never found it and no one cared. The scenery was stunning, and we were all amazed at how far it stretched, seemingly endless ruins from an ancient mythological monkey war.

We drove in a pack, sporting sunglasses and (comical) bad attitudes, and discovered the mysteriously-destroyed bridge some kilometres from town. There was a ferry here, too, but instead of the usual passenger boat it was a large black concave saucer-like craft, designed to shuttle two motorbikes across the river at once; we made a note of this and carried on.

The gang followed Uri's plan of searching for a fabled village of dwarves he'd read about: these dwarves were part of mythology, but there was supposedly a real-life settlement where nearly everyone was a little person. We were skeptical, but it was something to do.

Our gang drove far off the main road and up a mountain made of boulder-shambles where there was a bit of a trail. We found two children, a young boy and an older girl of about twelve; she asked for a ride up the mountain and I let her jump on the back of my bike, which struggled under the added weight. But we made it to the top with the others, where we found a temple and some monks and more kids, but no dwarves. The view was a nice enough reward and we took a break. Uri let one of the kids examine his expensive sunglasses, but the kid wouldn't give them back, and we all laughed as the little Israeli got angry and chased the boy around with various threats until the thief got bored and handed them over.

We climbed the boulders for a bit, exploring until we were tired enough to return to the bikes, where we found the children hanging suspiciously around our hogs. We fired them up and tried to leave, but some of the kids held on to the back of my bike; pathetically, my hog was weaker than they were and they prevented me from moving, even with the engine fully revved. The little girl was riding with me again and she tried unsuccessfully to fight off the boys. I reversed suddenly, scaring them, and we roared off with the nasal drone of the engine.

I let the girl off near a village at her request before the Desperados headed to the two-lane strip of varying material and quality called a highway. Uri led us to the next town, a larger settlement than Hampi, where we could get some food. By this time Brian, the older Brit, was getting cranky and frustrated at how no one was listening to his cries for food and drink. He also seemed unwilling to drive as fast as the rest of us (which wasn't very, since the hogs were more like piglets) and often got left back from the gang.

After refuelling with masala dosas in the town, we headed back in the direction of Hampi; but instead of turning to go home, we kept on in a new direction, through another unknown village and up to a reservoir in the hills where a river had been dammed. We found a smattering of white tourists on the rocks, sunning, swimming, drinking. Three of them were rock climbers (due to the surrounding landscape, Hampi is a prime destination for climbing) and we watched them scale an absurdly tall, smooth rock formation to dive into the water from at least twenty metres. Where we were standing was already a ten-metre plunge, and some of us elected to take a swim; Brian, unsurprisingly, declined.

A few dives into the cold lake refreshed us, but the hot sun was still strong. Brian pointedly voted to head back home for a nap, and everyone but Tom and I went with him: we had noticed people with inner tubes down below the dam, and we got dressed and ventured down the road.

Some enterprising locals were running an inner tube service, whereby a flat fee would get you a four-kilometre-ride down the river, plus a tuk-tuk shuttle back to the starting point. It cost two bucks, and an American girl and her Austrian boyfriend joined Tom and I for a float; it was a perfect summer day.

We drove back to our hotels for a late-afternoon nap before reconvening with the other Desperados for more drugs, beer and food while bullshitting and playing cards; this was to be the thematic backbone of my time in Hampi.

Not unlike Goa and Pushkar, Hampi can often be more Western than Indian if you so choose: a place overrun with high school graduates and college kids more interested in chilling out and smoking pot and eating pizza than exploring another culture. Why they fly halfway around the world to do the same thing they'd be doing in their parents' basement at home is not for me to say, but I suppose not having their parents around is part of it.

Dropping out wasn't my goal, and guilt settled in on me after a few lazy Hampi days filled with bowls of subpar pasta and evenings of cards and movies. But it is a seductive life: all your slacker dreams come true for the lowest possible price, and the ability to tell everyone for the rest of your life that you've been to India.

What kept me there longer than a day was the gang, the Desperados, and the friendships that were formed. Besides, tooling around aimlessly on scooters is a fine way to explore and discover, as we proved the next day.

Brian elected to stay home, and no one particularly missed his bitching. The rest of us headed straight away for the big concave saucer ferry, which floated our bikes across the river two at a time for a small fee. Uri again directed the gang, mostly because the rest of us didn't much care where we went and we knew Uri was happiest when he felt in charge. He had heard of a guru in the hills nearby: an old Italian hippie who had come to Hampi as a young man in the 1960s and never left, instead growing his hair long and turning himself into some kind of a wise man based out of a temple or commune. It sounded like bunk, but it was something to do.

Amazingly, Uri found him. We were invited in by one of the guru's underlings and brought up to a small sitting room in the spartan concrete building. The old man came in with light steps and a graceful manner. His hair was white and long, as were his robes, and he seemed messianic in that strange cramped house. He spoke softly in English and asked his underling to prepare some tea, and the young Indian scurried quietly out of the room.

The place was a temple of some sort: the icons and artwork were vague and simplistic, appearing to my untrained eye as somewhere between Buddhist and Hindu. There was a large colourful rug on the floor and we sat on it with the old man. It wasn't clear what he thought his role was or why he was living there. He coughed hard and often, and apologized and said he was very sick.

We threw questions at him, respectfully: how old was he (Very old.) Where was he from? (Milan.) What did he do in Italy before coming to India? (Cryptic non-answers.) What languages did he speak? (There were six: Kannada, Hindi, English, Spanish, French, Italian.)

The tea came and it was very good. The old man packed a large chillum with marijuana and offered it to everyone. He said it helped his cough, though it seemed to make it worse; I declined the pipe, wary of riding on two stoned wheels on the highway. The guru began speaking softly about the universal spirituality of mankind and the life of self-denial and sacrifice required to achieve enlighten- ment. The more he talked, the more he coughed, and he seemed to be drained of energy as he fell silent near the end of our visit; perhaps he was just stoned. It was time to move on. Uri was prac- tically bowing at the guru's feet and had to be dragged away from this holy-ish man.

Back at the ferry, we watched as locals made their way through the shallowest part of the river, stepping carefully on the rubble of the fallen bridge with all sorts of objects balanced on their heads. They moved in single file, and the water soaked the lower parts of their clothes as they calmly but carefully moved along narrow beams and smashed slabs of concrete.

The Desperados drove aimlessly for a while, following an irriga- tion canal in search of Uri's missing dwarf village. We soon mutinied against our leader and decided to start back in the direction of the hotels.

I was the only gang member who was not a hobby photographer with serious equipment: the others had been rising at dawn each day to go take pictures of the landscape; now they were in search of portraits, so we stopped at a random village on the side of the road, parked our bikes and ventured in.

We found ourselves greeted warmly by a gang of children. Uri spoke Hindi reasonably well, but it wasn't the native language in this southern region. We got by with a little Hindi, simple English and hand gestures. The kids brought us to older boys, perhaps seventeen years old, and they took us to an elderly lady holding a small child. The photogs had their cameras out and were snapping shots right and left. Indians in general love to have their picture taken, espe- cially children, so there was no shortage of faces waiting to be captured.

A game of cricket broke out, as often happens on the subcontin- ent, with Bhavesh and Tom joining in while Uri and Matt hunted for photos. The village couldn't have housed more than forty children, but they all seemed to be out and swarming us; many of them were wearing blue school uniforms.

After an hour, we decided to move on, to the great disappointment of the children. Even the adults bid us fond farewells as we rode off back to our hotels to consume and amuse in a world they would never see.

BANGALORE

The return of Jenny

After a handful of days I felt a need to get back on the road. The Desperados had decided to move on as a group to a party town north of Hampi, but I had gotten a message from Jenny that she was travelling alone again, moving in a circle in southern India. She planned to be in Bangalore for a day or two, which was the only place our paths might intersect. The city, a modern success story filled with IT workers and a burgeoning computer industry, was five hours south by train; I resolved to meet her there for a day and see what would happen. That kiss in Bombay was still on my lips and I hoped there would be more to come. So I whooped it up with the Desperados one last time and hit the road again.

The majority of Bangalore is a stereotypically Indian city: loud, crowded, dirty, chaotic, polluted. I had been in so many places just like it that it blurred into the background of my mind. I felt little inclination to explore, and my only reason for coming was Jenny. I found a hotel room for the night and wandered around the neighbourhood, waiting for five o'clock when she would meet me at the train station. She was already in town, staying just out of the city with an older couple she'd somehow befriended. Now that I had arrived, she told me she only had a few hours to spare, not the full day promised to me before I had agreed to come.

But a few hours was still time together nonetheless, and I was hopeful to spark any physical connection I could. I found her on the street outside the station and she embraced me warmly. I suggested we head to a restaurant near my hotel; but when we got there, it was dark and dingy and she didn't like it, so we left and went to the entertainment district many kilometres away, which was in close proximity to the bus station she would need to get home.

We took a cab and then walked down the street, which was reminiscent of that other Indian bastion of new money, Bombay: Western shops, bars, restaurants, concrete sidewalks, and four McDonald's in six blocks. It struck me as a sick sight, like watching your friend die of a disease he caught from you.

We ducked into a bar of some sort, which was playing bad music too loudly, mostly American '80s pop hits. I bought her a drink, and she bought mine: gin and tonics, our old usual. We talked and laughed and, yes, flirted. But our time ran out, and she let me hold her hand as I walked her to the bus station, where we found her bus ready to leave. It was an abrupt parting, and she seemed very aware of the crowd of locals we were standing in. There was a kiss to be had, but we let it be this time, and I watched her bus drive away as I stood on the platform with staring Indians and a confused sentiment for this very pretty girl I never really got to know.

I took a bus back to the hotel, poured a glass of Old Monk, and immediately began planning my escape from Bangalore for the following morning.

MYSORE

The paranoiac shambles of the Raj,
and the glories of gobi manchurian

My thirty hours in Bangalore were more than enough to strip me of any desire to explore the city further, and I boarded a train to Mysore in the morning with great gusto and a bounce in my step despite not having gotten any satisfaction, if you will, out of Jenny.

Thanks to a delayed train, I spent the whole day in transit and arrived by rickshaw at a hotel in Mysore late in the evening. Once checked into a hotel, I took a walk around the streets of the old town, soaking in the sights, smells, sounds and myths of yet another Indian city.

The incense market and opulent palace notwithstanding, the best thing to do in Mysore is wander around aimlessly. The palace is impressive, especially on Sunday nights when they light up the joint with one hundred thousand bulbs (my first impression of the city, as it happened). But the most memorable thing Mysore can offer is an atmosphere: take a walk at dusk and observe all the old Raj-era buildings with their faded glory somehow becoming more glorious in the dying light. Only certain streets still retain that feel (or rather, give off that vibe): a sense that Mysore is still haunted by the Raj, still defined by it; not unlike the country as a whole in some ways.

Streetlights were few and far between in the central area I was staying in, particularly on the main boulevard lined with the worn

British façades of four-storey buildings from a different time and sense of future. In the evening dimness, the place was beautifully decayed, like walking through a painting or photograph or tragic novelscape.

I turned a corner and found a late-night food market: vendors selling Chinese stir-frys and dosas and gobi manchurian (the latter is deep fried balls of cauliflower with sauce). There must have been thirty street stalls on wheels and a hundred Indian men eating, but those were the only three things on offer.

I opted for a plate of gobi manchurian, which was twenty rupees and pure fast-food miraculous. While standing and eating, a man approached me and started speaking in decent English. I chatted with him for a short while, answering all the usual questions for foreign men, until he asked me what I was doing that night. I said I was going back to my hotel; he asked if I wanted to smoke a chillum. My spidey senses told me straightaway that he was a drug pusher, not simply a friendly and generous guy; but I had nothing to do so I went along.

I paid for the manchurian and the man motioned to a rickshaw parked nearby: its two drivers were standing and smoking beedis, and they scurried into the tiny front seat as we climbed aboard. As we rambled down the road, the man asked my name and I gave a fake one. I asked his name; "Master Blaster," he told me.

M.B. asked if I had been to the market or seen incense being made (the two things Mysore is known for). I knew this was a sales pitch, but I said I hadn't and, what's more, I would like to.

In my experience, it is sometimes worth your while to go along with these touts; I have seen many artisans at work, many experts demonstrating their knowledge, and had many free cups of chai offered to me. They do all this with the hope of making a sale, but they will do it all the same for the mere opportunity to pitch. Perhaps travelling alone at night with a probable drug dealer in a town I didn't know at all would seem foolish to some; but I didn't fear for my physical safety and had little of value should I be mugged.

In any case: we drove to a small shop and I was led inside. An old man was sitting on a couch, but he was beckoned to come and demonstrate incense production for the foreigner. After watching him roll several sticks in various powders, I thanked him and was led into another room. On one wall near the door was an old photograph of a young and powerful bodybuilder flexing.

"Do you know who that is?" asked Master Blaster. I said no. "That's Mr. India. He is very famous, and very loved."

I nodded appreciatively. Master Blaster pointed at our host, who had his back to us as he arranged bottles of oil on a table; then he pointed back at the photo, and I understood.

"You were Mr. India?" I asked the host, who was in his fifties but indeed had the physique of a former bodybuilder.

"Yes," he said, "a long time ago."

I asked him when the photo was taken, and he said maybe twenty-five years ago; I pressed him for an exact year, but he shied away and turned the topic to his expertise.

"Give me your hands," he said; I did and he clasped them in his, feeling them thoughtfully for a moment. "Why are you so cold?" I shrugged and said I wasn't; this piqued his curiosity and I immediately regretted it.

"Take off your shoes," he ordered. I sat and removed my sneakers and socks, and he took one of my feet in his hands, feeling my pulse. He counted it and announced the number with shock after counting a second time.

"That's normal," I said, assuring him that my doctor was aware of my low heart rate. But he was not convinced: Mr. India lectured me on diet, specifically advising me that I should eat more cucumbers and peanuts to gain energy and weight.

Finally he got to the point, the reason I was brought in to begin with: his oils. About thirty glass bottles stood on the table beside him, and he dabbed samples on my hands and arms of about twenty of them, explaining what they were and what they were used for: repelling insects, calming the mind, arousing the libido. Most of them smelled pleasant. Next came the sales attempt: I was handed a price list as he pulled out empty plastic vials of myriad sizes to show me that I didn't have to buy a great amount. But I had no use for oils, and they were pricey anyway, so I thanked Mr. India and scurried out with Master Blaster.

We drove to a tea stall and had a cup while smoking two of my cigarettes. It was there that he got down to his own business for the first time: he said ganja would cost five hundred rupees for five grams. I said that was outrageous; I also said I wanted to sample it before buying, which must have signalled to him that I wasn't an idiot. The bargaining ensued, and I got him down to three hundred. M.B. paid for our chai and we hopped back into the rickshaw. He tossed me a package of dried green leaves, which had suspiciously little smell. I told him this and he grabbed the package and fashioned a makeshift joint using one of my cigarettes as we drove. We both smoked it and it wasn't long before I was stoned, thus confirming the business transaction. As Master Blaster put it with a smirk, "It's not papaya leaves."

We went to my hotel and M.B. waited with the two drivers while I went up to get the money. I came back and as I handed it over to M.B., I asked the strange man at the wheel his name; he spoke as if he was James Dean, but he came off as a quiet, frightening fellow who might do frightening things at any moment.

"McDowell's Whisky," he said with a sinister smirk.

"McDowell's Whisky," I repeated. "Master Blaster." M.B. nodded and smiled. I pointed at the other driver. "Don't tell me: you're Old Monk."

They laughed uproariously at this and started teasing Old Monk for his rum namesake as I left the scene. I deposited the ganja and my room, then left the hotel and walked in search of another plate of gobi manchurian.

India at night is a remarkable experience, usually slightly different in every city but especially odd in Mysore with a head full of drugs. The busy market street that my hotel was on was crowded, even at this midnight hour. People were buying and selling all kinds of things: clothes, junk, trinkets, everything. It seemed I was the only white person in town, and as the ganja descended further onto me the fear began to set in. When you are a large pale man in an Indian town, people stare at you; when you are under the influence of paranoia-inducing drugs, that shit turns real evil real quick.

Everyone was looking at me. I was convinced that they all knew I was funny and would lock me up or report me or possibly mug beat rape me in a dark alley. I put on my sunglasses so as to hide my eyes, thus becoming a large pale man wearing sunglasses at midnight, which doesn't help to avert attention.

The streetlights seemed to be burning incredibly bright in this crowded street market and I began to panic. I frantically turned down a smaller pitch-black alley that served as a shortcut between one main road and another. At first I thought I was the only one on this four-hundred-metre-long stretch of darkness, but as my eyes adjusted I saw people sleeping on doorsteps and a group of men standing and talking quietly; they glanced over at me several times as I walked, so I stopped for a while and collected myself, keeping an eye on them in case they decided to mug beat rape me.

I saw shadows move. There! What was that! Holy God, there's another one, on the left. My head swivelled from side to side, trying to catch the fast-moving shapes in action as they swooped in and out of my peripheral vision.

What was that ganja laced with? I wondered. I had never experienced fear and paranoia like this with any sort of hallucinogen: I caught myself ranting and raving terrified things inside my head in a frighteningly similar vein to Raoul Duke on his nightmarish trip; and all I'd had was a mysterious joint.

The creepy ghost town dead-British vibe of the place added to my fear. It was like a horror movie: Indian zombies in a crumbling post-apocalyptic town, standing in groups in the darkness, talking softly until an unsuspecting tourist wanders down the wrong dark alley...

I hustled back to the brightly-lit street and made my way to the gobi stall, where I ordered two plates of the magical fried crap and wolfed them down before scrambling back to my hotel room, bolting the door and hunkering down in my heavily-fortified bunker until the violent waves of ugly fear subsided.

UDAGAMANDALAM

**Ootylicious, corneal ulcers,
and a strange Italian hipster girl**

I wandered around Mysore for a couple of fear-free days before booking a seat aboard a tiny eight-seater minibus bound for Udagamandalam, a small town in the mountains of the state of Tamil Nadu. The former British masters favoured it as a quiet, scenic place to escape from the south Indian heat; they also noticed that the climate was exceptionally well suited to growing tea. But the name was a bit unwieldy, and it morphed into Ootacamund and then to simply Ooty, which is now the dominant English moniker among Indians and tourists alike.

The distance from Mysore to Ooty is quite short on a map, but the twists and turns of the mountain-face roads are not taken into account by this measurement. After many hours of swerving up up up the steep ascent—back and forth around tight corners at, of course, the maximum possible speed—we arrived in the centre of town and I scrambled off and tried to find my bearings.

Ooty baffles me: it's warm and open, but cold and lonely at night; it has few attractions or activities, but I was never bored; it's British and it's Indian and it's stuck up in the mountains so you can't find it easily. Above the busy streets and markets, the town's houses orderly curve along the face of steep hillsides to form perfect convex rows that pop out of the lush green surroundings with wonderful colours. I had to stop on the street to enjoy the view, soaking in the bright pinks and blues.

Ooty is a hill station, and if you don't like hill stations, then you probably won't like Ooty. But it's very seductive in its casual beauty, with the mountains and hill mansions and fruit markets often over-powering the standard noise and filth of any subcontinental settle-ment.

I picked a decent-sounding and cheap hotel out of the guidebook (not feeling much in the mood for adventure, what with a pain in my skull centred behind my right eye that had started to trouble me a few days earlier). I walked the two kilometres there, past an amuse-ment park with a bizarre and slightly creepy statue of a large cartoon cat holding a baby kitten, which was in turn clutching a heart-shaped sign that said I Love You.

I found the place and talked down the price of a fairly decent room with a squat toilet and bucket shower. It was late in the after-noon, so I promptly pulled out my bottle of Old Monk and my pack of rolling tobacco and set up shop on the communal balcony near the outdoor stairs.

It wasn't long before a slim woman with black hair pranced up the steps. She glanced back at me sitting there on a red plastic deck chair with my rum perched on the railing; she smiled at me before heading to her room.

Ten minutes passed: I smoked and drank and soaked in the enjoy-able sun, which was warm but not scorching hot at that high altitude. The lush green park across the quiet road partially obscured a fenced-in pond. The black-haired lady, good-looking and around thirty years old, emerged from her room.

"Hi," I offered from a distance.

She waved oddly and walked over. "Hi."

I held up my pack of rolling tobacco. "Cigarette?" She shook her head no and fished out her own pack of Gauloises. Her name was Roberta and she had a weird energy, very free and unique and confident; fairly nuts as well, but certainly an interesting personality. I gleaned all of this in about three minutes of conversation, along with the fact that she was travelling alone and had been in Ooty for one day.

She accepted my offering of rum and we sat and talked and

drank: her quirky and slightly playful, me trying to gauge the possibility of bow-chika-bow-wow.

I soon suggested smoking a joint; she readily agreed, and we went to my room. My large backpack was on the only chair, so we both sat on the bed and I rolled the magical and spooky Mysore marijuana.

We smoked the joint and had some more rum and then decided to go for food. By now it was about eight o'clock, and I questioned whether many places in the sleepy town would still be open, so we opted to go to an eatery just down the road from our hotel. Of course, we were completely goofy out of our heads, which was not conducive to proper behaviour in a public setting: we had a difficult time not laughing hysterically at every single little goddamn thing.

The restaurant was completely empty and the lighting was very dim. Roberta and I ordered and ate, but the food was lousy, so we amused ourselves with jokes and absurd, mildly-disruptive behaviour. Any conversation with the gruff and impatient waiter was difficult for both sides, and once we had finished our meal they hustled us out of there as quickly as possible.

We walked briskly down the dark cold road to our hotel, where we went back to my room and sat on the bed. More rum followed, along with bizarre and non-sensical card games devised on the spot by Roberta. She seemed smart but silly, cute but beautiful, innocent but slightly dangerous somehow, very unpredictable. As we sat on the bed together with cards between us, I detected an energy in the air. I leaned forward to kiss her; she pulled away with a wrinkled nose and I retreated into my own space. She looked at me for a moment, before continuing to shuffle the cards. Our awkward moment seemed over before it started, and our strange childlike playfulness resumed.

"Red or black?" she demanded suddenly, holding up a card with its backside to me.

I held out my hands with outstretched fingers and waved them magically at the card. "Black." She turned it over and I was correct.

This new game was repeated over and over, and I was correct every time. It was funny at first, but after a while it just started freaking me out. The paranoia started to return, creeping in through the effects of THC in my body. The odd Italian was amazed; I had no explanation. I stopped the game after about thirty correct guesses in a row, beginning to fear for our lives.

She bade me good-night and went to her own room without any hint of awkwardness between us; like it never happened; like we were old friends.

The nights in Ooty are damn cold: no worse than a Canadian autumn, but when you've been ensconced in the heat of India for three months, it's a shock to the system. I slept little, just enough that I had to wake up, which I did in considerable pain: the discomfort behind my eye had escalated to the point where it was clear that this was not a simple headache or mild strain that would vanish on its own; this was a problem.

Roberta and I went into the town centre for breakfast on the street, then set out to find me a doctor of some sort. I stood in line at a physician's office only to be told that I should seek an ocular specialist; and so we wandered around the town, looking for such a thing, finding nothing.

Ooty is a town that was once (I'm told) quite lovely and peaceful, but seems to have grown too large for its britches: the traffic is endless and horrible and the streets are often densely packed even by Indian standards; this is the result of the mountain town becoming a popular tourist destination for middle-class Indians in recent years. There were plenty of tour buses and hotels everywhere, but very nearly zero white people.

Miraculously, we happened to stumble upon an eye specialist's office. I went inside and made an appointment for that afternoon, and then Roberta and I set out to kill some time.

A portion of Ooty is built atop the rolling hills of the area, and high above on a mini-mountain was a long low white building with a huge sign advertising a tea factory. It seemed an obvious destination, so we climbed the streets in that general direction until we came to a residential settlement in our path. There was no obvious direct route, nor any fences or private yards to obstruct us. We became lost several times and received non-English directions from residents, who were more than happy to have us pass through their yards. Finally, we discovered a worn path that led up the steep hill.

We entered the tea factory and opted for the inexpensive, self-guided tour, following along and observing the various processes involved in converting raw fresh tea leaves into the prepared product ready to consume. The threshing, cutting, drying, toasting were all very much automated and mechanized: it was quite an elaborate endeavour. But the best part by far was the complimentary cup of tea at the end, brewed from a recently harvested crop. We headed back down the hill rejuvenated.

Roberta and I sated our hunger with a quick lunch before making our way back to the eye specialist. My eye was very much throbbing, worsened by the fact that I was wearing contact lenses so as to wear sunglasses (to my tender eye, the sun seemed a worse burden than the lenses, but it was all a matter of degrees).

There were many people lined up in the tiny waiting room, but I was ushered in immediately. The entire office was about ten by seven metres, and that included the waiting room. But inside the dim examination room were myriad medical devices, all apparently clean and fairly new. The physician was a well-groomed man of about fifty who spoke English well and changed his gloves and mask before examining me.

A perfunctory check-up of my eye revealed the problem: a corneal ulcer. I was told that the cause was likely the lack of oxygen suffered from the contact lenses, which were of the 'Sleep in them for thirty days!' type. I had thought they would save me the hassle of carrying bottle of solution, as well as reduce the number of times I would expose my eyes to my dirty-India hands by rarely removing them; instead, I now had a lesion inside my eye in a small mountain town in a developing country.

"Come with me," said the doctor kindly, and the female nurse led me behind him around the corner into an equally tiny second room with a gurney, upon which I was told to lie down. My contact lenses were removed and he gave me eyedrops without permission or explanation, then stood there waiting. I assumed we were pausing for them to take some sort of effect, and I was right: they were anaesthetic, which was necessary for what would come next.

The doctor produced a white cotton ball and held my eyelids open, again without a word as to what he was about to do. What came next is simple to describe, but the words must be believed in order to appreciate the experience: he scrubbed my eyeball.

I felt the action, but no pain followed; it was a strange and uncomfortable sensation. When he had finished, the doctor put two more types of drops into my eye and then nodded to the nurse, who patched it up with gauze and tape.

As I lay there feeling very strange and somewhat violated but also grateful, he told me that I would have to wear an eyepatch for two weeks and put the two types of drops in my eye every hour. He wrote me a prescription and I thanked both of them and left.

Roberta was sitting outside and she tried not to burst out laughing when I sauntered out looking like a rather flamboyant pirate with a white patch.

The rest of the afternoon was spent trying to search out a pharmacy that had the drops in question, which was harder than I expected; but we got them, plus a self-prescribed bottle of rum. On the dark walk home in the early evening, Roberta descended into silliness once again, dancing in the street with me, and singing nonsensical things. It all seemed like low-level flirting again, but I knew I must have been mistaken after what had happened the previous night. Then she grabbed my hands and placed them firmly on her breasts with a devious smile; she held them there a moment before spinning and dancing on.

Who is this girl?

We got high again that night, which made my eye feel better. The drops were hideous creamy things that made a terrible mess of the gauze patch, forcing me to change it regularly. Roberta kept flirting and eventually I, confused, made a move again, and was rebuffed without awkwardness once more.

We decided over rum and ganja that we would move on to Kochi the next day. Our transport would be the toy train: a small gauge railway built by the British to take them to their favourite mountain resort, since the wider track of the primary railway couldn't navigate the steep, winding passages; this would take us out of the mountains to the main train line and thence on to the Arabian Sea.

Roberta and I ate breakfast together before splitting up for the morning: she went to get train tickets while I braced myself for one more eye-scrubbing appointment. When I joined her at the station, she told me that the tickets were fourteen rupees for general class or one hundred for first class; we spoiled ourselves, and the two dollars was worth it for the leg room alone.

The view from the endearingly-small train was spectacular: the Nilgiri Mountain Railway runs along the edge of cliffs, with a sheer death-drop straight down alongside it. The panoramic views of the tea fields and rolling green hills were breathtaking. We chugged along for ninety minutes until we reached Coonoor, the de facto terminus since a recent landslide had closed the lower portion of the railway, cutting us off from the main rail system; we only discovered this when we bought our tickets in Ooty, and now a quick readjust-ment of our plan was needed.

Finding a bus out of Coonoor was a nightmare. There was a patch of dirt on the side of a main road where all buses would stop to pick up travellers: a sort of unofficial bus station that was swamped with people clambering for the state-operated vehicles that couldn't come fast enough to move the crowd out. Eventually, after waiting and watching full buses pass us by, I talked our way on to one (with a little bit of pushing and shoving, as is customary) and we arrived in Mettupalayam, just outside the bigger city of Coimbatore. This was merely half the battle: now Roberta and I needed to find a way to out west across the country to the coastal city of Kochi; as usual, we had no plan and very little solid information.

By a rare stroke of luck, the bus station we were dropped off at was across the road from the railway station, where the regular broad-gauge train to Kochi departed from. But there just happened to be a state-operated bus leaving in seven minutes, so I bought us two tickets (paying extra to reserve seats) and we scarfed down some chai and fried things before climbing onto yet another vehicle. The drive took about six hours and we arrived in Kochi late at night... correction: we arrived in Ernakulam, the more modern section of

Kochi, which was across the water from our intended target of Fort Cochin. Roberta and I weren't expecting this, but we were booted off the bus anyway and had to find another, which we somehow managed to do by hollering enquiries at people on the busy, dark road and getting half-English, fully-shouted answers in return. A bus pulled up and a lot of people boarded, so we followed them.

It did indeed take us on the hour-long trip to Fort Cochin (which is much faster over the water, but the ferries were closed for the night). The bus stopped in the centre of the tourist district, near the waterfront, and we disembarked and began searching for a large, loud white man.

KOCHI

Lonely Sebastian's homestay, and the dark triumphant return of Conway

I n the interests of good storytelling, I have held back some key details from the chronological timeline; with apologies, permit me now to jump backwards in the narrative in order to explain what comes next…

While I was en route to Bangalore to see Jenny, I received a message from another ghost from the past. Conway was still travelling ahead of me in a roughly similar southerly direction. We hadn't spoken much since Diu, but he contacted me to say he was leaving India to move on to Malaysia, and he asked where in the world I was at that time. Through amicable exchanges, we agreed to time our movements so that we would spend a couple days in Kochi together before he flew out of that city.

And so there I was, arriving in the middle of the night in a strange city with no map, no bearings, an odd childlike Italian hipster who made me touch her boobs but wouldn't let me kiss her, and no earthly idea of where to go. It all hinged on Conway, who had sent me a text message an hour earlier to say he had arrived and found accommodation for us, and would meet us at the bus drop-off in Fort Cochin.

But he was nowhere to be seen. It was midnight, and there wasn't much action on the street: restaurants and shops were all shuttered; a handful of locals strolled in the darkness, but no Conway.

Roberta and I stood around looking like fools for a while, waiting for an unreliable man in a foreign city. Then, suddenly, he appeared out of nowhere, indeed as ghosts do. His voice hit me first—"You ugly bastard! Welcome to Kochi!"—followed by a big meaty paw on my back.

I introduced him to Roberta and we set off walking through the dark city. Conway had found a room for him and I, but Roberta elected to find her own accommodation for her one night in town. Relieved of our baggage, the three of us went for dinner at one of the few restos still open, across from our hotel, where Conway and I immediately set about arranging for some after-hours whisky (which cost us thrice the price, but was worth it when we were told the bottle had been stolen from the local barracks of the Indian Navy).

Roberta seemed to tire of our male camaraderie quickly, and she politely said her good-byes midway through the meal: a hug and a kiss on the cheek and she was gone.

No matter: the long-lost Conway and I picked up where we had left off some six weeks ago, swapping stories for shots of whisky and filling in each other's timeline. We had followed similar routes in our time apart, but we had travelled very different roads. The old wounds had healed, the grudges had been forgotten, and the friendship was laid bare for rediscovery.

❖

Kochi is an old and important city in south Indian history. Long a key spice trade centre due to its natural harbour on the Arabian Sea, Fort Cochin became the first European-colonized site in India when the Portuguese seized it in 1503. The Dutch and British later took their turns as rulers, and the resulting mix of cultures produced a unique architectural and culinary landscape which, set against the picturesque seaside backdrop, makes Kochi a very seductive tourist city.

Conway had only arrived a few hours before I did, so when we woke up late and discovered our newfound hangovers, a team effort was required to find food, chai and cigarettes. I got a sense of the city, which seemed built expressly for the purpose of taking it easy, and reminded me of a more urban Diu.

Still sporting the pirate look, I was quickly running out of eye-drops. That mission occupied much of our day as we ventured from street to street, popping in at every chemist we found, invariably being told that they didn't have what I needed. Having exhausted Kochi, we decided to take the ferry across to Ernakulam.

If Kochi is yin: laid back, beautiful, historic, touristy; then Ernak-ulam is its yang: modern, hectic, commercial, sprawling. The two cities are often referred to as including the other, and are separated by a two-rupee, twenty-minute ferry ride over a large expanse of water.

By the time we boarded the ferry, the mid-afternoon sun was beginning to show signs of falling towards the horizon, and the stun-ning scenery seemed to glow faintly orange as we drove across the water. Houses and shantytowns and huge hotels and palm trees lined the bays and inlets leading to the harbour, where we found enormous container ships from all over the world.

We arrived in Ernakulam and managed to track down relatively quickly a pharmacy that happened to have my drops. Conway and I hustled back to the docks just in time to catch the final ferry of the day back to Fort Cohin. When we arrived back at our room, Sebastian was waiting for us.

Sebastian is an old, lonely man who lives at and operates the small homestay owned by his son. (The term 'homestay' is a stretch, since the entire operation consists of four rooms rented out from a neigh-bouring homestay. There is no sign for the Little Flower Homestay; there is only a sign for Prem's Homestay at the end of the driveway that leads from the shared property to the road. Sebastian relies on poaching wandering travellers before they can get to Prem's door, and on the superfluous tourists offered to him when Prem's is full.)

Sebastian is seventy-six years old. He is thin and always dresses himself in slacks and a short-sleeve dress shirt, untucked. He has little to do during the day, so he sits in the three-square-metre common area shared by his room and two of his rental units. He might doze off there, or walk to the road and chat with the tuk-tuk drivers, or have tea with Prem. Sometimes he has cause to go to the bank or the market, opportunities for which he seems thankful.

Sebastian is a lonely man. He has a wife, who lives in his house four kilometres away; he has grandchildren who sometimes come to visit him on the weekend; but most of all he has the Western tourists who come to stay with him. These poor souls are the victims of his kindness and generosity, which know no bounds. He will latch on and smother with offerings of food, train bookings, theatre tickets, more food, always food—whatever he can do to be useful and of service. He will chat with you about anything. He will pull out the huge binder he keeps under the coffee table and show you the photocopies of foreign passports he is obliged by the police to keep. Most of the faces he remembers, some he doesn't, a few he speaks of with deep affection and longing and admiration. (You'll see your own passport as he flips through the stack, and you wonder to whom he'll show it, and how he'll speak of you.)

Once you enter into a conversation with Sebastian, you're trapped. It's not that he's a boring person—he used to fix bombers for the Indian Air Force, and he has a wealth of knowledge about south India and the state of Kerala—but the sheer length of these talks is numbing: it's as if he wants to make the most of this chance to kill some time.

But he is a good man, and a kind man, an unfailingly loyal man, and it breaks your heart to push him away.

Upon our return, Conway and I do the Sebastian Shuffle: he talks to the old man while I go to the room and grab my bag of ganja, then I ask Sebastian a leading question about something to allow Conway the chance to grab the bottle of gin to go with our juice. We extract ourselves from the grip of this lovely man and head to the roof, where we waste the rest of the day in low-slung chairs above the palm trees, marvelling that this was what our lives had been leading to all this time.

✿

Our reunion had been trouble-free up to this point. More than that: it had been pure fun to remember—amid a hazy backdrop of smoke, liquor and profanity—why we had been friends in the first place.

Gin-soaked and nicely toasted, we headed back to ground level at dusk in search of sustenance. Now sapped of our exploratory energy by sun and drink, Conway and I sauntered across the street and into our previous-night restaurant.

We sat down and ordered beer and food. Even the nights were hot and humid in the south; our conversation about the nature of this trip and its value to us did little to cool us down. I sipped my beer and listened to Conway explain how superior we now were to everyone we knew back home.

"…and I don't just mean our eyes are open. That's part of it, but there's more. Man, we fucking did it. That right there should mean something. But a trip like this <u>changes</u> you, and all those smug bastards back home never did it, so what does that tell you? When we go back, no one can tell us what's what in the world. They've never played cricket in a slum, they've never seen the things we've seen, and they can suck it. Hey," he said to our passing waiter with a few snaps of his fingers, "hey, two more beers." He turned back to me. "I don't think he heard me. Man, what's wrong with this country? Nothing but stupid monkeys."

More than anything else, I think that moment changed the tone of the night for me. Everything else was just Connie being Connie; but that was something even he wouldn't have said six weeks earlier, not with the is-he-joking? casual sincerity he looked at me with as he lit his cigarette.

I didn't say anything about it until we went back to the room, many beers later. My mind hasn't retained the precise transcript of what was said, but if you'll permit a few liberties, it likely read something like this:

> Conway (drunkenly): I love India, man…
> Me (passive-aggressively): Yeah, sure…
> Conway: Hey, why so passive-aggressive?
> Me: I thought Indians were stupid monkeys…

Conway: Uhh, what-huh?...

Me: In the restaurant, you snapped your fingers at the waiter, and then you said that all Indians were stupid monkeys.

Conway: What? No way...

Me: You always say shit like that, about lazy Indians, begging instead of working...

Conway: ...

Me: ...it doesn't sound too enlightened.

Conway: I...

Me: ...and now you're better than everyone back home! Like balls, you smug bastard.

Conway: (proceeds, drunkenly, to launch into an attack on my own character flaws, which I in turn deny regardless of veracity and thus do not now recall...)

Me: (rolling a joint) (following self-defence, my attack begins once more until, all grievances having been aired and the joint smoked away...) You know, Connie, sometimes you make it really hard to be your friend.

I watched him, sitting cross-legged on his bed as I sat on a chair. He looked past me, then at me, then nowhere in particular. Never, anywhere, had I witnessed something get to him, affect him, shut him up so profoundly. I realized I had gone too far; but I decided to say nothing and simply went to bed with that statement hanging in the air, up there above us with the cloud of smoke from the cigarettes and ganja.

◦

By the time we'd slept off our hangovers, both of us had somehow found enlightenment, or at least some contrition. Conway was flying out that day, leaving India for Indonesia, one road for another. It meant that there was little point in allowing any continuing animosity to cloud our final day together; but it also signified the end of our trip somehow. We had come to this country together, and even when our partnership dissolved in Diu, we were both exploring India. Now he was leaving and I was staying. My own road had no end in sight; but, still, this felt like a conclusion to something: it was, by absurd cosmic coincidence, three months to the day from our arrival in Delhi.

We walked, had breakfast, chatted, joked… and then that was it. Conway collected his bags and I stood and waited with him for the bus that would take him to the airport. One last cigarette together before the bus pulled up and we hugged and said thank-you and swore at each other fondly and he was gone, off to another land; and I realized then, perhaps for the first time, that despite whatever faults flaws shortcomings he may have, he was always a true friend: a rare and valuable thing, in my experience.

✿

I was wandering through an unfamiliar part of Kochi—exploring on my way home from a shawarma, pondering which town to move on to next—when I ran into Kristi.

We hadn't seen each other since Diu, and once we finished marvelling at this happenstance meeting, we each recounted our travels since and plans for the future.

"I'm taking the train down to Varkala in a few days," said the sweet little Estonian voice, "chill out on the beach. Oh, Jenny's down there, did you know that?"

Ah, the elusive Jenny. The book never fully closes on us, does it?

After contacting Jenny, who confirmed that she was in Varkala and was thrilled that I would come, I had supper with Kristi, packed my bag, tore off my eyepatch, bade Sebastian farewell in the morning and caught a train to Varkala, where my future would be shifted in unforeseen directions.

VARKALA

**Too many women,
the legend of the pineapple pancake,
and drinking to moving on**

I t's easy to miss your stop on the train to Varkala: there is no real uniqueness in the people or station or landscape when you roll in; no boatloads of tourists, no stunning beaches unfolding before the mighty sea. It's just another dirty blip in a country filled with them, a village stop on the rail line.

A five-kilometre rickshaw ride out of the actual settlement lands you in the midst of mid-range rustic hotel territory, colourful signs dotting the road with palm trees towering overhead. The roads are unpaved, and the alleyways and paths from here are jagged and twisting and confusing, even in the daytime. But somewhere in the mess is the golden road that takes you to the edge of the cliffs. Hold your breath and grab onto something: the view when you emerge from the semi-jungle is staggering, surely one of the most stunning knock-you-on-your-ass sights anywhere in the world...

But first, I must take you back (with apologies) to Kochi for a moment, to share one brief but crucial anecdote: I was waiting for the ferry that would take me to the train station in Ernakulam, where a train would take me to see a girl in Varkala. But it was the girls in front of me on the dock who had my attention: two blondes, one tall and gorgeous, the other more plain-pretty. I struck up a conversation with the pair, who were British and who happened to be on their way to Varkala by bus. We wagered a drink as to who would arrive first, and we parted ways after the ferry without exchanging any contact details. Even before I had begun my journey to see Jenny, I had begun arranging my backup plan...

Back in Varkala, where no girls anywhere were on my mind as I emerged from the semi-jungle and rough collection of shack hotels onto the clifftop pathway and ran smack into the view of a lifetime.

Varkala is staggering: the Arabian Sea unfolds before you with one-hundred-eighty degrees of ancient blue indifference, stretching out like a salty unstable azure field that you could walk across to Africa. The red rocky cliffs tower over the beach below, demonstrating with terrifying grandeur the former heights and depths of the ocean and the forlorn power of nature. Above all this, foreign tourists sit in clifftop restaurants and drink cocktails and eat overpriced seafood; on the beach, they sun themselves or cower under umbrellas from the unforgiving Keralan sun as the waves, some as tall as a man, crash down in front of them.

I walked along the seemingly endless red-dirt pathway, a wall of thatch-sided shops and restaurants on one side and the majestic seascape on the other. Jenny and I had arranged to meet at a café, and I soon found it and her.

Hugs. Greetings. Sit. Have you eaten. No. Some food: calamari and beer to share. It's beautiful here. Yes, it is. How was Kochi?

And so it went as we felt our way through the start of our third Indian meeting, once again back on the sea. There was uncertainty between us, hesitation peppered into the familiarity: we both had things we were not yet saying.

It was late afternoon when we walked down to the beach, which was emptying as many of the tourists left in search of food and drink. Jenny and I walked down to a secluded, empty section of beach where the waves crashed against the rocks with such impact that we had to almost-shout to each other. We held hands as we strolled. She said she didn't want things to get weird; perhaps 'complicated' is what she really meant, though complicated is what we were. Still, she was leaving India to go back to the UK in three days, and she preferred to maintain the rather ambiguous status quo. I did not.

"Why did you kiss me in Bombay?" I asked. That was all it took: she dropped my hand and took up her sword, launching into a tirade about my unfairness. I thought the question was perfectly reasonable, considering it was me she had kissed without warning or explanation. If there was to be no further romance between us, so be it; but I needed to understand her motives and feelings for me.

But she was angry and petulant: it seemed I had no right, she said, to ask why, despite all her insisting on a platonic relationship, she had suddenly kissed me that night.

In honesty: I wanted to get with Jenny; if that wasn't going to happen, I still liked her and her company. But in that moment on the beach, she seemed a child to me, unwilling or unable to determine the nature of our relationship as adults might do. As the sound of the surf overcame us, I walked away from her without saying a word.

❖

A few hours later, wandering along the clifftop pathway looking for anything magical, I happened to run into the two British girls from the Kochi ferry. I had won the wager, but we all took turns buying each other drinks at a nearby restaurant. The three of us hit it off immediately: the beautiful leggy one was called Lois, her friend was Racquel, and they were both caustic and sarcastic and hilarious people to drink with. Lois was a dream of a woman, but since we were all staying in Varkala for several more days, I elected to play it cool. There would be time, and I would make the most of it.

❖

I didn't see Jenny the next day: Lois and Racquel and I went to a quiet, remote part of the lengthy beach, and I happened to know that Jenny's hotel was at the opposite end.

The main beach is unfairly divided: the north half, which we were even farther north of that day, is the sandiest, the most even, the most lovely and open and scenic—and is unspokenly reserved for the foreign tourists in bikinis and speedos. South of this, in front of Beach Road, lies a far smaller patch of uneven sand where Indian pilgrims come to worship and bathe in the sea and indulge in their various Hindu rites (such as sending wooden shrines out on the water, which inevitably wash back up on shore). Occasionally white folks will wander down there, cutting through a group of local worshippers en route to the shops or their hotels, sometimes in bikinis or holding hands, sometimes showing deference and keeping a clear distance.

There are also a few Indians, mostly young men, who go into the water purely for pleasure. But swimsuits are not necessary: either they will simply roll up their trouser legs and wade in (often becoming completely immersed while horsing around), or else strip down to their skivvies and run and bathe and laugh without a trace of self-consciousness.

But we three were alone on our remote patch of beach, and I was less interested in observing local culture than in keeping my eyes on Lois, whose bikini confirmed my suspicion that she did indeed have legs out to Armageddon.

We spent the day on the beach swimming and sunning and discussing female authors. When the afternoon brought the intolerable sun we scurried back up to have lunch at a restaurant (and some beer, why not). I was having fun with both of them, but subtly flirting with Lois, trying to gauge her interest. Now, sapped of energy from the sun, we all agreed to go home to our respective hotels to shower and rest, and meet for supper later.

As we walked out of the restaurant together, I saw Jenny strolling on the path, alone. She looked at me talking and laughing with my two good-looking companions, and I ignored her as we moved past her on our way.

❖

The nap served me well and I woke up hungry and full of optimism for the night ahead. I dressed as sharply as I could with my limited wardrobe and set out for the restaurant where I found the girls, both of whom looked far better than I did.

We ordered drinks and dinner, in that order of priority. The sun was down already, and though we were on the second storey of a building on the cliffs, the sea sky horizon water were completely black, the vast Arabian Sea having vanished into the night: a narrow shimmer of moonlight and the distant scattered beacons of small fishing boats were all the view we had left.

A pile of seafood arrived at our table, along with more drinks. Once all was consumed, additional beverages were ordered. Lois and Racquel and I sat there for hours drinking beer and rum and talking and laughing. These were easy-going gals, perfectly suited to my uniquely damaged sense of humour, and I to theirs.

The restaurant closed surprisingly early, and we had to walk a ways before we found another establishment. More drinks, more jokes—and then Racquel said she was tired and was going to head home. That was how Lois and I came to be alone and drunk together in a Varkala bar.

Two drinks later: "Do you have a boyfriend back home?"

"Well, it's not exactly serious yet, but I did just start seeing someone before I left London."

I wasn't quite sure what that meant for my purposes. "Does that mean I shouldn't try to kiss you later?" She smiled and blushed, literally and otherwise. "No, I think you shouldn't."

Two lesser people would have become uncomfortable at this point, remaining just long enough to escape under supposedly unrelated auspices. But Lois and I had a real connection, and we spent the next two hours drinking heavily and playing truth or dare. I continued to flirt with her and she continued to blush, and suddenly the bar was closed with us still sitting on the dark patio, the only people still awake in Varkala at four o'clock in the morning.

"I guess we'd better go home…"

"Well, my hotel is a long way away, and it's dark…"

"You're welcome to stay at my place. I'm just over here."

"Would that be okay?"

We staggered to my hotel where she made a point of reiterating that nothing was going to happen between us while stripping down to her skivvies in front of me. My God, she was beautiful.

I followed suit and we jumped into bed together and passed out tangled up in each other in a hot and sweaty Keralan hotel room.

❖

When I awoke, I discovered a text message from Jenny: 'I feel sad about us and I'm not sure why.' She added an invitation to meet for lunch. Of course, I still had a nearly-naked bombshell passed out in my bed as I read this; so first things first.

Lois got up and threw her clothes on and we stumbled back to the clifftop road to meet Racquel for breakfast, looking like two people who had been awake all night battling djinns (rum, in our case). At breakfast, Lois seemed flirtatious at times, while Racquel was clearly getting bored with my presence. My sincere hangover was confounded further by the mixed signals coming from Lois (be they real or imagined), and I did not have the clarity of mind to process or interpret them.

Once we finished and parted ways, I immediately headed for the beach, where I was running late to meet Jenny. I moved quickly between and among the piles of toasting beige skin, searching for her, squinting at faces under umbrellas in the hot hot sun until I saw a slender blonde figure half-wrapped in a sarong walking towards me. Seeing her in her swimwear brought back flashes of Diu: the sarong thinly hinting at what it covered, her straw-blonde hair falling on her shoulders above her blue bikini top.

It was a long walk before either of us said we were sorry: slow steps down the beach, up the narrow rock-cut stairs, along the dirt clifftop path, hot and sweaty while ducking into an open-air restaurant for respite, and then…

"I don't know why I kissed you," she said without meeting my gaze. She was confused, torn, never thought she'd see me again, still didn't want to sleep with me. "You should have told me you had questions before you came here." Now she was looking at me.

I said fair enough (though I wasn't in complete agreement) and apologized for my childish reaction to her childish behaviour. We ordered gin to celebrate our reconciliation, and then another. Jenny asked the time and I told her, and she mentioned that Kristi was due to arrive in Varkala shortly, which was news to me.

Less than ten minutes later, the little Estonian plunked herself down at our table with her backpack in tow. It was the first time since Diu that we had all been together, mere minutes after Jenny and I had made nice, six hours after I had woken up with Lois in my bed. Varkala was becoming a strange place indeed.

❖

After we finished, Kristi followed Jenny back to the hotel room they would share while I took my notebook down to the empty beach for the last few hours of daylight.

I stood on the shore of the Arabian Sea, a thing I once never imagined I'd see, my eyes fixed on its straight blue distance dropping off an unimaginable curve to Africa…

…and as my eyes stared straight ahead my mind wandered and was filled with thoughts women: of Jenny and Lois and Ruby and Finnish Ellen and Roberta and the nubile Austrians and the ones in Canada and elsewhere, love found and lost and set aside, pursued and lusted after endlessly, to what end? …

…and I was suddenly completely and purely and surely convinced of my failings and flaws and inadequacies, and what felt like my own personal inevitable doom.

While these thoughts saturated my mind and the sea air inflated my lungs, I sat on a rock and opened my notebook and wrote: 'I believe in self-redemption and I know that I can be saved, if only I will be saved, and the burden will be mine, and the weight will be steady; but such is life and such is the lot for us all.

'Bring me the love of a good woman and let me drown and be reborn.'

°

I spent the next two days bouncing between groups of women: breakfast with Lois and Racquel, lunch and beach with Jenny and Kristi. Each pair was aware of the existence of the other, but they never met, and perhaps I liked it that way.

Jenny and I had advanced our relationship as far, it seemed, as it would go: one day as we talked in her room about us—I wanting more, she ever-hesitant—I sat down next to her on the bed with honest, casual intentions and said I wanted a middle ground of some sort; she agreed, but we wondered what that was. As we sat, I touched her back, she put her head on my shoulder, I kissed her... and without knowing and without trying we found the middle ground ourselves: more than friends, less than lovers.

The human contact with Jenny was, of course, nice (and worth enjoying for what it was, since she was leaving shortly anyway), but my unusual, sarcastic, raw sense of humour was often misplaced with her and Kristi. And so I would seek refuge in my other group, who were just as dry and biting and outlandish, and wonderfully well-read as well.

I was spending a small fortune in Varkala: the restaurants were delicious but expensive, to say nothing of the amount of booze I was drinking each day. But it was during a moment of relative sobriety that I made the decision to begin sleeping on the beach as a way to stem the bleeding of money.

The sand was mostly empty at night, save for a few squatters, but the main beach area was very open and unsheltered. On the south end, past Beach Road where the Indians ritualized, there was a rock formation that blocked dry passage when the evening tide was in. Past here I found a few more squatters and hippies, but beyond them was plenty of sandy expense to isolate myself in. I checked out of my hotel, left my backpack at Jenny and Kristi's, grabbed my rolled-up mosquito net for a pillow and a towel for a sheet and headed down to my new bed after dark.

There was no one anywhere near me in either direction, and no electric lights or campfires either; just me and the sea. I stripped naked and went crashing into the papansam waters, which Hindus claim will wash away all the sins in a person's life. I emerged into the warm night air and, once dried and dressed, sat on my hard sandy bed with the sea and stars in my eyes until I had to lie down and fall asleep.

Enter the Minx

A round seven o'clock in the morning I awoke to the sight of Jenny crouched over me. She had come, as planned, to wake me for an early-morning swim and walk. It was her last full day before leaving, and after two days of making out and petting, she now pulled her hand from mine as we walked, saying she was uncomfortable. Over the course of a half-hour walk I brought her back on board and it was as though nothing had changed from the day before; but her continuous vacillations were pushing my patience. I was gaining new insight into how her mind and heart worked; yet I was also beginning to realize that her continuing uncertainty was resulting in my becoming more emotionally detached than her, as demonstrated by breakfast.

Jenny took me to a place on Beach Road for our morning meal, a little hole-in-the-wall with plastic lawn furniture outside to serve as the dining area; the only other patrons were a couple with a young child, and a darkshorthaired svelte young woman. We took the table next to her and she smiled at us as we sat down. A man came outside and handed us laminated menus.

"What's good here?" I asked Jenny.

The darkshorthaired woman leaned over just then: "Try the pineapple pancake, it's amazing."

And so that was how we met; and it wasn't long at all before Jenny and I invited the young woman to pull her table over to ours and join us. Jenny had the pineapple pancake; I did not order it that day, but I would soon.

The young woman was Norwegian and something of a live wire. She was, like myself, a journalist, as well as a DJ, filmmaker, and a half-dozen other loose job descriptions. She spoke quickly but well, in fluent English, and there was a strange seductive energy about her, though it wasn't entirely sexual: it was some kind of charm, a type of cheerfully manic current running through her every move and word; like a minx on speed. I was instantly attracted to her, and she seemed to be everything Jenny was not.

The three of us sat talking for over an hour, and then Jenny excused herself to go buy coffee beans from the shop next door to take home on her flight the following day. I pounced the moment she was out of sight, asking the Minx for her mobile number; perhaps she'd like to get together for a cocktail sometime? Yes, she would.

Jenny returned and we bade the Minx farewell and headed back to the beach.

"You know, once I leave," she said playfully as we walked hand in hand, "you're going to have to find some other girl to harass."

"You think so?"

"Sure." She looked back in the direction of the restaurant, now far behind us. "Maybe her."

❁

It was our last day together and we spent a good chunk of it alone (which is to say, without Kristi) in Jenny's room and wandering through the streets and back alleys of Varkala, making out wherever possible.

Given that it was our last night together—this time undoubtedly so, since she had a flight to England to catch—I, ever the incorrigible optimist, held out hope that we might finally consummate our non-relationship. Since she shared a room with Kristi, I invited her to spend the night with me on the beach; she refused, and I was never sure if it was because she quite fairly didn't want to put herself in that position, or if she just found the idea of sleeping on the beach entirely unappealing.

She did, however, come find me early in the morning at my sandy resting place, and we swam and walked and talked and kissed. We made our way to the pineapple pancake restaurant from the day before and met up with Kristi and some of Jenny's friends who happened to have arrived that day. We ate and told stories, and then it was time to go. She hugged all her friends, crying when she embraced Kristi, and then solidly turned down all offers to have the group escort her to the train station. They were insistent, and she practically had to beat them off of the waiting tuk-tuk, but she got her way, and I will say this for her: though she was immature and uncertain when it came to romance, Jenny knew that she wanted to spend the little India time she had left alone with me. After politely telling everyone else to shove off, she looked at me with great clarity and I jumped into the tuk-tuk and we sped off.

We had nearly half an hour to kill at the train station, so we sat and talked about everything except 'us'—partly because Jenny always said she hated to 'complicate' things; partly because, at that point, we'd both have been hard-pressed to define what 'us' was.

The train arrived and we stood and watched it slowly creep into position along the platform. We found her car and she took her bags on board, then came back and kissed me until the train started moving. I can't recall if either of us said anything before she turned and climbed on board. She stood at the open door and I walked alongside her until the train picked up speed and she pulled ahead of me, rattling north into the Keralan jungle.

It would take me weeks and months to fully digest and dissect my relationship with Jenny; but in that moment as I walked the length of the platform towards the exit I counted at least three distinct emotions in me, the quality and depth of each I leave to you to judge: sadness, at having bade farewell to a friend and companion I cared about; poignancy, as I felt the closing of another chapter of my journey; and relief, that the constant quest for common ground, the absurd battle to win her affections and her physical love, was over.

Exiting the train station, I realized I had left my sunglasses at the restaurant. I boarded a local bus that snaked through the town on its way back to Beach Road. Sitting there when I arrived, on a plastic chair at a plastic table, alone drinking coffee, was the Minx. Salutations and greetings, followed by the retrieval of a sunglass case, an invitation to sit, and the handing-over of a menu.

"Did you try the pineapple pancake yet?"

"No, it sounded too sweet for me."

"Trust me."

We spent two hours talking over pineapple pancakes (which were, in fact, astoundingly delicious), sitting on patio furniture on the roadside, discussing everything: India, politics, my background as a journalist, her background in various artsy things as well as a transient and former squatter, Canada versus Norway, and so on. Most of all, though, we talked about her; for nothing pleased the Minx more than informing someone about the details of her life. Fortunately the stories she had to tell—be they true, imagined or exaggerated—were more interesting than most.

Her original plan before I arrived was to have a quick coffee and then head to the beach (she had her swimsuit on under her clothes), so we went there and I swam in my boxers and it seemed we would never run out of great conversation.

But even if we had, her beauty was such that I would have happily settled for simply staring at her: long and thin but feminine, eyes that seemed to tell you such wonderfully naughty things as to cause you to lose your train of thought.

After spending most of the day in each other's company, we parted ways for the standard afternoon nap-and-shower (I was sleeping on the beach, but my bag was living at Kristi's, and she was happy to let me use her hotel facilities).

Nap-and-shower was inevitably followed by food-and-drink. Kristi and I were joined by the Minx at one of our favourite restaurants; the Minx's local yoga teacher also arrived some time later. I introduced the group to pineapple juice and rum, which we enjoyed copious amounts of over the course of several hours, along with the usual fantastic seafood at tourist prices (which is to say, expensive for Indian sensibilities, cheap for Western ones).

Suddenly, seemingly without warning, it was quite late. We all parted ways and, since the Minx's hotel was near the beach in the same direction as my squatter's plot, I offered to walk her home.

The tide was coming in as we walked along; the dark empty beach, and the stars above us were so bright and clear and true that one felt guilty for looking anywhere but up. We stopped and took in the night view for a few moments. The first time we kissed, it was my lips that touched hers and not vice versa; but her reply made it quite clear that I had beaten her to the punch by a fraction of a moment.

We stood there on fire, the Minx and I, under the stars with the surf in our ears and precious little space between us. When we pulled apart she took my hand and we continued walking to her villa-style hotel: there was no discussion about the destination; there was no need for an offer to come in for a drink when we arrived. All pretences were dispensed with. She opened the door and I stepped into the Minx's world. I would stay longer than I could imagine.

º

It probably goes without saying, but I woke up the following morning feeling rather sanguine, quite pleased with myself and the world.

Part of that, of course, was the result of making love to a beautiful woman on a warm night and sunny morning in a south Indian paradise. But it was more than physical pleasure: after spending what felt like ages chasing Jenny, who didn't want to be caught; who shied away from affection and attention; who could never make up her mind as to what it was she wanted… after chasing a girl, I had found a woman.

The Minx knew what she wanted and had the confidence to go get it, both in the bedroom and beyond. The more time I spent with her, the more I laughed at myself for ever becoming involved with a girl who neither wanted me nor was right for me.

Despite these relevant thoughts, Jenny was already becoming background noise in my mind, and she had only been gone twenty-four hours. The Minx and I spent our first day together (or second, depending on how you define 'together') in the usual Varkala fashion: split between the beach, the sea and the restaurants. Kristi wandered in and out of our world, no doubt feeling like a third wheel despite our genuine efforts to include her. At night, more food and drinks, followed by a walk along the beach back to the Minx's hotel (I had upgraded from the beach) during which she mentioned that she had been sleeping with her local yoga teacher (whom I had met; who had a supposedly-serious German girlfriend abroad; who seemed to me to be something of a pseudo-spiritual snake-oil charlatan) up until a day or two before she met me.

I don't know what compelled her to tell me, other than a driving desire to talk about herself. But I wouldn't have particularly cared, except that she mentioned how it all started: after a few lessons, Arun (the teacher) told her that there was a cosmic energy between them, and that it was blocking their yoga progress, and in order to dispel it they would have to sleep together.

How much of that nonsense factored into her decision to go to bed with him, I was never sure (and it was none of my business), but from that moment on I began to question the mindset of the Minx, and possibly her mental stability as well. But I was having far too much fun to care much, and I went to bed with her again that night feeling as far away from all problems, people and prisons as ever.

✽

We wake up and make love and shower together and go down the road for some coffee and pineapple pancakes, and that's when the Minx asks about—more like suggests—accompanying me to my next destination. It was my last day in Varkala: the train ticket in my pocket said 'Kanyakumari' and '0945' and had the next day's date on it. The Minx and I were still getting along far more often than not, and I liked the sound of this new adventure; I readily agreed. And so the rest of the day turned into a combination of preparation, celebration and savouring our final hours in that strange paradise.

Kristi was leaving that night, so we all had lunch and drinks together and then my sweet little Estonian friend was gone. Everyone was drawn back to the road eventually, either by necessity or desire: friends came and went and were rediscovered and disappeared once more; nothing ever stood still.

(Perhaps it was no coincidence that I received a plethora of emails that day from former lovers. The timing and synchronization was incredible; I don't get so many messages on my birthday. They wrote me from Japan and Montreal and Calgary and Saskatchewan and England and Finland, with varying intentions and purposes; but the salient point is that I had no less than eight women on my mind when we went for dinner that night…)

The Minx swore by this seafood restaurant right on the beach near her hotel, and so we went there for our last hurrah. Then, a surprise: she had invited Arun along as well, which was news to me. One he arrived and joined us, something became apparent: the Minx had not informed him of our newfound romance.

And so there we were, two men who were not quite clear on the nature of the other's relationship with the woman they both coveted, who sat there uninclined to shed much light for either man's benefit.

I was quiet and sullen, partly because of the situation before me, partly because of the other seven women in my head. But Arun and I were civil if not friendly, and the food was good and the drinks were plentiful.

Following dinner, which finished quite late, we all began walking to the Minx's hotel. Knowing that Arun didn't know about us (which was apparently how she wanted it), I was curious about how this would work: should I blatantly go inside with her and make evident my intention to stay? Or should I keep up appearances and pretend to go sleep on the beach (despite the fact that my bag was now in her room, since Kristi had left)?

I could not know how irrelevant my dilemma was until we arrived and the Minx made some crack about how we could all fit in her big bed before going to use the washroom. A dark thought suddenly hit me and, now alone with Arun, I asked him if he intended to stay: he did.

I don't know if she was hoping for some sort of multinational ménage à trois, or if she simply thought we'd all get along swimmingly together for an innocent sleepover; either suggestion seemed ludicrous since she knew I had no patience or fondness for Arun.

The Minx emerged to find me collecting a few things from my backpack. "Let me borrow a towel," I grumbled, "I'm going to go sleep on the beach."

"No, don't," she said cheerfully. "You can stay here."

I grabbed a towel from the bathroom with violence, gave the Minx a long, hard, flesh-searing look (long enough to make them both uncomfortable) and stormed out.

I was beyond anger, beyond outrage, as I walked down the hill to the beach. Part of it was the fact that I felt completely blindsided by this, as well as my assumption that she intended to sleep with Arun again. We had only known each other a few days, but our connection and our newfound travel plans seemed reason enough to expect that she would keep me in the loop about a sleepover for three.

Smoke was still pouring out of my ears when I reached the beach. As I turned left to go find my usual plot, I saw a beautiful and frantic woman in a red dress come racing down the hill. I stopped, looked at the stars, saw no indication in them as to my next move, and decided to wait for her.

The Minx apologized profusely and tried to explain; I kept myself from yelling but spat my words at her just the same. She was completely lost, this I could see: hopeless and bewildered.

According to her, Arun lived quite a ways away, and he had told her hours ago that he would stay over after dinner. She, for whatever reason, had frozen and neglected to say no; she allowed his presumption of their situation to stand.

She was close to tears with apology and self-hatred. Against my better judgement, I allowed her to live. I let her kiss me and I went to sleep on the beach, still fuming.

The anger was still there in the morning when I returned to her hotel as agreed. Arun was gone, but I found the Minx being chatted up outside by some Italian tourist punk on the road. I ignored both of them and went inside to pack. Once she dispensed with the punk and came inside, I voiced my anger and disappointment again, much more calmly than before. She was visibly torn up and apologized a dozen times, saying it was stupid and ridiculous, and she won my forgiveness.

She didn't offer an explanation, and I didn't press for one. I had

spent my time in Varkala chasing one girl or another (often simultaneously) and, though I felt a sense of betrayal about whatever had
happened last night, I knew I couldn't begrudge her too much.
After all, as the Minx and I hustled to the train station to return to
the road together, we both knew that our partnership was merely a
vehicle for hedonism.

KANYAKUMARI

A new adventure begins
at the end of the world

I had spent a week in Varkala (my longest stop yet aside from Diu) and the Minx had stayed nearly two (her first and only destination, having just begun her trip). I, for one, was tired of the Western tourist scene, which had begun to feel like a cop-out, to say nothing of the drain on my finances. I wanted back into India, and Kanyakumari seemed the perfect place.

Set on the southernmost tip of the subcontinent, Kanyakumari is not on the foreigner's roadmap. There is little of compelling interest unless you are a Hindu coming for pilgrimage purposes; it sounded like precisely what I wanted.

We arrived with no plans: no hotel booking, no map, not even any vaguely helpful information in the guidebook (which was, of course, geared to foreigners). As at any railway station in India, there stood a herd of tuk-tuk drivers all clambering for our attention and money. Ordinarily, there would be an auction to determine who among them was willing to take us to our destination for the lowest fare.

But these men not only know their towns inside-out, they are also offered commission from many hotels for every non-reservation customer they bring in, which is then factored into the cost of your room. This is a great system, if you use it to your benefit.

I told the men that we needed a hotel, which certainly got their attention. "How much?" I asked, standing still as they all tried to

motion us towards their chariots on three wheels. I negotiated as far
down as I could (having no idea, naturally, of how far we'd be driving). We told our lowest bidder how many rupees we wanted to pay
for a double room, and he drove us to three different ones, patiently
waiting at a distance while we inspected the premises and price; if it
was no good, on to the next. Eventually we found one that was suit-
able. We took the room, I paid the driver, and (out of my sight) the
hotel paid him his commission, which I was actually paying for with
the room, but which didn't matter since I got a room I liked for the
price I wanted.

The train had been slow and hot and we were exhausted. But,
more importantly, we had made nice on the train following the Arun
fiasco, and so we immediately christened the bed with what had to
have been some of the greatest most sensationally high-energy violent frenetic passionate copulating two people have ever survived.

Then we showered and went out for a stroll. There was nary a
light-skinned face to be seen. The skin tone in India is very much
geographically structured: quite pale in the north, darker than Afric-
ans in the south. And we were as south as south could be, surrounded by locals and Indian tourists in a shop-and-market-filled dingy
little town.

The Minx and I strolled for a while, browsing the shops, running
errands. We ate at a canteen by the road, where five heavy-set sari-
clad women sat together on one long bench at a different table with
their backs to us. We kept walking, we got lost, we found. It was
late in the afternoon, not quite dusk, when we arrived at the huge
open square at the bottom of the world.

We were standing at the southernmost part of the southern most
town in the country; before us, sprawling forever and without evident divisions, were the Bay of Bengal Indian Ocean Arabian Sea. To
my left, past an invisible Sri Lanka, were Malaysia and Indonesia; at
about ten o'clock was Australia; directly to my right was Somalia; and
straight ahead was Antarctica. Nothing between I and them but
waves and wind.

There are many Hindu myths involving this place, but I was more
amazed in that moment with my own story: I had started in Delhi
almost four months ago; my route was meandering, my road was

strange and lurid, but it had always been in a southerly direction, moving down and down and down. Now I was standing at the bottom with no more southbound road ahead of me; all there was left to do was to turn around and keep going.

The Minx and I sat for a while, and she indulged my soaking in the moment (she had only just arrived in the country, and she found far less symbolism there). We walked some more and discovered a lovely and quiet harbour and some beautiful churches and temples. Then, in the rapidly growing darkness, we paid five rupees each to enter a huge temple courtyard set on the water so we could jump the high perimeter wall when no one was looking and climb down to the huge rocks jutting out from the ocean.

I sat there with my Minx for a long time, until night fell, looking into the void and talking about life and love and hockey. Then she leaned over and whispered into my ear some things she wanted to do to me. "I guess we'd better hurry home before you change your mind," I said.

She leaned back and laid down on the rock we were sitting on. "Why bother," purred the Minx, "when we're already here?"

And so, under the stoney gaze of the enormous Thirukkural statue, with the waves from three bodies of water lapping at our feet, with the whole of India northwards, not-quite-in-view-of Somalia and Australia, there, on a warm dark rock, the Minx and I contributed our own mythology to an ancient land already teeming with them.

❉

An argument in the hallway outside our room woke us up unreasonably early the next morning. But the Minx was an amateur photographer, so we headed out to make the most of the best light of the day: back to the water, where short, squat, beautifully coloured buildings lined the road that ran along the harbour. Most of them were perfectly white with a bit of bright colour thrown here or there, but the white shone in the morning sun like hottest fire.

Along the beach that served as the sandy dock for the harbour, rows upon rows of fishing skiffs sat with only the brightest, loudest, happiest colours painted on them. And the breakers: long slender pile-o-stone fingers reaching out into the sea, protecting the skiffs from the surging waves.

We walked out to the tip of a breaker and looked back at the post-card-lovely town, and I thought about the day that the breakers failed to protect anything: 26 December 2005, when a faraway tsunami made its way to this very exposed place on the edge of the world. I stared at the idyllic scene and visualized the thirteen-metre-high waves arriving, and I was frozen with emotion as I grasped the unimaginable horror of that day for the first time.

Jutting up magnificent and stately from the background several blocks behind the waterfront was a tall snow-white cathedral spire. After photographing everything we could, the Minx and I made our way there. It was closed, so we stood silently and soaked up its architecture.

Then: wailing and shouting, and two women ran into the square we were standing in; one was carrying a small, limp body in her arms. There were a few young men standing around and some of them immediately ran to see what the trouble was. The men, the women and the limp boy all converged directly in front of us.

The woman holding the boy was too distraught to do anything but flail, so the other woman spoke to the men, one of whom quickly waved and shouted to another man on a motorbike, who zipped over. The boy had no visible signs of life. The man who had waved got on the back of the bike and the woman handed the boy to him and they sped off. There was evidence of a mother's grief in the emotion of the woman who had carried the boy, and she was led away slowly by the other woman, into the shadow of the church and then around the corner.

There were a few young men left standing with us, and I asked them what was said about what had happened.

"Water." He said it flatly, without any inflection in his voice or emotion on his face; water is what happened.

For all we knew, these people could have been family, friends or complete strangers. We never found out if the boy survived.

MADURAI

**A tenacious tout,
troubles in paradise,
and a midnight-hour escape**

It was after dark when we arrived in Madurai later that day.
The majority of hotels listed in the guidebook were concentrated very near the train station, so we elected to investigate
on foot.

After finding only full or filthy lodgings, our hunt was still on
when we ran into a tout who started flapping his arms and waving
around, talking a mile a minute about great hotels and cheap prices,
the best you've ever seen! All the usual bullshit. We tried ignoring
him, speaking sharply to him, crossing the street; but he would not
leave us.

The Minx and I went inside a hotel and he followed. I asked for a
room, the manager said certainly. The tout started speaking over my
shoulder with the manager (in Tamil, of course), and I—tired
stressed pent-up—lost it.

"I don't know this man!" I shouted. "I'm not paying for his
commission!" I turned to the tout. "Get lost, you punk!"

"No commission," the manager said firmly, shaking his head,
trying to convince me that what was happening wasn't happening.

"Get him out of here!" I hollered as the tout kept babbling. The
manager quickly produced the room key and had someone lead us
upstairs. It was fine enough for our state of exhaustion: a dump with

no shower, but comparatively clean.

I went to try and negotiate the price down, but the manager was having none of it. I saw the tout standing outside in the street, still hanging around. "No commission," I said again. The manager was becoming upset with my accusations.

"Sir, we don't pay touts here! No commission! Same rate!"

I didn't believe a word but took my receipt and walked slowly up the stairs; once I reached the room, I immediately rushed back down.

Sure enough, the tout was back in front of the desk and the manager was writing something in a ledger. The tout saw me coming and whispered to the manager, who innocently put the ledger aside and folded his hands on it.

"Aha!" I cried victoriously. "What's this? What's that! You're paying his commission!"

"Only once a year, sir!" said the manager indignantly, missing the point entirely. I glared at the tout and he produced his driver's licence as some sort of argument; I glared harder and he left, flapping his arms once again.

❁

The first order of business in the morning was finding a new hotel: the Minx wanted a room with a shower; I just wanted to leave on principle.

We found one two blocks away called New College House, which was a huge complex: three or four hundred rooms arranged on four storeys around a spacious courtyard, plus a cyber café, restaurant and canteen on the premises The room was the same price as the other place but far nicer. It was only nine-thirty in the morning when we checked in, so we headed out to see what we could see.

Madurai is one of the oldest continuously-inhabited cities in the world, making it a treasure trove of cultural artifacts and history. But the beauty of the Meenakshi Amman temple is in a class of itself, and it was our first destination.

The tallest of the temple's fourteen gateway towers is by far the highlight of the complex, possibly the greatest architectural achievement in south India. Tall, rectangular, tapered towards the top, it is the pinnacle of a unique south Indian style of tower architecture featuring elaborately carved relief figures in bright colours, normally depicting gods and deities. The southern tower is the tallest at fifty-two metres, but it is not the height that stuns so much as the detail: the relief work on the four sloping façades is impeccable, impossible, immaculate; the colours are not merely bright and lovely but sublime, almost tangible, approaching perfection. Hundreds and thousands of carved three-dimensional characters surge out from the stone, large near the base of the tower, tiny at the top. The amount and agree of craftsmanship is staggering (to say nothing of maintainance: the myriad colours were so vivid that it was clear the paint had been restored as needed, a horrifyingly painstaking task).

After a few more sights, the Minx and I continued our habit of following visits to religious sites with carnal exercise and alcohol. We washed some laundry in a bucket and hung it on the hotel rooftop, then went out for dinner, followed by a bar where I opened my big mouth.

The bar was in a basement, fully designed in a spaceship motif: everything was either cold steel or looked like something out of The Jetsons. After four or five beverages, I was loose enough to speak my mind: about how Arun was a fraud and she put too much stock in his nonsense; about how it seemed she didn't talk to me so much as bring up highlights of her career so I would take her seriously. I didn't feel I was attacking her, but she certainly did. I managed to stop myself before I did any lasting damage, but it was a long walk home, and enough of a fight that what followed when we returned home (after much apologizing) would count as makeup sex.

But while tension in a relationship can be accommodated and addressed, a strain on a prophylactic, particularly a lousy Indian-made one, will result in failure. And so, for the second time together, we found ourselves with a broken condom on our hands (so to speak), and we went to sleep together mumbling about finding a doctor who could get her the morning-after pill.

✿

When we awoke, we headed first to the train station to book our tickets onward, since it was nearby and wouldn't long. But it turned out to be a disastrously scattered process unlike any other station in India: we were sent from one place to the next looking for the foreign ticketing office, across the tracks and back again and back once more, to vaguely-described buildings that turned out to be closed. It took us three and a half hours to get our tickets, and now we had a new problem: it was nearly one o'clock when we returned to the hotel with our tickets for a train that evening; but the hotel used a twenty-four-hour checkout system (wherein your checkout time is the same time you arrived at) and we had checked-in at nine-thirty in the morning. The Minx continued onward to find a doctor while I went to the hotel reception to try and sort things out.

I gave the man at the desk the key with a smile and said we'd like to check-out, please. Some jokes, some chit-chat, questions about cricket, hoping to distract him. But he looked in the ledger and realized I was late. He wrote up a bill without a word and handed it to me; he was charging me for another full day, which was the norm in these situations.

"Look, I'm sorry I'm late," I said in soothing tones, "but we were held up at the train station, you see…"

"No, you pay!" He jabbed the bill on the counter with a crooked finger.

"Well, it's only been a few hours extra, I'll give you a hundred rupees…"

He started shouting at me in Tamil, and also at another man next to him who joined in to insist rather angrily that I pay the full amount.

I had no argument to stand on, and it was our own damn fault we were late, but they were so quick to anger and so rude and unreasonable that my will became reinforced tenfold.

"Look," I said, grabbing the receipt I was given earlier with the hotel rules on the back, "it doesn't say twenty-four-hour checkout anywhere on here. (True.) How was I supposed to know? (We were told upon check-in.)" They yelled some more, very little of it in discernable English. "Outrageous!" I yelled at them. They spat syllables back. No one was budging, this I could see. I slammed my hand down hard on the counter as I took the bill and stormed out. I had no plan, no solution, but I didn't want to boil my blood with these two angry men any longer.

I went up to the room and started packing. The Minx returned empty-handed: the chemists didn't know what a morning-after pill was, and she couldn't find a doctor on the weekend. I filled her in on our hotel situation and suggested what I saw as the most reason-able solution: skip out on the bill come nightfall. We had already paid in advance for the night we had slept in the room, so I felt no guilt about stiffing them for a night we had no intention of staying for.

Without hesitation, the trusty Minx declared she was in, and we set about planning our caper with all the detail of the invasion of Normandy.

✤

The hotel office was next to the main gate, which led to the central courtyard. Our room was on the fourth floor, far away from the office. Our stairwell landed on the ground floor between the restaurant and the computer café, both of which had doors onto the courtyard as well as the public street. The restaurant was farther away from the office, so we chose it as our escape route.

That night, we had a late supper at a rooftop restaurant nearby. No one at the hotel said a word as they watched us come and go without our baggage: they must have thought I'd caved and decided to spend another night.

Our train departed at midnight, so at eleven-twenty-five we grabbed our bags and started down. During the day, I had made a point of walking between the inner courtyard and the outer street via the restaurant a few times, passing through to make sure the staff would recognize me.

I was somewhat nervous as we walked down the stairs, mostly because I could guess what would happen if we were caught: the police would be called for a shakedown, and probably an expensive one. But the Minx and I encountered no one on the stairs, and we said a cheerful good-bye to the restaurant staff as we walked out casually with our backpacks. They said good-bye and waved.

The shortest route to the railway station ran past the hotel gate, so we took the long way, walking briskly and silently in the dark; we said nothing until we were several blocks away.

I was still nervous about being discovered when we arrived at the station: what if they happened to check our room and logically sent someone to look for us here? It didn't help that our train was twenty minutes late. I sat and paced and read train maps and stared at the clock. Only when it arrived and we got on and it pulled out of the station did I sigh in relief and kiss the Minx.

"That'll teach the bastards."

RETURN TO OOTY

Rat bastards

After three weeks in India, all of them in coastal towns, the
Minx was ready for a change: her sexy Scandinavian blood
wasn't accustomed to the constant taxing heat. I told her
about Ooty—that quaint little town set amongst the mountainous tea
fields, where sweaters were a necessity in the high-altitudinal evenings—and she jumped at the idea.

And so, after having just begun to travel north along my most
logical route after hitting the bottom of the subcontinent, I made a
sharp detour to accompany the Minx west. As with most decisions
made on the road, both the immediate outcome and the most distant
reverberations were entirely unpredictable.

We arrived and made the short walk from the bus station to the
hotel I had stayed in previously. It was cheap and decent, but after
one cold night and frosty morning with no hot water, the Minx
insisted we upgrade our accommodation.

I agreed, mostly to keep her happy, though Ooty wasn't in any
case the mountainous paradise I had promised: for whatever reason,
the congestion in the city, which had been a problem before, had
increased to the point where much of the town was a never-ending
traffic jam resplendent with honking a-plenty and crowds galore. I
was disappointed, and the Minx seemed to swing between frustration and exhaustion.

We hunted for most of our first full day there, going from hotel to hotel with our backpacks dragging us down. Eventually, we found a place that was dumpy-but-acceptable at the high end of our price range. We took it mostly to have a place to sit.

Our mutual exhaustion meant that sleep would be no problem, but we still drank a bottle of Old Monk before lying down. Too tired to fool around (a rarity), we simply curled up together and drifted off.

Within twenty minutes we were awakened by horrific squealing and chirping: there were rats—bloody rats!—in the room... and in the rest of the hotel and outside: we could hear them everywhere!, running and scurrying and probably screwing and using foul language.

I got up and turned on the light, and the room instantly fell silent. The loudest sounds had been coming from under our bed, but I couldn't spy anything there, so I investigated the bathroom, and it was only then that I noticed the hole chewed through the bottom-left corner of the door. Inside the bathroom I found another hole, a two-inch circle cut through the wall with a pipe leading into the alley: it was designed to serve as a drain for the shower, but with no grating it was a perfect rat pedestrian tunnel.

Just as I came out from the bathroom, the Minx managed to frighten the bastard under our bed out from hiding. She yelped and it squealed and bolted for the bathroom, plowing straight into my foot in the process. The rodent recovered and made a ratline for his escape pipe: gone.

I stuffed a rolled-up magazine into the hole in the bathroom door and we went to bed quite satisfied with our efforts.

Not two minutes later, a horrible chewing-scraping sound began at the door. The rodentious bastards were back, munching noisily on the magazine. This would not do; I turned the bathroom light on and listened through the door as the vermin hustled out. We left it on, which kept them away, though the thousands in the alley and dozens in the hotel were perfectly and horribly audible throughout the night.

Average everyday chaos,
and trusting our lives to a madman

The toy train was our method of egress from Ooty the next day; having found nothing but rats and disappointment, we were ready to flee. After spending a much more relaxing night in Coonoor (which was still serving as the terminus for the toy train as the railway had yet to be repaired since the landslide), the Minx picked our next destination out of her guidebook: another tea-filled mountain town called Munnar, not far from where we were, but reachable only by bus.

We exited our hotel to find a bus bound for Coimbatore with plenty of free seats that just happened to be waiting at the bus stop outside; this fortuitous moment was to be our last taste of transportational simplicity for the day.

The bus didn't travel more than ten kilometres outside of the town before the damn thing died and everyone was told to get off. We all stood around for twenty minutes until another bus appeared and the Minx and I clambered on to secure seats: we were told that this bus would take us as far as Mettapalayam, where we would have to change buses again to get to Coimbatore.

I got off to wander while we were waiting to leave; only by chance did I casually ask the conductor of our original broken-down bus if this bus we were on was the right one. He said no, no, we should get off and wait for the proper one. As he spoke the driver fired up the engine and I raced around to fetch the Minx while the conductor shouted for the driver to wait for us to get our bags off.

The proper bus did come and we got back on the road. Once we arrived in Coimbatore—sweaty, hungry and wide-eyed—there was some confusion as to where we should get off. I had assumed that the bus would terminate at the same bus stand I had arrived at before with Roberta. But we stopped at a different, much larger terminal instead, and the Minx and I grabbed our luggage and disembarked with uncertainty.

The bus station was hectic and filthy, a perfect replica of every other bus station in India. I spied a booking office on the far side and we headed straight for it. Inside was an older man in a khaki uniform unpacking his lunch; I realized how hungry I was as I asked about a bus to Munnar and he shook his head. "Not from here," he said almost sadly. "Come, I will show you."

He walked to his desk and took a scrap piece of paper and started scrawling names and numbers connected with arrows. A few other officials arrived and joined him, curiously watching what he was writing, advising him on things, telling him to change this-or-that.

Finally, I was presented with the diagram: the man explained in fine English that we needed to take a local bus (route 130) five kilometres to a different bus terminal, from where we could catch a bus to Udumalpet, another seventy kilometres away. There we would find many regular buses to Munnar, another eighty kilometres away. The kicker was that there was only one bus leaving the other station for Udumalpet and it departed in one hour. We thanked the man and his advisers and rushed out.

After some frantic confusion, the Minx and I found the correct stand for route 130, and the bus came and we made our way to the other station, another circus of noise and filth and chai-wallahs where we once again sought out the booking office and asked about the 2:35 bus to Udumalpet. The man pointed straight out the window of the office at a green bus and told us that was our chariot.

We scrambled aboard, the bus left ten minutes ahead of schedule, and we were on the road once more, this time to a place we had never heard of. The seventy kilometres to Udumalpet were lovely, mostly flat and winding with a canopy of grandfatherly trees shading the highway between villages.

When we arrived two hours later, we repeated our well-honed habit of seeking out the information office, where we found an overly cheerful man who was happy to lead us directly to the place where the bus to Munnar would come. There was a large crowd waiting there, but only a fraction of them boarded our bus, and it was a rare relief not to have to fight for a seat.

The road to Munnar ran through a protected park in a mountainous area and the scenery was stupendous once we gained some ground. The driver was a small man in his late fifties with wire-rimmed glasses who looked like he might be an erstwhile jeweller or mild-mannered hotel owner. He was also mad, mad as every other driver in India, and he bounced that bus and swung it around tight mountain hairpin curves without letting off the accelerator, let alone touching the brake. Whether ascending an incline or flying down towards a valley, his speed was constant and it was fast.

The road was only three metres wide and snaked along mountain faces with the short and soft shoulder giving sharp drop to the cliffs below. But the madman refused to slow down: he raced around the bends with fury, taking wide turns, swinging the nose within inches of the rock face and letting the back wheels kiss the cliffy shoulder as he bent and wrapped the bus frame again and again around curves. Cranking the wheel left and right rapidly, swinging the passengers along with him, he often had to put his clutch foot up on the metal dashboard next to the steering wheel to give himself leverage and stability as he careened around a turn.

I loved it: I had been on enough wild bus rides now to know that madmen are indeed professionals. The other passengers, all Indians, sat swaying with blank expressions. The Minx was tense with the fear of the uninitiated. I looked at the driver's face: it looked bored. He drove this way because he had to, because he had driven this road a thousand times. He didn't drive like a lunatic because it was exhilarating or empowering: he flew that bus around every bend at top speed because the sooner he reached the end of his route, the sooner he could go home and eat his dinner and screw his wife and go to bed and wake up the next morning and do it all over again for the rest of his life. And as night came and the beautiful scenic valleys below were shrouded in darkness, his driving seemed all the more frantic and mad, mad like every other driver in India, like the professional ones who have taken their mad art to the level of genius.

As we skittered around corners or squeezed past oncoming trucks with borrowed space, our shadow hanging off the cliff, all we passengers could do was put our minds somewhere safer and wait for either our arrival or our doom. At least the scenery was lovely.

MUNNAR

**Ebb and flow,
a faraway hockey puck,
and the day the horns of Kerala fell silent**

Munnar is a small settlement, much less spread out than Ooty, so the Minx and I decided to hoof it to a hotel once we arrived at the bus station after dark. We had a few options in mind, cribbed from the guidebook, but we happened to run into a young American couple heading to the bus depot. They strongly recommended the hotel they had stayed in, and we headed straight there.

It was a real find: spacious, bare-basic rooms, clean and cheap, centrally located with friendly staff. The Minx and I christened the room and immediately passed out.

In the morning we found a glorious masala dosa place and made our way to the edge of town for a hike. The city was relatively quiet and relaxed, especially compared to the chaos of Ooty. We soon noticed that this was another destination for middle-class Indians, and we were the only foreigners in town.

We escaped the city on foot quickly, moving in an arbitrary direction to find postcard-lovely scenery: rolling hills covered in perfect rows of low tea bushes, forming an impossibly beautiful pattern that captivated the eye as it stretched through the valleys.

But there was tension as we walked; not between the Minx and I, but as a result of our looming situation: she had admitted to me the previous morning that she was now several days late for her period, a piece of news made all the more foreboding when our two broken condoms in the past ten days were taken into account. We had not been able to find her a doctor or clinic, let alone a morning-after pill. If, God forbid, she turned out to be pregnant, she feared she would have to suspend her long-dreamt-of five-month India trip only a few weeks into it. An abortion in a developing country is not a particularly comforting thought.

These scenarios ran silently through our heads as we walked hand-in-hand amongst peaceful tea fields, wondering and worrying about the future.

✿

I had another problem weighing on me, admittedly of a very different nature. The Vancouver Olympics were winding down, which meant it was time for the biggest and most sacred event: men's hockey. It was Canada versus the United States in the final, potentially one of the defining games of my generation, up there with the 2002 Salt Lake Olympics when Canada won its first men's hockey gold in five decades, or the 2004 NHL Finals when a wildly overachieving Calgary team became the first Canadian team in a decade of even having a sniff at the Stanley Cup, falling one controversial non-goal short of the prize. These are games of such national significance that even non-fans are obliged to watch, and hockey faithful recount to each other years later where they were while watching the game. Now Canada had a chance to win its first hockey gold on home soil, against the Yanks no less, and I was halfway around the world in a tiny mountain town.

The Minx did her best to placate me with rum and fresh pineapple juice, but I was anxious and grumpy when we went to bed that night. In the morning I received a text message from my mother: '3-2 OT' was all it said. I furiously typed a reply, demanding to know who had won, who had scored in overtime, what had happened!? No answer came, so we went for breakfast.

Sitting over masala doses and chai, watching me rub my hands and check my phone every few seconds, the Minx stayed quiet, not bothering to try and console me or take my fixated mind off of a puck on a faraway sheet of ice.

An hour passed. Then another. I felt like I was losing my mind; India was meaningless to me that morning. Finally, my phone beeped and I grabbed it with the narrow beedy eyes of a junkie to read the message: 'Crosby from Iginla in OT'.

I yelped loud enough to frighten everyone in the restaurant. They must have been reassured, if confused, when they turned and saw the pure joy on my face.

❂

We spent the next several days eating, drinking and shagging in Munnar, with the in-between time dedicated to wandering, exploring, hiking, reading and generally relaxing. The guidebook turned us on to a true gem that became our favourite restaurant: a bit of a hike, set on the edge of the town in a somewhat rundown area, this place was found only if you knew to look for it (the other establishments nearby had signs with name so similar to the real deal that they would face legal action in a Western country; when your competitors start pretending to be you, you know you're doing something right).

Simple tables, simple menu on the wall. This being something of a working class joint, the most popular item was a south Indian dish uncreatively called a 'meal': several small bowls of different curries and pickles served with a crispy papadum and an unlimited amount of rice.

Leaning to eat curry-and-bread with one's hands is a challenge fairly easily met by adventurous Westerners; eating curry-and-rice with one's hands, however, is a very different and far messier beast. When I attempted it for the first time in Madurai, I first watched the locals for style tips: it seemed everyone had their own method, starting with dry or soupy curries, scooping or pinching or shovelling, mixing different things with the rice, crushing the papadum and

231

sprinkling it on top. They key is to find what works for you, and to not be embarrassed.

The whole meal was thirty rupees, about seventy cents, and was different every day, but consistently among the best food I ate in India.

For drinks, we befriended a man who ran a juice stall in the market near our hotel. He gave us a good price for a whole pine-apple, blended into sweet liquid oblivion and poured into large empty water bottles to transport the juice home where we mixed it with Old Monk rum.

At night we drank and went out to the evening food market, which appeared every other day. There were paranthas—flaky fried bread—transformed from dough to delicious right in front of us. Curries and fish and chai were all prepared to perfection, and huge long tables with plastic stools were set up for a communal meal. It might have been paradise.

Then one morning I awoke to find the Minx already up and smil-ing. She had gotten her period. It also happened to be my birthday.

We celebrated both events with breakfast, and then bought some fruit in the market and wandered out of town in a new direction. We came across a beautiful valley scene, picturesque in every way: tea rows, mountains, and some boys playing soccer down below us. We spent hours sitting there with our fruit and our books and each other.

On our way back into town, we came across some road construc-tion being down entirely by human labour: nothing exceptional in itself, but the workers were all women, mostly middle-aged and older (though this was a guess, and perhaps a flawed one, as a great many Indians are much younger than they look, their manual labour and often-hard lives having weathered their faces well beyond their years). They were dusty and wrapped in working-woman's rags, but they were more than happy to be photographed by the Minx. They all but ignored me, and I was happy to stand quietly nearby, this being a very fine and human moment between women.

She snapped shots of the women working, and had them pose for close-up portraits; the Minx showed one of them women her beauti-ful dirty brown dignified face on the camera screen and the reaction was priceless: a timeless laugh and a toothless grin and happy words to her colleagues.

That night, we bought two bottles of rum and a great deal of pine-apple juice and spent our time in the room. There were no bars as such in Munnar, certainly none that a white couple could go to without creating a fuss, so the Minx put on a lovely dress for my birthday and did her hair and make-up, and we danced together in our three-dollar-a-night box, far away from our frozen countries, two strangers briefly sharing the road together.

❉

Birthday rum makes for a long, hard sleep: when we awoke mid-morning, we only had time enough to pack our bags and dash out with limited hopes of breakfast before we were due at the bus station.

There was a small market between our hotel and the street, and it was unusually quiet as we walked through it in search of a chai-wallah. Ordinarily there would have been a crowd of people at every stall, buying fruits and spices and haggling loudly; but the stalls were all shuttered and there was no one in sight. And there was something else wrong, some absence, some void that I could not identify immediately; India is too full of colourful details to notice a missing detail upon first glance.

The Minx and I walked to the street, and the scenario shifted from odd to downright eerie: the town looked deserted, devoid of human presence except for a handful of bored-looking men gathered around a makeshift chai stand. That's when I realized what felt so wrong, so unsettling: there were absolutely no vehicles in motion on the road, and therefore no horns being honked; it struck me that this was the first time I had experienced a city without engines and horns in four months.

We examined the deserted streets in bewilderment until we arrived at the bus station. There was no one there, and the office was closed. So were all the restaurants and shops and, literally, everything. The only signs of life were a handful of chai stands scattered about, and I asked the men standing at one for an explanation: a general strike, they said, to protest the increased taxes on petrol. Some restaurants might open in the late afternoon, but most things—including bus service—were shut down until the following morning.

And so we were trapped in Munnar for another day, resigned to eating nothing but fried dough from the chai-wallahs and exploring a bizarrely peaceful ghost town as the Minx and I began the countdown until our paths diverged again.

Exit the Minx

T he buses were indeed running the next day, and we boarded one to Kochi. Munnar had been good to us, and good for us, but my sexy partner and I had each developed separate plans and itineraries-for-one before we crossed paths.

The Minx was heading north along the western coast, eventually hoping to reach Nepal. I, however, was running out of time: her adventure was still young, but I had not planned on spending as much time as I did in Varkala, nor had I intended to return to Ooty and Kochi; I only had about a month left on my Indian visa, and I had yet to reach the east coast, let alone Calcutta and Sikkim. If time was not on my side, money was even less so: India may be cheap, but one can only live so long on savings. That as much as anything dictated my next move after Kochi.

The bus from Munnar to Ernakulam was uneventful, and getting from there to Fort Cochin was painless my second time around. We arrived in the early evening, and the look on Sebastian's face when I walked through his door without notice was terrifyingly welcome, the sort of kindness and generosity that makes you want to run for cover. He was especially pleased that I had turned up with a lady-friend, and he gave me a clandestine wink as he showed us to our room—across the hall from where Conway and I had left smoke and words hanging in the air over a month ago.

We went out to get some Portuguese food nearby and returned with full bellies ready for our bottle of rum. We didn't have any pineapple juice this time, but one last drink was in order, if only for posterity. The Minx and I were far from a perfect couple: there would be no talk of a future, no dreams of long-term bliss; there had been enough non-physical friction between us to preclude any such thoughts. But we had met each other at the perfect time, when we both happened to be exactly what the other needed. It was the quintessential road relationship, and it was nearly finished. All that remained was black rum, some more wild sex, a heavy sleep wrapped in a foreign lover's arms, and a train speeding into the jungle.

°

Morning. Shower, pack. Sex. Shower. Farewell, Sebastian, no time for breakfast. Backpacks on, out the door. Find a tuk-tuk. Railway station, please. How much? No, thirty! Okay, thirty-five. No-no, turn around, other railway station! No, same price! Yes, same price! (tick-tock, tick-tock...) Okay, forty-five, just drive!

...Arrive late, but the train is delayed. Sit down, I'll get us some food. Okay, you get the chai. Yessir, one of those, two of those, make it three, and two of those. Thank you. No update on the scheduled postings about the delay. Sit down. Eat. Drink. Talk.

It seemed we had little left to converse about (which was poor timing as my train was an hour late), but we made do with a combination of our future plans and recalling memories from our time together; when you don't want to talk about the present, you're left with what's ahead and what's behind.

My train pulled into the station and I hauled my bag on board to claim my seat. Then the Minx and I ducked into a train restroom for a two-minute make-out session in a haze of hot piss fumes. The train started moving, and we exited the restroom hastily as it shuddered forward, much to the amusement of a nearby man. The Minx jumped off the train, stumbled as she landed, then caught her footing and started running after me. I leaned out of the door as she came nearer and we kissed briefly. She slowed her pace and waved, and I waved back.

Then she yelled something and started sprinting again, moving impressively fast, catching up to the train even as it was speeding from the station. I grabbed the handle bars beside the door tightly and leaned precariously out of the car and kissed her for the last time. She stopped running. I waved. She waved back. I held her eyes as she walked along the platform before turning up the stairs to the exit.

The Minx and Pineapple Slim: two people, equal parts fact and fiction, who built their own mythology out of rum and blended juice at the bottom of the world; finally, inevitably, forcibly separated by the road. I turned my head in the same direction as the train, south, forward, next please.

AMRITAPURI

Amma, meet Pineapple Slim

The Minx was staying in Kochi for a few days before heading north. I, however, was southbound once again, heading unexpectedly for an ashram where I was told I could find a room with included hot meals for pennies a day. I was not particularly interested in meditation or some hippies' idea of spirituality; in fact, considering I was emerging from a rum-fuelled south Indian sex romp, the strict rules about clean living would be a challenge, albeit an inherently beneficial one. Conway had stayed there weeks earlier and was unceremoniously kicked out after two days for getting high and mouthing off to everyone about Amma, the founder and spiritual leader of the ashram.

My reasons for going to Amritapuri, however, were less about inner peace than cold hard numbers: I needed to rescue my bank account from the sizeable hit inflicted by the good life in Varkala, and a week of low-cost spartan living seemed just the ticket.

I disembarked the train at Kayankulam, the nearest stop to the ashram, and a rickshaw driver immediately approached me and asked, "Amritapuri?"

I said no, and he looked at me dubiously but moved on. I had heard there were regular local buses direct to the ashram, which would be the cheapest option. I followed the crowd down the platform and noticed the palpable feeling of many eyes on me, something I had not felt since north India, at least not to this extent:

I was the whitest thing around despite this being a landing pad for the ashram, and the curious brown eyes could not help but watch me.

I avoided the rickshaw stand and headed for a Kerala state bus at the far end of the station. There was no driver present, so I asked the few people on board if it would go to Amritapuri. An old man told me it would go to a bus station in the town where I could find the bus I needed; I thanked him and sat down.

The rest of the folks on the bus began speaking to each other in Malayalam, and the few English words I caught—'bus', 'station', 'Amritapuri'—conveyed to me the group's doubt about the information the old man had given to me. Without a word, he left the bus and walked to another that had just arrived, on the side of which were painted the words 'Educational Institute'. Two white women appeared to be discussing something with the driver of the bus, and when the old man approached them I could feel their rudeness from a distance. The man came back to our bus.

"I think those women are in your group," he said. "That bus is going to Amritapuri, but they wouldn't talk to me."

I assured him that I did not know those women, apologized for them anyway, thanked him for his help and carried my things off the bus towards the women, who were now yelling at an Indian man trying to carry his luggage on board.

"This is not a public bus!" they cried. "This is a private bus that we ordered!" I stood nearby with doubts about my chances, but then they just yelled at both of us to get the hell on board; I hadn't said a word.

They were obviously in bad moods: the exact sort of bad moods that befall unsteady or unready people who travel in India. I had seen it countless times in fellow travellers, and once or twice in myself. They ignored me and continued yelling at the man for bringing too many suitcases on board.

"We are picking up a group of thirty with a lot of luggage," the middle-aged woman with her dark hair in a bun said angrily. "Sir, there's no room for your bags!"

"Just kick him off," drawled the other one from inside the open hand she had rested her face in. She was in her early sixties with a bone face and too-big eyeballs. She seemed the most bitter of the two, and her bitterness seemed free to extend to the entire world around her; she shot me acid looks despite the fact that I still had not said a word and had only gotten on because they told me to.

Tired of arguing with the Indian man, who was now himself becoming irritable due to being yelled at constantly, the middle-aged woman asked me to move his bags to the back. I watched the man's reaction as I slowly picked up the first bag, but he didn't protest; in fact, he started passing me the rest of his luggage.

More white folks started arriving, and I became in charge of packing all their luggage at the rear as well. And there was a lot of it, at least two bags for every person, most of them huge heavy suitcases and backpacks, and the sweat poured from my face. But I didn't mind: if I was useful to the cranky women, perhaps they wouldn't yell at me.

Once all the bags were packed and everyone was on board, we set off. I didn't mind standing on the cramped bus, but a seat was insisted upon me, so I took it. I sat next to a Dutch woman in her sixties who had been living at the ashram for twelve years. I learned that the group had been travelling with Amma on her trip to the north and had just taken a long train ride from Bombay, which explained everyone's tired state.

"How long are you going to stay at the ashram?" she asked.

"A few days, maybe a week."

"Did you come to India for the ashram?"

"No, I've been travelling in India for four months now."

"Oh." She let this register. "So you're not on a spiritual journey? You're not on a tour visiting ashrams?"

I decided to avoid the first question. "I haven't been to any ashrams before."

"So you're not on a spiritual journey, then?"

"Well, I'm on a journey of some kind, I suppose." She smiled and seemed to accept this, and she turned to look out the window as the bus rolled through the town of Kayankulam. A minute later she began singing to herself in Malayalam.

I looked at the rest of the group on the crowded bus: they were all clad in white, mostly robes, and they were evidently from various countries and spoke myriad languages; some were silent; some were boisterous; everyone but the Dutch lady ignored me.

"So how long will you stay in India?"

"One more month," I replied. "Then I go to Thailand."

"And then?"

"Laos."

"And then?"

"Vietnam."

"And then?"

"Cambodia." I turned away before she could continue her game.

"You're travelling alone?"

"Yes. Well, I started out with a friend, but we split up."

"It didn't work out."

"No, it didn't."

"That happens sometimes."

"I guess it does." We rode in silence for a few minutes.

"So what brought you to the ashram?" I asked.

"Amma." The word was quick and without hesitation; the pause came when she considered how to explain. "I felt greatly drawn to her. I've never known anyone who laughs, who talks, who walks, who lives like she does." She looked at me. "She's a wonderful person."

"Sure is."

"I felt so drawn to her that I had no problem leaving behind my life, my job, my family to come here."

"Were you married?"

"No."

We fell back into silence until the ashram came into sight. She started telling me about the different buildings, about the university, about the sea shore and the temples and all of it. I nodded and smiled politely at every enthusiasm.

And then we arrived. After helping unload the luggage, I grabbed my own and headed for the international accommodation office.

The ashram was like some strange village with people milling about but seemingly not going anywhere or doing anything. Most were sitting or standing, talking in pairs or groups. Two women played with a baby; a few people read books. The buildings were painted pink and in good condition, though apparently several years old. The apartment complexes would not seem out of place in a mid-range hotel. There was a swimming pool. It felt, more than anything, like a mediocre resort.

The international accommodation office was closed until nine o'clock that night, so I was directed to the Indian office where I was given a card with a room number and a lock combination and pointed to a nearby building where I could find my temporary room.

The room was on the fifth floor in North American parlance, the fourth in British terms, but the sign outside the elevator said 6. It was a standard basic double room with no furniture: instead of a proper bed, a thin foam mattress lay on the floor; eleven others were stacked nearby. The toilet was Western and there was a cold-water shower. It was a corner room, and the windows looked out onto the ashram buildings and the courtyard below. In the near distance I could see the Arabian Sea. The sun was setting in that direction, lighting the palm trees with a fiery glow as a voice began singing from the temple.

I had spent the past two weeks guzzling rum and pursuing carnal delights with a beautiful mad Minx all over south India. This gig was bound to be tougher. I braced myself as I stared out the window and prepared to be spiritually cleansed.

✿

DAY 1

Registered with the international accommodation office. The girl gave me a standard form to fill out; then: "You know Amma's not here, right?" Pause. Smile: "Well, she's here and she's not here."

My roommate is a forty-something Englishman named Dave. Dave is a panchakarma patient, which means, he apologetically explained, that he must avoid sun and wind and fans, which means, he's very sorry, that he can't have the fan on at night, which was the impetus for his previous roommate's departure earlier that day.

Found the canteen: watery rice and vegetable curry, three times a day at no cost; fairly tasty and unlimited. There is also a Western canteen which serves pizza, etc. for a price. Not interested.

Second roommate today, a young German guy named Felix who is only staying one night. Dave roped him into a conversation about Amritsar...

> Dave: The Gold Temple is, for me, the most beautiful building in India.
>
> Felix: More so than the Taj?
>
> Dave: Oh yeah. The Golden Temple is all about happiness. The Taj is all about death and misery. Plus, it was built with slave labour.
>
> Felix: Really?
>
> Dave: Yeah, it's not something they tell you on the tour.
>
> Felix: Huh. (pauses) Just like the pyramids. (chuckle)
>
> Dave: (hesitates) Yes. Well, if you believe that the pyramids were built by humans... then, yeah, sure, I guess.
>
> (The room is silent for several moments.)
>
> Dave (cont.): I mean, we don't even have the technology to build something that grand today. I have a hard time believing it was all done with hands and carts.
>
> Felix: (laughs nervously)
>
> Dave: Some people will believe that, though. The people who watch television for eight hours a day will believe that. I think people who believe that are the most ostrich-ized people.

Dave then went on to explain about the head-in-the-sand and the ostrich, demonstrating that he apparently was not trying to say 'ostracized'. I read my book and ignored them; they are both moving out tomorrow.

DAY 2

The apartment building has an open-air emergency exit stairwell near my end of the hallway, and I set up shop there today with a chair, my bottle of water, some books, a notepad and a word processor. Spent seven hours there with words, the Arabian Sea on my left, the Keralan backwaters on my right, and nothing but a carpet of soaring palm trees as far as the eye could reach. I broke from words and work only for meals—my own personal brand of meditation.

People don't seem to be particularly joyous or in a state of zen-like bliss here. On the contrary: in my short time thus far, I've already seen several examples of bitterness and exasperation and general pettiness, usually among the most dedicated ashramites, who are distinguishable by their white robes. Whether it's interactions between people or conversations overheard in the canteen, there is plenty of anecdotal evidence to discount the ashram as a source of enlightenment or personal growth.

DAY 3

Amma has her own branding, her own logo, her own tagline ("Embracing the World"). Her face is everywhere in and around the ashram, usually the same photo of her looking over her shoulder with a carefree and genuine grin, like some celebrity caught in a moment of humanness—except that her celebrity spawns <u>from</u> her humanness, her smile, her 'happy'. There must exist somewhere photos of Amma scowling or yelling or looking angry and disappoin-ted; she can't always be happy, like the photos suggest, because that would make her into an impossible Christ-figure, something to aspire towards and never attain. Then again, He's done pretty well for himself, so maybe it's not such a far-fetched gimmick.

More reading, some exploring today. Avoiding conversation with anyone lest I catch whatever whatever mysterious ailment causes them to dress in white robes and worship a chubby Indian lady.

DAY 4

Today I finally went to the seva office. Seva is volunteer work, except it's mandatory. In order to keep the ashram open and highly affordable, everyone has to pitch in with the operation: sweeping, cleaning, cooking, washing dishes, hauling trash, etc. The seva office was literally a closet, with a one-metre wide desk that took up the entire room. I sat down in front of a young blonde girl with dorky-chic glasses who was peering at a laptop. She asked how long I was staying; I said a few more days and she wrote down the details of a man who needed help cleaning out a storage locker of some kind.

I was supposed to meet him in front of the temple at one o'clock. He never showed, so I went back to the stairwell with my books and my view.

DAY 5

Dave, who had moved into a special panchakarma room in the same building, appeared on my stairwell/balcony/office today. He proceeded to tell me a ranting tale about trying to rent a guesthouse outside the ashram and being told he wouldn't be allowed back in to continue his treatment—or something; his Northern English accent made him impossible to understand. In any case, he concluded his rant about the ashram administration thusly:

"…But I know that Amma is a truly special and wonderful person. I know that, even though I've never met her. And she helps the poor on the street and in Africa and feeds 'em and all that.

"But if you're going to do these things right it needs to be on the straight and honest, d'yknow wot ay mean? And I think, really, that this place is one of two shining lights in the world for us, this place, one of two, one is Buddhism, centred in Dharamsala, the Dalai Lama's residence, and the other one is here, Amma. But some of these people are just dishonest and deceitful. It's a shame. Their karma, not mine."

Today I wandered outside the ashram for the first time. Immediately outside the gate was a man with a cart selling cigarettes, which Amma has banned. I bought a pack and secretly smoked them in my bathroom by the window while my headphones played Billie Holiday. Don't ever let anyone tell you that vices and enlightenment don't mix.

DAY 6

Went to the tiny computer café to try and book a train onward, but the internet is down until further notice.

There is an old lady in the room next to the stairwell, and she comes out from time to time to do yoga or eat lunch. She doesn't speak any English, but she always looks unhappy with my presence. Perhaps she had the balcony all to herself before I came along. Whatever the reason, I feel an awful lot of indignation coming my way.

Two gay roommates today, both from France. They step lightly around the room and whisper in French as though they are worried about disturbing me. They never said they were a couple, but it is fairly obvious: I asked if they were travelling together and they hesitated awkwardly, glancing at each other before one of them said yes and smiled. Nice guys.

There is a sign in the ashram: O Amma, let everything I do be a prostration unto you.

DAY 7

Considering that seva is mandated, and that the powers that be confiscate your passport upon arrival, I thought I should try again to get a job. I was assigned to work two hours in the recycling centre sorting through garbage and carting the unsalvageables over to the incinerator and burning them. Not a bad job: it felt good to be useful again. My inner socialist is pacified.

No internet again today. Wondering how I'll ever get out of here.

Most of the time at meals I pick up a clean metal plate and spoon from the pile, rinse them, get in line to collect my food, then walk past the people congregated around the three long rows of tables that stretch nearly the length of the open-air auditorium. I walk and walk, past the white robes and hippies and hipsters and Indian men eating in groups. I keep walking down the line until I am alone, except for a few other people who also want to be alone, and they're all right with me. My people.

Snippets of conversation overheard in the canteen:

"I think it's cheesecake…"

"…you do that, you've got a perfect setup for worms…"

"When you're studying, Amma leaves her body and comes to help you. That's true."

DAY 8

Internet! My escape plan is finalized: a boat from here to Alleppy, then bus to Ernakulam, then train to Pondicherry. The soonest I could book for was three days from now. Patience is a virtue.

Today, as usual, the old lady came out onto the stairwell balcony while I was writing on my laptop. She hung out her laundry and ate her lunch and threw me the usual bad vibes, but said nothing. Then, just now, she came back out carrying a small steel plate with three big slices of pineapple. I politely refused as I leaned forward and eyed the deliciousness: I hadn't had any fruit at the ashram at all, and the bright yellow flesh stirred memories of my now-suppressed alter ego. I reached for the top piece and she pushed the plate forward to indicate that the entire dish was for me. I took it and thanked her, slightly bewildered as one usually is when one's presumptions are dispelled.

There is a rule (one of many) in the pamphlet given out to new arrivals that 'strongly advises' residents to 'avoid the village'. Today I walked outside the ashram again, this time at greater length: past the wide-open steel gates with the disinterested guard and his newspaper, across the footbridge and over the backwaters.

The other side is no different from any of dozens of sleepy, sparse communities I've seen in India: the rickshaws lined up, their drivers occasionally offering their services to you; the the rows of single-unit shops along the blazing roadside; the women walking that roadside with various parcels balanced perfectly on their heads. It was India, <u>real</u> India, and it was right next door.

The ashram powers-that-be advise ashramites to avoid the village out of 'respect' for the locals' 'very traditional' values. What they really mean is that this large conspicuous group of comparatively wealthy white people can't be trusted not to make fools of themselves when exposed to a foreign culture. Sadly, this is probably true, especially given the sort of genuine weirdos this place seems to attract. But they'll never learn how to behave in foreign cultures unless they are exposed to them; and the whole tired idea of finding personal salvation by wrapping yourself in the ancient spirituality of India doesn't work well when you lock yourself in a resort: technically in India, but safe from it behind steel gates.

DAY 9

More writing, more reading. The old lady brought me a mug of chai. I think she likes me.

Then, still on the balcony, a bald eagle flew up and landed on a

concrete ledge above me. It stood there for several minutes, preen-
ing its feathers and surveying the view below. It never once looked
at me. I watched the talons on it closely, thinking that they looked
large and sharp and sure enough to take down a baby cougar. Could
I take down a baby cougar? I wasn't sure. I was therefore wary of
the massive bird and we respected each other's space until he departed.

Now, on the rooftop of a different building below me, I see a
woman in her mid-twenties come out carrying a child, both of them
clad in white. Wait, that is no child! That is a doll, an Amma doll,
and, yes, she goes and—sweet God—gets a plastic chair and sits
down facing the sea (I can't believe this) and puts the <u>doll</u> in her <u>lap</u>
and kisses its hair! There they are now, they perfect picture of
madness, of childishness, of refusing to grow up and see the world
for what it is, what this doll is. (Ordinarily, I would allow for the
possibility that this is a tragically mentally disabled person; however,
my time here forces me to admit that this is typical, albeit extreme,
behaviour for Amma-followers.) This may or may not be exactly
what Amma wants her disciples to be.

DAY 10

Finally, after seemingly endless days of the same meals, of nothing
but reading and writing, of strange roommates coming and going, of
being locked in here with these strange personality-cult worshippers
who frighten me and force me to sneak verboten cigarettes in my
bathroom with Billie Holiday, finally, it is time to leave. I don't
regret my time at the ashram: I saved a lot of money and got a lot of
writing done; but, most importantly, I never would have believed the
truth about Amritapuri without seeing it for myself.

In the early afternoon I hop on a boat outside the ashram bound
for Alleppy and watch the giant mural of Amma next to the dock
diminish as we pull away from the lunatic shores of Amritapuri and
chug north back into the glory of India.

The enduring curse of Amma,
and the French connection

The boat was uniquely outfitted with two storeys and a noisy motor, but was of the same provenance as the majority of vessels on the backwaters: it had begun life as a barge used for hauling rice before tourism became a booming industry in Kerala. We cruised along the wide backwater channels fairly slowly, and I arrived in Alleppy later than I expected. Hustling to the bus station in the dark, I had to hunt for the route to Ernakulam. There were buses everywhere, all with destinations posted in the window, but all written in Malayalam. No one could answer my questions; the information office existed in name only. One man pointed to a particular bus; I went to it and asked a man sitting on board if it went to Ernakulam; he said yes. With relief, I climbed on and took a seat and within twenty minutes we were on our way.

Most government and some private buses work as follows: you board without a ticket and, once en route, the conductor comes around and asks you where you want to go. He punches it in on a little electronic device (similar to the mobile credit card machines in restaurants) and it quickly spits out a receipt-like ticket with your origin, destination and fare printed on it. You then pay him and he moves on to the next person. It's actually quite efficient, and watch-ing him move through the crush of an Indian bus is impressive in action.

I was at the back of the bus, which wasn't full but had enough passengers so that it took the conductor some time to reach me. I told him Ernakulam; he looked at me strangely, so I said it again. This wasn't good. He looked at the other passengers within earshot for help, one of whom told me in broken English that this bus didn't go to Ernakulam; moreover, it was heading south, not north.

By the time I jumped off at the next stop, flagged down a rick-shaw, caved in to a ridiculous price and returned to the bus station, I had long since missed the more timely bus to my train. I was cutting it close, but I had no choice but to wait an hour for the next bus. It was jammed from front to back as we stopped at several more stations in the vicinity, and I wound up sitting on the floor at the front next to the driver with my back to the windshield; I didn't need to see the reckless manoeuvres he was attempting at high speeds.

I couldn't find a rickshaw at the bus station, as unbelievable as that sounds. It was fate, it was karma, maybe it was Amma: the one time I needed a rickshaw, any rickshaw, at any price, there were none to be found. It wasn't a proper station so much as a dark street somewhere, but I judged from familiar landmarks and highways which way the train station was and started hiking with my backpack, chain-smoking along the way as though that might make me move faster. My train was due to depart in seventeen minutes; meanwhile, I was crisscrossing alleys and streets in the pitch dark, trying to find one that would take me in the direction I thought I needed to go. Suddenly I broke through the darkness and saw it there at the end of a row of shops, bustling with people and glowing in the night, the most beautiful train station in the world. I rushed towards it, arriving with three minutes to snare. Then I found out that my train was thirty minutes late, so I went and had a masala dosa and cursed Amma in every language I could manage.

 ✿

You'll have to forgive me for one minor exaggeration (a rarity, I hope, through all these stories), one tiny not-quite-truth: my train was not bound for Pondicherry but for Tiruchirappalli.

Almost always referred to as Trichy by everyone these days, this was as far as I could manage to book rail passage; any connecting trains were booked solid. What's worse: there are no direct trains to Pondicherry, only to the town of Villupuram forty kilometres outside the city, which connects via a spur line to the larger city. Thus I woke up in Trichy with as many problems in front of me as I'd had the night before.

Somehow, as usual, I managed to cope: I squeezed my way onto a train that I knew would be stopping in Villupuram en route to Chennai; unreserved cattle class would do for this leg of the journey.

I couldn't get a seat, unsurprisingly, so I stood at the front of the cramped, dirty car. I noticed a white girl sitting in a window seat, late-twenties, curled up with her feet underneath her, trying to sleep on a foam pillow against the steel bars of the window. She was quite attractive, and I kept glancing over to her once she woke up, trying to catch her eye. There was a man sleeping on the luggage rack above her, curled up with his back to the world; I didn't realize it was a person for the first hour of the trip.

Shortly the girl rose and collected her baggage, thinking it was her stop. It wasn't; but she stood next to me long enough for us to strike up a conversation. Her name was Caroline, she was French, and she also happened to be travelling to Pondicherry. Caroline was with her sister, their friend and the friend's boyfriend, all of whom she was avoiding by sitting in a different carriage. We talked for a while until we reached Villupuram and met up with the rest of her group.

I said I was taking another train into Pondicherry because the rail station there was central while the bus station was in the suburbs. Caroline wanted to stick with me, which may have been because she saw the logic in my plan, or solely because her sister et al. voted for a bus. They were—and this was apparent immediately—a highly dysfunctional group.

We all waited for and caught the train, and Caroline and I sat on the floor by the open door and smoked and watched the world go by; just me and another pretty girl. She mentioned that she had an awful lot of weed and, since she was flying home in two days, would I be willing to help her smoke it and inherit the leftovers?

I had a feeling I was going to enjoy Pondicherry.

PONDICHERRY

Haziness, visa pleas, and The Rub

The first priority was getting rid of our baggage—and not only the things on our backs. Caroline's crew were insufferable, annoying and, worst of all, useless. The four of them had spent one month in India, almost all of it in the softness of Varkala. They knew nothing about trains or rickshaw hustlers or finding hotels or the importance of reading maps before you arrive. They might as well have just stepped off the plane from France that day.

Caroline was equally inexperienced but more courageous; and if she didn't know the best course of action, she was happy to defer to me. The rest of the bunch debated everything endlessly in French, which they must have thought I could not understand.

We all walked along a side drag checking out hotels until Caroline suggested we simply abandon her sister and friends and get our own room together. Well, okay.

Her and I jumped in a rickshaw and told the driver to find us a room for cheap. The group shouted at us and Caroline waved and said she'd see them at the airport in a few days.

The first place we tried turned out to be a damn satisfactory dump, with a balcony and dingy-but-functional shower and no paint on the walls; two-fifty a night. Sold.

We immediately started smoking the pot, almost before the bags hit the floor, two joints back to back. We explored the town for a bit and got some food, but carefully maintained our condition with regular top-ups.

Caroline was somewhat disappointed with the Indianness of Pondicherry (which would have been a brutal shock if all you knew was Varkala) but I couldn't have been happier to flee the ashram for this world again: there I was, back in the chaos and smog-filled madness that is the real India just hours after escaping Amma, and accompanying me was a lovely girl I had been checking out on the train who, it so happened, wanted to share a room, just her and I and her drugs. Someone up there must think I'm doing something right.

The ganja made the night markets something else entirely, something big and bright and incomprehensible, like wandering through a funhouse as a kid, where everything is strange and wonderful and a new experience. It was getting late by the time I bought myself two cans of beer as we headed home to smoke again. Caroline passed out and I finished my beer and consigned myself to one side of the double bed.

✿

Pondicherry is a former French colony, one of just a handful in India and certainly the largest and most renowned. There are French cafés and quaint restaurants on quaint streets; these are, of course, part of the tourist-oriented Old Town, which is removed from the very Indian bustle of the surrounding areas.

Our first full day consisted of: street chai followed by expensive coffee and pastries at a Western bakery; wandering around town until we reached the botanical gardens; exploring and relaxing in the quiet shade and strolling the tree-lined pathways; street lunch; nap; street supper; music and cards. All these activities were interspersed with marijuana, and I was beginning to see that Caroline had a bit of a problem (or at least an obsession). But she was leaving the next day, and she was good company, so I went along with her vices, happy to have any once again.

I was having trouble getting a read on Caroline, specifically her sentiments and possible intentions regarding me. She was flirtatious but not bodacious; friendly but not overly inviting. The haze of ganja made getting a read all the more difficult, and I couldn't decide what to do, so I played it safe and complimented her liberally without making a move. The following day, however, did nothing to dispel my confusion.

After lunch and a walk, we smoked up back at the hotel and had a nap. I slept for an hour but Caroline was out cold for four… well, that might not be the most accurate statement.

I was sitting up in bed reading while she slept; she appeared to be dreaming, breathing heavily with a strange expression on her face. Then she rolled onto her back and slipped her right hand inside her stretch pants. She started masturbating, her hand moving down below, picking up speed, and she started to wiggle and rock.

I was a foot away from her, high as a kite. What's a boy to do? I was frozen in shock at first: disbelief mixed with excitement, that too-good-to-be-true feeling. I waved my hand in front of her eyes. She really seemed to be sleeping, and I couldn't imagine her to be the type of girl to use this as a come-on. I began to feel bad, dirty, creepy, uncomfortable, despite my unavoidable arousal: she didn't intend for me to see this. So what to do? Wake her? No, that would embarrass her. Leave the room?

The dance with herself lasted a minute or so, building in intensity until she abruptly stopped (without evident climax) and rolled over away from me. I had gotten up to leave, but now returned to my side of the bed and tapped her shoulder, spoke her name, said we'd be late for dinner if she didn't wake up. She turned her head to look at me, but it was clear she couldn't see: her eyes were glassy, her stare entirely blank. She slept for another hour. When she rose I asked her how she'd slept; very well, she replied.

"Did you dream?"

"Yes, I think so," she said after considering, "because I wake up happy."

After a subpar squid curry at a French/Chinese/Indian restaurant, Caroline and I headed back to our drugs at the hotel. We smoked as we lay on the bed, and, after doing the math in my head (eight hours until she left, worst-case scenarios…) I made my move.

The kiss caught her off-guard: after a few moments of silence she spoke in French—"I think it might be better if we…"—with a gesture for separation. I apologized and we agreed we were still amigos, and that was that. So much for mixed signals.

She left the next day, travelling to Chennai alone where she would catch a flight to France with the rest of her former group. I inherited what was left of her greenery, which was only about two grams or so, but it had been an interesting few days with that odd stoned French girl.

And now I was alone. This was expected, and normally not a problem, except for the date: 17 March. Indians have no clue about St. Patrick's Day, so I scoured the markets and quaint streets and beaches for a pale-fleshed drinking companion; none was to be found.

I went to the bottle shop and, though dreaming of Guinness, bought a large plastic vessel of awful Indian whisky and headed back to the hotel after dark. The friendly hotel manager was at his desk when I came in, and I asked him if he'd like to join me on the balcony. Any friend would do.

We stood and drank and told stories; I told him about St. Patrick's Day, he told me about his family. We talked about nations, sports, politics, religion, all the usual subjects that flow out when you remove the cap from a bottle of spirits.

I noticed something strange on the street below: two policemen, one on a motorcycle, the other on foot, were moving from building to building. The man on foot would run inside while the other waited; moments later, he would emerge and they would move to the next place. I asked the manager what they were doing.

"Every two weeks they come. We must pay. Or else…" He trailed off and shrugged with drunken resignation. "Excuse me." He left and went down to meet the cops and pay them their fort-nightly protection racket money.

I handed him his drink once he came back, and we stood in

silence for a minute or so. Then . . .

"You can get me visa? For Canada?"

"What? No, no, I don't..."

"Yes, so I can come. I come and work."

"I can't do that."

"Please, yes?" He looked at me with a desperation I had never seen in anyone before. "Please."

I poured him another drink and told him I was going out for a walk. He persisted, begging, pleading. I gave him several sympathetic-but-stern no-nos and slipped out with my bottle.

A couple hours later, I quietly snuck back in without him seeing me and spent the rest of my final night in Pondicherry reliving better St. Patrick's Days past, drinking three-dollar whisky in a four-dollar room.

KOLKATA

**Walking through history,
and booze and pills and shouts in the night.**

I covered more ground in the next two days than I had in the past month combined. A train to Chennai followed by a train to Calcutta, and I was suddenly out of the south and, for the first time, high up along the eastern coastline, not far from Bangladesh.

I had about two weeks left on my visa and I had to start prioritizing the remainder of the country; Calcutta, Kolkata—city of culture, of history, of Mother Theresa, the once-upon-a-time capital—was a must-see.

The trains were exceptionally long and boring, more than thirty hours in total (though dirt cheap, naturally, for a sleeper class bunk). But as I prepared to disembark at my final destination in the middle of the night I happened to meet a British fellow named James who asked if I would like to split a taxi.

The driver took us across the bridge into the city and dropped us in the middle of the central tourist district. It was just before four o'clock in the morning, and everything was pitch black except for the rare streetlight on every other block. We knocked on a few hotel doors before we came to one that would answer us. A double bed with attached bath cost four hundred, and James and I took it rather than argue or keep searching.

My first view of the city was from the bathroom window just after daybreak, and I immediately got dressed and bounded down the stairs to street level.

There are some experiences that feel seminal at the very time of living them: visiting the Eiffel Tower, for example, one appreciates the significance of the moment in one's life; the Taj Mahal has the same effect; and, for me, for whatever reason, Calcutta did as well. It felt like walking through history everywhere I went; but a specific type of history, distinctly Raj, highly British, and yet Indian; but more: Calcuttan, very much the product of this once-great city, still distinguished as it continues to redefine itself after nearly a century of human despair. This was also the home of the centre of the Indian drive for Independence (and, not-coincidentally, for the eastern partition of the subcontinent).

Founded by the British in the late seventeenth century, Calcutta (or Kolkata; it suffers from the same multi-moniker syndrome as Bombay/Mumbai) is a strangely beautiful city: regal and elderly in its buildings and facades, relatively clean in its streets, it seemed, somehow, to be proud of its British roots. While other cities have Raj-era buildings, they seem to be somewhat resented by the surrounding structures; in Calcutta, they feel celebrated. These are, at least and no more, the observations I made as a pedestrian exploring that first day.

Much of my time in the city was spent hunting for the Thai consulate to secure my visa; this limited my time for visiting major sites, but my meandering search took me to parts of Calcutta I would have otherwise missed.

The culture and attitude seemed to feature more small courtesies than other Indian cities. In the metro, for example, people let those disembarking the train get off before they move on, rather than both sides simultaneously trying to force themselves through like so much cookie dough through a small tube.

James and I switched hotels the next day (after our manager, in a fit of drunkenness, tried to kick us out four hours earlier than our agreed-upon time; he threatened to call the police, but we—who were also inebriated—reminded him that he had failed to have us register in the ledger, which was required by law, and, after daring him to phone the authorities, we settled the matter by slamming the door in his drunk face). Our new place of lodging was down the street and significantly cheaper, though we were sharing a dorm-style room with ten other people.

James seemed a bit of an odd duck, though a decent guy. He'd had his luggage stolen from a train the previous week: clothes, passport, money, everything; a traveller's nightmare. We'd split up during the daylight hours, him to the British consulate, I to the Thai, and then regroup in the evening to compare notes on the machinations of our respective bureaucracies over pitchers of draught beer—the first I'd seen in India.

One night, after a few pitchers, we went to the bottle shop and picked up a couple of mickeys of Old Monk, which we smuggled up to the dorm (liquor was prohibited). We drank the rum neat while lounging on our beds. I played some Beatles on my laptop and everything was nice and easy.

Around eleven-thirty I decided to call it a night: everyone else in the dorm was in bed, though the lights had been left on. James had taken some sleeping pills after complaining about his lack of rest, but he also wanted to keep listening to music, so I loaned him my MP3 player and earphones. I switched the light off and crawled back into bed.

"Enjoy your sleeping pills," was the last thing I said before rolling over to sleep.

Ten minutes later, James started yelling "Yeahhhh!" at the top of his lungs in the dark, presumably in favour of whatever song he was listening to. The others in the dorm angrily shushed him as he continued, and I told him to be quiet. He brushed us all off with yelps and hollers. We hadn't had that much to drink—I was borderline tipsy—but his behaviour fit the description of a man fallen into the deep end. Eventually I became fed up as he continued his shouting, and I grabbed the music player from him. He was appalled and accosted me in slurred English for a while. He kept mumble-shouting nonsense, and people kept shushing him, but to no avail.

After one particularly loud exclamation, I swung an arm and slapped him on the shoulder, not very hard. "Why would you do that?" he half-shouted in a pitiable voice. His finger appeared in front of my face. "Why would you do that?" he repeated. "You want to take me on? I'll knock you out."

I didn't want to escalate the situation, but, sick of having his fingers stuck in my face, poking my nose and jabbing my cheek, I grabbed them and twisted his arm around until he was almost thrown out of bed. I relented and he lay back down, and I made sure he got the message that people were sleeping and he needed to be quiet. But it didn't get through: he continued on, completely non-sensical, mumbling in normal volume and occasionally shouting various things and noises. The shushing continued, and I waited for someone to go complain to the manager and have him thrown out, but no one moved; everyone suffered through it until he finally shut up around a quarter to one.

But nothing lasts forever, including silence, and he was back at it at a quarter past three. I'm sure people must have been awakened by his yelping, but everyone stayed silent. He continued for half an hour before taking another break, only to fire it up again around dawn. But this last episode was short-lived: upon hearing the muezzin's first few words of the call to prayer, James fell silent, perhaps curiously listening to the noise made by someone other than him, perhaps simply content that the void of intolerable silence was being filled.

I awoke at nine-thirty and saw James completely passed out, look-ing very peaceful as he lay sleeping on his back. I also noticed the half-empty blister pack of diazepam on his bed. (When I saw him later before leaving town, he was extremely contrite and apologetic, asking me to explain what had happened; he'd been told that he'd been an asshole, but had no recollection of any of it: it had indeed been the combination of booze and pills.)

I wandered the markets for a while before going to book my last two train tickets on the subcontinent: one to Darjeeling for that evening; one for a week later, back to Calcutta. I was down to my last seven days.

While walking back to the hotel in the late afternoon to collect my bags, music—Für Elise—began blaring through an unseen loud-speaker somewhere, audible everywhere, echoing, it seemed, through the entire city, perhaps all of India. The song played over and over as I walked through the old city streets in the dying of daylight, the faded Raj all around me in the buildings and elsewhere, the Indians filing along the roads to their homes and metros and taxis and buses, the sadness of the city—history and people and death and decline—coming over me so soft and sweet with the music, tempered by the foreign song, made sadder with and because of it. And yet everyone moved on, pushing forward as the notes floated through their city from some unknown source. Calcutta will live and survive; she always has.

I passed a bare concrete wall with a faded metal sign posted: "Calcutta is your own, leave her walls alone."

DARJEELING

Shrouded beauty,
and the glories of pork fat

F ilm buffs will be disappointed to learn that there is no such train as the Darjeeling Limited. There is, however, the Darjeeling Mail, which sped me north from Calcutta—a city that had infected me with its charms; a city I wished I could spend more time in—towards the Himalayas.

The main railway runs as far as New Jalpaiguri, more commonly referred to as NJP, from where one can choose between a shared jeep-taxi to get to Darjeeling, or the Darjeeling Himalayan Railway, another narrow-gauge mountain train, reportedly very uncomfortable, very long, and inconvenient with only sporadic departures each day (though the scenery was, supposedly, worth it).

This latter choice was my plan until we arrived later than scheduled, meaning I would have to sit around NJP for hours waiting for the next train while my India clock ticked down.

I met a young Korean couple upon waking up on the overnight train, and we quickly found a jeep together. It cost us one hundred rupees each, and there was already a nine-person family inside, including a little girl who kept throwing up out of the window.

The trip took three hours on hairpin mountain roads, with construction backing up traffic in tiny villages along the way. The views were likely spectacular, but everything was completely obscured by the mist and fog once we left NJP and climbed into the grey air of the mountains above.

More than anything, I noticed the temperature. Going from Calcutta, where it was roasting hot until the wee hours of the morning, straight to NJP was already a noticeable and welcome change; but the jeep ride into the mountains was a far more dramatic shift: wearing only an undershirt and long pants, I sat next to an open window as the jeep raced around corners and the Koreans put on jackets; I basked in it. I had forgotten what it felt like, this 'cold' they have in other countries. Brisk. Cool. Non-sweat.

We moved with the labourious flow of traffic until we entered Darjeeling, a hill station that holds a charm that Ooty must have lost long ago, or perhaps never quite had. There is traffic and a few horns, but only along a stretch of road downtown, and certainly not on the level of other towns.

We were dropped off and the Koreans and I hiked up one of steep roads to find a hotel listed in the guidebooks. The three of us took a 'dorm' room, which had only three beds for eighty rupees apiece, and we marvelled at the jaw dropping views the hotel would surely provide when not socked in by fog: high up on a ridge, with a lovely balcony looking down on the valley below and the mountains beyond, it was an impossible paradise.

I was starving, so I headed back down the hill to the main drag and found a small Tibetan restaurant where I ordered pork curry, the first pig flesh of my time in India. The meat was tender and the sauce was nice, but the highlights were the huge chunks of pork fat thrown into the mix, succulent and juicy and pure unexpected joy.

✲

It rained steadily for the first two days, and the thick fog refused to reveal the mountains as we hid indoors. There weren't many people around the hotel: I spent much of my time alone reading books and drinking Tibetan tea next to the fire in the communal area with the hotel's resident cat on my lap. A few people came and went, ordered food and drinks from the kitchen, sat, talked, left. I did, however, meet two women within hours of each other, both of whom would come to define my last days in India.

The first was Silvia, a Polish girl in her mid-twenties. Silvia was, in every sense of the word, odd. Her English wasn't great, but she loved to play cryptic games when speaking to someone. She was almost childlike in her carefree optimistic disposition; but just when you might be ready to dismiss her as living in a fantasy world, she showed her biting humour with a wink. We met on the balcony, watching the rain, and hit it off immediately.

Later, again by myself sitting by the fireplace, I met Sonia: tall, wearer of lovely long skirts and sensible, warm, flattering gypsy clothing, Sonia was from Prague. She was pretty, but her face was especially lovely: full of inherited character, strong and bold; perhaps comparable (in a kind way, I assure you) to an old Czech grand-mother... but youthful, bright, beautiful; like a confident warrior princess. She spoke English well and was smart, but it was her unique good looks that drew me in immediately.

Neither girl was staying at my hotel; they had each come for lunch while out wandering in the rain. I invited them both, separately, back for supper and drinks that evening, and they both came, and we formed a group. Polish and Czech are related languages, so they were able to communicate with each other, which made them greatly happy: native English speakers are spoiled, since our language is used nearly everwhere; try finding two Czech speakers in Darjeeling.

The rain stopped the following morning and the three of us headed out together for exploration. Darjeeling is, like most Indian cities, a jumbled mess of roads and alleys, and the steep mountain slopes mean that a wrong turn usually results in an exhausting hike. The city has one hundred thirty thousand residents, but carries the soul of a much smaller settlement, and we explored the peaceful town until the rain returned and we scurried for the safety of my hotel for more Tibetan tea and fried bread.

Darjeeling is on the edge of the Himalayas, the world's highest mountain range, which separates the subcontinent from Tibet and the Tibetan Plateau. Everyone knows Mount Everest is found here, but the range taken as a whole is equally impressive: the tallest mountain outside Asia is Aconcagua in the Andes, standing six thousand nine hundred sixty-two metres; the Himalayas have over one hundred mountains above the seventy-two hundred metre line.

But Darjeeling, though high up in the hills, is slightly sunken in a valley for protection, rendering the majority of the most spectacular peaks obscured. This is why each dawn dozens of jeeps ferry hundreds of tourists to Tiger Hill, the summit of the nearby station of Ghoom. A renowned tourist experience for its breathtaking sunrise views of Everest and other peaks, Tiger Hill is something one simply must do when in Darjeeling.

But we were concerned about the unseasonal bad weather blocking our view, and the trek was postponed daily by Sonia, Silvia and myself until we were down to our penultimate day in town. We decided it was now or never.

I awoke around three o'clock in the morning and roused the Koreans as planned. The three of us dressed and headed down the road to collect the girls. We found Sonia walking up the hill towards us to report a problem: Silvia had been taken hostage by her hotel.

We arrived to find the little Polish pixie on the unfortunate side of a locked iron gate, clutching the bars sadly like a captured cartoon villain. She rang the doorbell for the manager's suite repeatedly, but there was no answer. She tried everywhichway to escape, even attempting to climb down from the rooftop balcony. We were pressed by time: the jeeps would leave Darjeeling by four o'clock. I banged on the door of an apartment attached to the hotel, believing it to be the owner's, but instead I roused an old lady who was inno-cent of the whole situation. She did find it amusing, thankfully, and produced a mobile phone to call the manager, who promptly sent the boy to unlock the gate. We were on our way.

We found and hired one of the last jeeps waiting for tourists. Ghoom is not a long distance from Darjeeling, but the climb up to Tiger Hill is winding and treacherous. There was an endless caravan of jeeps making the trek, and once we came close, the road was lined with vehicles parked and waiting until their tourist cargo finished with the sights. Our driver let us off as close as he could, and both he and we agreed to remain monogamous to each other.

Daylight was coming, slowly: enough to see where we were walking, not so much that we feared we'd missed the show.

The 'show' turned out to be a disappointing but laughable hour on the summit surrounded by fog and tourists with cameras. No one could see a damn thing: the fog was actually far worse at the higher altitude. We waited and hoped and watched, but nothing changed. It was bitterly cold and none of our group had much in the way of winter clothes. Frost nipped at exposed skin; a local lady sold milky tea and cigarettes and made a fortune off of the shivering tourists. Any time the sun—now risen behind the clouds—threatened to break through, a loud cheer erupted and people raised their cameras into the air en masse, hopeful to make something out of their early morning. But nothing ever came. Eventually we gave up and found our driver, who dropped the three of us—Sonia, Silvia and I—at Ghoom so we could walk back and explore some of the monasteries along the way.

The sun came out as we walked, and the sky cleared, and we were hot and sweaty in our layers of clothes. The monasteries were beautiful and ornate, with artwork and sculptures depicting Siddhartha Gautama and other Buddhist figures and mythology. They were mostly quiet places, but we happened to enter into a room at one of them where a large group of young boys dressed in bright orange robes with shaved heads were seated cross-legged in front of a row of similarly-attired men who were leading them in some sort of prayer-song-chant ritual. We lingered awkwardly in the doorway at first, not wanting to intrude, but one man gestured with a smile to invite us in; we stood at the back and watched as the routine continued, these young monks earnestly filling the room with their young-but-sure voices. We stayed for half an hour, watching and listening in fascination, before leaving them quietly.

The three of us carried on down the road, soaking in the spectacular valley views now revealed by the departed fog. There were no other tourists here, all of them having gone directly from Darjeeling to Tiger Hill and back again. But the monasteries were worth the hike; and, at the third one, while Sonia was off by herself, I kissed Silvia for the first time.

I couldn't say why I chose Silvia over Sonia: both were lovely and attractive to me. Perhaps I found Silvia more receptive in our short time together. Or perhaps it was because I was trying to convince her to continue on with Sonia and I: all three of us were headed to the state of Sikkim next, but Silvia was torn between coming with us or heading to Gangtok first to meet some other friends. In the end, she would choose the latter, and Sonia and I would move on together; so perhaps that kiss was intended to express something we were going to narrowly miss. If so, the fact that she kissed back would imply that she knew it, too.

✿

We made it back to Darjeeling in time for lunch with the Koreans at a fast food stand in the city centre. It was grand: all of us sitting on a long wooden bench in front of a happy woman operating the grill, all of us continually ordering more fried treats and cups of chai, sharing everything with each other at our last meal together.

Sonia and I said our good-byes to the group—Silvia kissed me on the cheek—and we hurried to collect our things from the hotel before buying our tickets for the final jeep of the day to Jorethang; time, for me, was running out.

SIKKIM

Connections missed as the clock ticks

S onia and I arrived in Jorethang after an uncomfortable hour-and-a-half jeep ride. Jorethang itself appeared quite dull, and we had designs of finding onward transport. But there didn't appear to be any: the bus station had buses but they all seemed disused and abandoned; our driver had let us out on the side of the road, and we saw no other jeep stand.

Sonia went down the street in search of options, while I found a soldier and asked where we could find a jeep to Pelling. He suddenly started shouting and waving with great urgency at the street behind me, and I was certain that somebody was about to get shot.

I turned around to see an Indian man of about thirty years dressed in an undershirt and trendy thick-rimmed glasses with long greasy hair and a big grin: he had stopped his jeep beside us at the soldier's command.

"This jeep go Pelling," said the man in uniform. I called Sonia and we were on our way.

The nearly-new jeep had plush fake-leather seats and an excellent stereo system. We were the only ones in there and Sonia and I stretched out in the back as we reacquainted ourselves with the long-ago forgotten concept of an uncrowded modern vehicle.

Our driver was enthusiastic about everything. "You guys like Bengali rock?" he hollered, cranking up the tunes. Sonia started singing along with one particularly catchy song, and her lovely Czech voice was a pleasant surprise. I asked if we could smoke; we could, and did, and I gave one to the driver.

Our jeep picked up a couple of people on the way and dropped them off before arriving in Pelling in the early evening. Sonia asked if I would like to share a room; I said yes.

The fog had settled in for the night by this point. Pelling is small in population, winding in area, alternately stoic and jovial in attitude: the town is situated on a mountain road that snakes back and forth as it descends. Thus you have Upper Pelling, where our hotel was, as well as Middle and Lower Pelling.

We were wandering down the road looking for a restaurant that would whet our appetites when Sonia stopped to buy cigarettes from a tiny bottle shop in Middle Pelling. I asked about local restos, and the woman at the counter said there was a very good one just down the stairs, in the same building as her shop.

We walked down the rickety steps on the side of the building and entered a small, spare old wooden box that hung off of the mountain while supporting the liquor store above it. It was the epitome of rustic: plain dry wooden walls, uninsulated despite the cold, dim electric lamps, hard wooden furniture.

We ordered momo, which are dumplings prepared in myriad ways, a Tibetan staple; and wai-wai, which turned out to be instant ramen noodles. We also ordered tongba, a local alcoholic beverage made from millet: after being sealed and stored for six months to ferment, the millet grains are collected and placed in a wooden container resembling a miniature barrel, to which boiling water is added; the concoction sits for five minutes before it is ready to drink through bamboo straws, which have a slit rather than a hole on one end to act as a filter for the grains. The stuff tastes something like warm sake, and works just as well. More hot water is added as needed until all the flavour and alcohol has been drunk.

And that we were as we stumbled out into the dark night, laughing and full of warm booze and dumplings, walking up the steep curved road wet with fog, hearing our laughter echo off the mountains.

۰

Our hotel room was decent but cold, and layers were a necessity for sleeping comfortably. The hot water heater was broken, which made for a rough morning. I awoke to find myself alone in the double bed; I peeked out the window and saw Sonia on the common terrace doing yoga in the morning sun as the foggy mountains looked down on her.

We got dressed and ate breakfast before venturing out of town: there was a monastery some kilometres away, but we also wanted to get into the mountains, to soak up the natural grace and bloom of West Sikkim.

Though the monastery was operational, the oldest and largest buildings were solely tourist attractions. The artwork and sculptures were beautiful, but the real pleasure was the walk: peaceful, rarely a car or soul to be seen, surrounded everywhere by mountainous forest and shrouded in cool mist. I had to wonder, I admit, when I had left India.

Sikkim is an oddity, but a beautiful one, fought over for centuries by the Nepalese, Chinese, Tibetans, Bhutanese, kings and prophets and dynasties coming to and going from this tiny corner of the world. When the Raj began in India, a then-independent Sikkim allied with the British against a common enemy: Nepal. When Nepal attacked Sikkim, the British invaded Nepal; eventually, as they were wont to do in those days, the British just took over the whole of Sikkim.

Fast-forward to 1947 and a popular vote in India rejecting Sikkim joining their newly-independent nation. It wasn't until 1975 that Sikkim—a strange, foreign place, so far as Indians were concerned: don't they speak Nepali and look Nepalese up there with their yak butter?—was finally accepted into the club.

So it is India, but not India; though, given the scattered and hodgepodge collective nature of the Indian Union, Sikkim fits in just as well as Goans and Punjabis.

Farther down the road from Pelling was the town of Geyzing, the capital of West Sikkim; with a population of eight hundred and change, it was several times larger than Pelling. Sonia wanted to buy a raincoat to keep out the constant dampness, so we continued down the steep winding road, coming to the quick conclusion that a jeep would be the most sensible way back to Pelling.

We had lunch in a small dive while the rain tried to start up again, then did some shopping. Sonia did not find her coat, and we were both tired and wet and ready to go home. We went to the jeep stand, bought tickets and sat in the vehicle, waiting to leave. A strange figure jumped from behind our view with a grin and a yelp; she stood for a moment as Sonia and I tried to process the sight before us; we told her to get in, and she did, and we all drove back to Pelling together.

Silvia had changed her plans of going to Gangtok at the last minute and decided to come find us instead. She took a dorm-room bed in our hotel and we all showered (separately) to celebrate the return of hot water before heading out for food. That night, we gathered in the hotel's common area with the common guitar and I played for the girls and the cats and drank Old Monk until Sonia went to bed and it was just Silvia and I. We sang and talked and flirted and, eventually, began kissing, which went on for an hour or so, but we had no room to ourselves, so we said good-night and went our separate ways.

The next morning was a lazy one: we had plans to head to Khecheopalri Lake, but we all took our time and missed the early jeep, which meant, naturally, that the next one would be late; we didn't hit the road until two-thirty, having added a loud Bristol hippie named Ruth to our clan while waiting.

Jeeps (not the brand, remember, but a catch-all term) hold, in theory, thirteen people; as in the rest of India, the rated capacity of a vehicle is considered pessimistically low. Our jeep carried: four on the front bench, including the driver; five on the second bench; six on the third, including children; our group of four on side-seats installed in the rear cargo area; and five young boys, aged around twelve, hanging off the back with their feet on the bumper; a total of twenty-four souls.

The rain had started before we'd left, drenching our uncovered baggage on the roof rack. The road was slippery, but the driver was driving reasonably by Indian standards. The rain no doubt made the metal bumper the boys were standing on quite slick; but that didn't stop the lads from pushing and shoving and wrestling and laughing and swapping positions with the ease of lemurs.

Once the rain became very bad, some of the boys stuck their heads inside, leaning and dripping over us. Sonia offered the youngest one her lap to sit on; he declined, but I have never seen a bigger grin in all my life.

We arrived at the lake, which is to say we arrived at a spacious patch of gravel surrounded by trees which blocked the view of the lake. There was a large map on a wooden board, and we found our bearings. Sonia was bound for a monastery in the hills; she said her good-byes with big hugs, and Silvia declared she would stay with Ruth and I.

The three of us tried a couple of hotels before settling on a homestay a short hike into the trees. The rustic wooden building high on a hill was modest but comfortable with eight double rooms, a small kitchen and dining room, and a fantastic view of the valley. The girls took a room and I took my own, and we headed back down to a shack restaurant near the gravel patch for momos and beer.

Silvia began confusing me, not that she had ever been straightforward: we had become accustomed to holding hands, but now she withdrew; same for kissing or affection of any sort. Always games, always cryptic, always fantasy-world. When we walked back to the homestay, Ruth went inside while we stayed out to look at the night sky. I tried to kiss Silvia's cheek but she pulled away; I asked what was wrong and she gazed at the stars silently. I stood for a while with her, then walked inside, and she followed at a distance and went to her room while I went to the campfire outside.

There I was alone. There was enough light from the moon to see the silhouette of the Himalayas; small clusters of distant electric lights signalled the location of houses and villages.

I was suddenly overwhelmed with a variety of emotions, and I stood staring at the dark scene for a long while as the fire warmed the back of my legs. I couldn't explain what I felt: the smallness of self that the mountains bring; the holiness of the place; ancientness and peace all around me; the sense that things used to be like this everywhere once, in one way or another; a feeling of loss and of being lost.

The young son of the owner came out and sat with me, as did a Polish couple who were staying there. As we all talked together, the kid told us to ask him anything, for his general knowledge was superb. He did not know the capitals of Canada and Poland, but he, could quote Abe Lincoln; he wrongly thought Ben Franklin and Alexander Hamilton were presidents, but he knew which currency notes they were on. We ordered rum and beer from inside and sat for hours.

It was late. I had been half-hoping Silvia would come find me, but she never did, and once I had finished my beer and cup of rum I decided to seek her out.

She wasn't in the dining room or on the balcony. She wasn't in her room or in the bathroom or outside. She was gone.

It was quite cold, so I went to my room to get a sweater. There, lying on my bed with her hands on a book on her chest, fast, asleep with the lights on, was she. I sat down and woke her gently. "What are you doing here?" I asked softly.

"Waiting for you," she said with sleep in her voice. She was a sweet girl, after all.

I brushed my teeth and climbed into bed with her and she fell asleep in my arms as I thought, and dreamed, about Sikkim.

✿

We woke early and Silvia decided she wanted to go to Geyzing for some shopping. I had to go back to Pelling to catch an early-morning jeep out of Sikkim the following morning—the first step of a day that would end with my departure from India—so I agreed to go with her. We spent the morning in a jeep and a few hours in Geyzing—holding hands, affectionate once again for reasons unknown to me—before going back to Pelling. We waited and talked for a while until her jeep came to take her back to the lake. She hugged me, and snuck a kiss in at the last moment. I waved good-bye as the jeep sped out of sight.

In the hotel I found a new batch of tourists, including some familiar faces from Darjeeling: Brits, Aussies, Swiss, Kiwis, even a Canadian girl from Ontario travelling with her boyfriend. We drank and
bantered and played cards and guitar until late. I went to bed and
thought about my departure the next day, about my time in India…
Until…

wait, what day is it?

I awoke with a start and scrambled for a calendar and realized I
had come back too early: my train ticket to Calcutta wasn't until the
day after tomorrow; I still had one full day left!

Time (or perhaps any one of the hundreds of gods in that part of
the world) proved to be on my side: I awoke to find the skies clear
and the Himalayas purely visible for the first time. There, above
everything, was Kangchenjunga, the third-tallest mountain in the
world. The sight was worth all the rain and dreariness of the preceding week.

After breakfast and a morning hike, I sat on the roof with the
hotel guitar until Valerie joined me. Val was a Swiss girl travelling
alone, and we hit it off immediately. Just as the Minx so perfectly
followed Jenny, Val seemed an attractive opposite to the oddness of
Silvia.

We sat and talked for a long while, then decided momos and
tongba were in order. Dusk was falling as we walked to my favourite
restaurant in Middle Pelling.

The manager/cook wasn't in, but his wife was happy to seat and
serve us. (She admitted later that she didn't know how to cook,
though the food was fine.)

The three of us talked openly, and our hostess told us about
herself: she was thirty-one with three children, the eldest of whom
was thirteen. She asked about us, and it came out that Val was going
to the lake in the morning while I would go to Calcutta.

"No!" said the woman, apparently shocked and devastated by this
news; she pointed straight at me: "You broke her heart!" I laughed,
and so did Valerie. The woman pressed for confirmation.

"That's right," said Valerie, looking at me (Val had a tendency to
stare into my eyes while talking, and even after she had finished; I

think we both felt a connection between us).

We continued talking for a while longer before heading back up to the hotel. There was some fast-moving chemistry building between Val and I, but there was no time to explore it: that night we would share the dorm room fat Korean guy, and the next day we would both be gone. I think she revealed enough to show me she felt something there, too; perhaps that's ego, but I don't think so. Either way, the road doesn't always provide sufficient time to explore alternative directions and detours.

Eventually, we retired to our separate beds and talked for an hour while the Korean read comic books on his laptop.

After a very early breakfast together, before anyone except us and the hotel cook were awake, Val shouldered her bag and hugged me fully and warmly with a kiss on the cheek. A twenty-four hour friendship on the road; we'll never meet again. I watched her walk down the road and around the bend and gone.

Not long after, I hauled my own bag into the jeep that would take me to the nearest rail station, in Siliguri, out of Sikkim. I rode with an Indian family on holiday who wouldn't talk to me much and we arrived in the early afternoon. I killed my last few free hours in the markets of the bustling town, walking aimlessly until I happened upon a restaurant serving masala dosas. I thought this would be an appropriate final meal: south Indian cuisine in the shadow of the Himalayas.

I smoked as I walked after my meal, trying to soak in the sights, sounds, smells, stares, enjoying everything like never before—except, perhaps, when I first arrived; but with a different appreciation, a more refined palate to taste the flavours. It felt, truly, like I was leaving home.

I went to the rail station and sat outside for a while, thinking about the plane I would board in Calcutta to begin a new adventure in another foreign place. That prospect was of little consequence, little appeal, in that moment. I had fled Moose Jaw with little fear or hesitation or regret; now I felt all those things and more leaving a country that was not my own.

Beggar children begged from me, wandering naked and filthy, perhaps by necessity, perhaps as required by their tragic profession.

I tried to drink everything in with huge fast choking gulps that threatened to at once kill and elude me: the rickshaw drivers, the food stands, the chai-wallahs, the horns, the grime, the spectacular saris, the <u>smells</u>. Three samosas and one of those little fried dal pucks and I boarded my final train in India.

I slept lousily in sleeper class, my mind unable to rest. The shifting, rocking train woke me just after dawn as it chugged into the outskirts of the city. The chai-wallah was already making his rounds, and I bought a cup and lit a cigarette and sat on the floor next to the open door, my leg dangling out of the train. The sun shone on the trash littering the tracks, specks of colour flashing up. Dogs sniffed through it all. Factories loomed and smoked with me.

I had not known what I was seeking when I left home, nor really what I wanted as I ate my soggy reuben in a café on Main Street many months ago. What I had found was the road. As I listened to the clacking rhythm of the train, that felt like enough. I bought another chai and lit another cigarette and watched the sun rise up through the smog.

THE AUTHOR

Taylor Lambert has written for numerous Canadian newspapers and magazines while also somehow finding time to visit 18 countries (and counting). He is currently a freelance writer based in Calgary.

Made in the USA
Charleston, SC
04 December 2013